THE
METHOD
OF OUR
MISSION

LACEYE C. WARNER

THE
METHOD
OF OUR
MISSION

UNITED METHODIST
POLITY & ORGANIZATION

Nashville

THE METHOD OF OUR MISSION:
UNITED METHODIST POLITY AND ORGANIZATION

This book is printed on acid-free paper.

Library of Congress Cataloging-in-Publication Data

Warner, Laceye C.
  The method of our mission : United Methodist polity and organization / Laceye C. Warner.
     pages cm
  Includes bibliographical references.
  ISBN 978-1-4267-6717-3 (binding: soft back / pbk. / trade : alk. paper) 1. United Methodist Church (U.S.)—Government. 2. United Methodist Church (U.S.)—Doctrines. I. Title.
  BX8388.W27 2014
  262'.076—dc23

                                                                              2014002113

Scripture quotations unless noted otherwise are from the Common English Bible. Copyright © 2011 by the Common English Bible. All rights reserved. Used by permission. www.CommonEnglishBible.com.

This edition has been updated to reflect changes made at the 2016 General Conference.

16 17 18 19 20 21 22 23—10 9 8 7 6 5 4 3 2

MANUFACTURED IN THE UNITED STATES OF AMERICA

This book is dedicated to the clergy and laity of the
Texas Annual Conference
from whom I first learned to love United Methodism.

– Contents –

– Acknowledgments –

It has been a great gift to reflect upon the polity of our denomination and to provide a guide introducing its governance and organization. I am very glad for the invitation from Abingdon Press to participate in this project. As an ordained elder and full member in the Texas Annual Conference, as well as an instructor of courses required of those seeking ordination in the UMC (United Methodist History, Doctrine and Polity, and Evangelism/Mission), I consistently depend on the pastoral and intellectual wisdom of others to sharpen my work and hold me accountable to standards beyond the world's. Among those are friends and mentors that gave of their valuable time and expertise to talk with me, simply listen patiently, or read some or all of the manuscript as it came together in the midst of many other tasks.

Encouraging conversations with Duke Divinity School colleagues Diana Abernethy, Jeff Conklin-Miller, Edgardo Colon-Emeric, Beth Sheppard, and Warren Smith, as well as Stephen Chapman, Susan Eastman, and Dave Odom, helped to provide momentum and to give shape to ideas. Greg Jones and Susan Pendleton Jones, Judith Heyhoe, Nathan Kirkpatrick, and Randy Maddox not only discussed but also read early drafts of the manuscript to offer thoughtful guidance. I also appreciate the time and consideration taken by Belton Joyner to read and review the text. I am grateful to Sujin Pak for granting me research assistance, and I am appreciative to each one for their work: Laura-Allen Kerlin, Robert Mason, and Laura Rodgers Levens. Laura-Allen and Robert attended their first General Conference while enrolled in United Methodist Studies. Laura Levens provided inspiration by

consistently demonstrating her love for the church—as it should be—
and students preparing for ministry. Thanks also to Bishop Kenneth
Carder for conversations and friendship over many years, including
coteaching a number of courses. Emily Chapman, a pastor in the Texas
Annual Conference, and Donna Banks, currently serving as a district
superintendent in the North Carolina Annual Conference, also read
drafts and offered helpful suggestions. Rebecca Hymes-Smith and
Cathy Germanowski helped in numerous ways—I am grateful for their
Christian witness.

I am also humbled by the time and consideration given to this
project by active episcopal leaders. Bishop Kenneth Carter Jr. read the
earliest draft and offered careful and earnest responses. Bishop Scott
Jones read the penultimate draft offering expertise to many important
details in need of attention. Thanks, too, to my bishop, Janice Riggle
Huie, not only for her incredibly capable and wise example but also for
making time for conversation and for offering that time so generously.

And, finally, I am deeply appreciative to family. It is a distinct privilege to share in the order of elders of the Texas Annual Conference with
my brother, Peter Cammarano, and my spouse of over twenty years,
Gaston Warner. With Gaston's support, encouragement, and humor all
endeavors seem possible. Among my parents and in-laws are successors
of many generations of Methodists, some lifelong Methodists themselves, who demonstrate an unfathomable depth of Christian faith.
May such witnesses provide a vision for the present and future of the
church, including our daughter, Ella Clare.

For these many lovely gestures—thank you.

– Introduction –

The purpose of this book is to provide a guide to United Methodist polity and organization grounded in the Wesleyan tradition. The chapters that follow interpret sometimes-complicated denominational policies and structure through a theological frame informed by our Wesleyan and Methodist heritage. This book introduces and helps prepare students for life as United Methodist professionals by explaining key polity and organizational components of the denomination. Though functional in nature, the polity and structure of the denomination facilitate our mission to make disciples for the transformation of the world. Important to understanding our polity is an awareness of the layers that undergird our mission. In the following chapters, dimensions of our experience of church—from doctrinal standards and ministry roles to conferences and councils—are considered in light of their interdependence to one another and location in the Wesleyan tradition.

An aim of this book is to connect denominational governance and organization to our beliefs—as well as our mission. Across mainline denominations there is arguably a crisis of identity and purpose leading to much discussion about polity and organization, even if those terms are not always used. As pressure intensifies on denominations, calling into question their likelihood of survival, the impact of that pressure can be seen in denominational governance and organizational structures in the form of persistent conflict with little if any constructive resolution. For example, the 2012 General Conference deliberated at length on proposals to restructure denominational organization. However, the proposal most seriously considered eventually was ruled unconstitutional by the Judicial Council leaving the denomination with little, if any, approved legislation after years of study and preparation.

Another aim of this book is to encourage current and future denominational leaders to understand their practices of administration and participation in polity as a theological endeavor and key component of their ministries. A clear understanding of our identity, as Methodists with Wesleyan roots, and our purpose, to make disciples for the transformation of the world, can help United Methodists navigate this landscape as present and future leaders.

Despite challenges faced by Christian denominations in the United States, there is much to celebrate about contemporary United Methodism. As a denomination it embodies the stability of an institution alongside its Wesleyan heritage as a renewal movement characterized by an agile responsiveness to the Holy Spirit's guidance. However, United Methodism also faces challenges of its past in its present and future. At times our forebears participated in systemic oppression including racism and other forms of exploitation. United Methodism has the opportunity to acknowledge its complicity in such less-than-faithful practices and to live more fully into our mission, boldly embracing our identity as a connectional church sent in ministry to the world. For example, at the 2012 General Conference, delegates participated in "An Act of Repentance toward Healing Relationships with Indigenous Peoples," and the 2016 General Conference remembered Methodists' complicity in the Sandcreek Massacre, acknowledging the church's role in the oppression of native peoples of all nations. The 2012 General Conference also entered into full communion with a number of historically black pan-Methodist denominations. The following sections describe various facets of United Methodism, select strengths as well as challenges within and beyond its structures that inform practices of polity and governance.

A Wesleyan Church

The theological commitments of John Wesley (1703–1791) and their embodiment in the practices of the early renewal movement provide important soil from which United Methodism grows. There are numerous other influences that have also informed and continue to inform Methodism in America, some of which are distinctive from Wesley's specific contributions and context. However, Wesleyan themes persist in framing many of contemporary United Methodism's strengths. These themes include doctrines/theology and practices as well as a distinctive integration of both.

John Wesley asked Methodists of his day, "What is the mark? Who is a Methodist . . . ?" And, as he often did, Wesley supplied a response: "A Methodist is one who has 'the love of God shed abroad in [one's] heart by the Holy Ghost given unto [them].'" This initial response was then followed by numerous marks identifying specific practices and values.[1] In the fifth volume of the *United Methodism in American Culture* series, Russell Richey with Dennis Campbell and William Lawrence survey Methodist history for similar occasions of articulating the distinguishing marks of Methodism.[2] Notable consistency may be found when considering these over time. As Richey and the others point out, "The official version of such marks can now be found in the prefatory matter in the Discipline—Constitution, Doctrine and Doctrinal Statements, General Rules, and Social Principles."[3]

As a result of their research, Richey, Campbell, and Lawrence discern four marks characterizing Methodist practices of church: connectional, disciplined, catholic, and itinerant.[4] According to these authors,

> [These] serve well to epitomize Methodism, particularly Methodist life together. And they link nicely and appropriately with what have been traditionally termed the "notes" or "marks" of the church, classic affirmations Christians make about the nature and purpose of the church. The church is one, holy, catholic, and apostolic. Individually and collectively these traditional ecclesial affirmations parallel the four Methodist marks.[5]

The process to discover deeper patterns in their research, which ultimately led to the distillation of these four marks with parallels to the traditional marks of the church echoed in the Nicene Creed, began with a larger list, following the example of Methodists from over the centuries. According to Richey, "We and they have characterized Methodism not with a tight creedal or confessional affirmation but with an array of characteristics embracing belief, practice, ethos, commitment, lifestyle, and mission."[6]

Their initial efforts composed the following list of Methodist marks as a summary of their research and as an "overview of Methodism" while "continuing Wesleyan commitments and practices": scriptural, episcopal, holy, oral/aural, itinerant, connectional, Arminian, sacramental, reforming/forming, evangelical/missionary, disciplined, and catholic/uniting.[7] A layer of categorization to apply to the latter longer list highlights four other marks that identify distinctive ecclesiological components of Methodism—reforming/forming, sacramental, holy, and episcopal.[8] Additionally, another four, argues Richey, may represent themes consistent with the quadrilateral in Methodist life as they "shape and form all the marks insofar as they work to give expression to a fourfold way of presenting, conveying, knowing, and apprehending": oral/aural (tradition), evangelical/missionary (experience), scriptural (scripture), and Arminian (reason).[9]

An exploration of distinctive marks of the Wesleyan/Methodist tradition may lead to a number of nuances as demonstrated by the discussion above. However, these also represent a basically similar and shared trajectory from a common origin—John Wesley's early Methodist renewal movement within the Church of England. Another formulation from John Wesley of his priority for the movement—specifically the importance of holding doctrine and practices together—is summarized in the following questions: "What to teach; How to teach; and What to do; that is, how to regulate our doctrine, discipline, and practice?"[10] From these questions Richey observes, "Surprisingly there seems to be little inclination among Methodists to go the other way, from the practices and polity of Methodist to their theological meaning."[11] In these questions we recognize a seemingly shared trajectory characteristic of the Wesleyan/Methodist movements over the centuries—a desire to hold together our belief, or doctrines, with our practice in ministry to and with the world.

A Missional/Evangelistic Church

Attention to evangelistic and missional issues thread through literature on ecclesiology or the theological study of the nature and purpose of the church. However, these topics are often subordinated to ecclesiology in discussions of the perceived grander concerns of ecumenism, nature of ministry orders, laity, and sacraments, even relationship between church and state. For contemporary United Methodism, its Wesleyan distinctive strength of disciple-making contributes to its character as a church.

United Methodism's heritage is one of a renewal movement within the Church of England resulting in ambiguity with regard to its ecclesiology as an institutional church. While John Wesley attended to some structural issues within the early Methodist renewal movement, he did not initially intend for Methodism to emerge as a distinctive institutional church. Despite this ambiguity, our heritage as a movement, characterized by a missional imperative to participate in God's reign, is the basis of our identity. While it has been argued that our origins as a movement are lacking in comparison with other ecclesial institutions, our roots as a missional renewal movement are at the heart of our ecclesiology.

Albert Outler, a significant Christian theologian and Wesleyan scholar of the later twentieth century, provocatively asked the potentially unanswerable question, "Do Methodists have a doctrine of the Church?" In Outler's essay of that name, he argues for Methodism's character as an "evangelical order" pursuing renewal in a larger catholic context, finding itself "detraditioned" as a movement turned church.[12] Despite United Methodism's lack of ecclesiology per se, resulting in confusion as to its appropriate contribution to ecumenical conversations, it does not lack an awareness of the primary means through which Christians make sense of faith and discipleship, namely by living into God's reign and gift of salvation. In the closing of one of his essays, Geoffrey Wainwright, another significant Christian theologian and Wesleyan scholar, alludes to the closing words of Outler's essay (mentioned previously), "Every denomination in a divided and broken Christendom is an *ecclesiola in via* [church in pilgrimage], but Methodists have a peculiar heritage that might make the transitive character of our ecclesiastical existence not only tolerable but positively proleptic."[13] Outler, in his concluding statement went on to claim, "what we really have to contribute to any emergent Christian community is not our apparatus but our mission." Outler, highlighting

5

Methodism's missional purpose and vocation as the primary characteristic of our identity, emphasizes, "This business of 'being a church' is really our *chief* business!"[14]

A Worldwide Church

United Methodism is a worldwide church stretching across five continents. One component demonstrating our worldwide nature is the changing demographics of General Conference delegates, including the speaking of numerous languages by those participating in General Conference. French, Portuguese, and Swahili are among those most often needing interpretation of the proceedings, in addition to Russian, among others.[15] Plenary sessions are also translated into Korean, Spanish, Russian, German, and American Sign Language.[16] The largest number of delegates ever from outside the United States—382 of a total 988 (or 39 percent from central conferences)—participated at the 2012 General Conference.[17] This is a number that continues to grow steadily with the increasing membership among United Methodism outside the United States, particularly in Africa, Asia, and Latin America, as well as the decreasing number of United Methodists in the United States. The impact of this worldwide trend on the denomination has been a focus of study by the Committee to Study the Worldwide Nature of The United Methodist Church commissioned by the 2004 and 2008 General Conferences.

The General Conference has continued to consider and work toward a number of proposals related to supporting and enhancing United Methodism's worldwide nature. According to a United Methodist journalist covering the 2012 General Conference, "as the denomination continues to see decline in members in the United States, rethinking policies and structures seems to be a natural step to help the church thrive in all parts of the world."[18] The 2012 *Discipline* included reference to a "Global Book of Discipline" that will expand development of and accessibility to policies and practices across the connection enhancing the existing flexibility extended to central conferences to articulate polity relevant to particular contexts. The 2016 General Conference continued consideration and work toward this "global" or General Book of Discipline, as it will be called. The Standing Committee on Central Conference Matters, initially mentioned in ¶101, in consultation with the Committee on Faith and Order, was charged with bringing "recommendations to the 2016 General Conference as to which parts and paragraphs in Part VI . . . are not subject to change or adaptation."[19] The 2016 General Conference made further recommendations to pursue additional efforts to be considered by the 2020 General Conference.

Another aspect of the 2012 General Conference's effort toward a worldwide nature of the church is the establishment of a Central Conference Theological Education Fund, ¶817, and the organization of Associations of United Methodist Theological Schools outside the United States. These developments support existing, and will facilitate further efforts in, theological education and pastoral formation in central conferences. Work to enhance our worldwide nature also includes plans to revise the Social Principles to better reflect the concerns of the broader connection beyond the United States. A central conference covenant litany, printed in the 2012 *Discipline*, ¶125, describes our shared affirmations and commitments to the unity of Christ, participating in God's mission as full partners in relationships of mutuality.[20] This is a crucial time in the life of United Methodism. How we respond as a denomination to the opportunities and challenges of our worldwide nature will have a significant impact on our ongoing Christian witness both globally and locally.

A Connectional Church

United Methodism embodies characteristics of a connectional church in its polity and organization. For example, local churches have roots in the religious societies in Wesley's Methodist renewal movement in both Britain and the United States that were connected with one another on a circuit within annual conference(s). Itinerating preachers appointed by an itinerating superintendency of district superintendents and bishops continue to serve local churches. Those annual conferences are now connected in jurisdictional and central conferences governed by the General Conference and supported by numerous general councils, boards, and agencies from the constitutionally created

Judicial Council and Council of Bishops to the Connectional Table and General Boards of Higher Education and Ministry, Discipleship, and Global Ministries, not to mention the General Council on Finance and Administration and The United Methodist Publishing House, among many others. The *Discipline* defines the term *connectionalism* when describing the general agencies of the denomination:

> [Connectionalism] is a vital web of interactive relationships (¶132) that includes the agencies of the Church, as defined in ¶¶701.2 and 701.3, with the purpose of equipping local churches for ministry and by providing a connection for ministry throughout the world, all to the glory of God. It provides us with wonderful opportunities to carry out our mission in unity and strength.[21]

According to the *Discipline*, "connectionalism is an important part of our identity as United Methodists."[22] More will be said in a later chapter, but general councils and agencies represent connectionalism as an expression of General Conference powers in their work to implement and fulfill the mission of the church.[23] The chapters that follow explore a variety of components of United Methodist polity and connection.

The language of connection—or "connexion"—dates to usage by John Wesley to describe the character of the early Methodist renewal movement. The early Methodist renewal movement seems to have relied on three convictions: "Christ died for all (so mission is the primary imperative), all are called to holy living (hence the discipline and the need for oversight), and there is no such thing as solitary religion (hence the societies and all that is designed to sustain them)."[24] Wesley used the term *connexion* to refer to at least three layers of relationships within the movement for which he was the center as well as the authority— members, societies, and preachers—with a later addition of the conference.[25] Several pragmatic attributes such as the development of band and class meetings, itineracy, rules, hymns, sermons, and *Notes upon the New Testament* as well as other publications in Wesley's Christian Library supported this connexion. Eventually, particularly for Methodism in America, the trust clause was carried over from Wesley's implementation of the deed of trust, ensuring the ownership and use of facilities would remain held in trust for the annual conference, building upon what are now called doctrinal standards including the Articles of Religion (revised and amended to twenty-five by Wesley).[26]

In the United States, Methodism's connection continues to represent multiple complex, yet related, themes, predominantly relationships such as itineracy, superintendency, organizational structure from classes to conferences, and discipline—eventually the *Book of Discipline* and worship practices.[27] For Russell Richey, United Methodism institutionalizes three competing structures of connectionalism from Wesley's time: superintendency and appointment-making, legislative decision-making authority of the conference, and organizational work in agencies.[28] In this way, connectionalism continues to lack a simplicity and clarity to inform a consistent use of the term and facilitate understanding of the concept it represents.

Methodists have continued to speak of themselves and their church as a connection even after a motion to expunge the language of connection from the *Discipline* at the 1816 General Conference (the first following the death of Francis Asbury (1745–1816), en route to the gathering). Richey argues this simple motion may "symbolize Methodists' inability and/or lack of desire adequately to draw out the rich implications of their connectionalism either for themselves or for the larger Christian community."[29] At our best, United Methodism embodies a connectionalism that is both organizational and functional as well as theological and eschatological—connecting the ministry and mission of the denomination to the unfolding reign of God.

Conclusion

It is my hope that by reading this book one may better understand United Methodist polity and organization as well as appreciate our eclectic roots. I also hope this book facilitates an ongoing connection between United Methodist governance and organization with our beliefs and mission enabling one to understand these through a theological frame. United Methodism's distinctive character, linking Christian belief and practice within its Wesleyan heritage as a renewal movement, presents significant opportunities for our shared witness in the world.

PART I

UNITED METHODIST BELIEFS: DOCTRINAL AND THEOLOGICAL FOUNDATIONS

– Chapter One –

The Nature and Mission of the Church

John and Charles Wesley did not intend the early Methodist renewal movement within the Church of England to become a separate ecclesial entity, which at times leads some to describe Methodist ecclesiology as deficient. However, at other times the emergence of Methodism in America is commended for its heritage as a renewal movement, particularly the claim that Methodism developed from a missional imperative rather than from doctrinal disputes similar to the origins of other Protestant denominations.[1] As mentioned in the introduction, Methodism's evangelistic character and missional heritage contribute significantly to its identity as church, or ecclesiology. When considering the nature and mission of the church, this evangelistic and missional character also shapes United Methodism's distinctiveness. This chapter describes the heart of United Methodism's identity as church—its nature and mission—offering a constructive theological commentary for faithful ecclesial practices of disciple-making.

Nature of the Church

The nature of The United Methodist Church can at times seem elusive. According to Bishop Scott Jones, "One of the least well-defined areas of United Methodist doctrine is its ecclesiology."[2] United Methodist ecclesiology exhibits tensions between our mixed heritage from Catholic and Protestant roots—namely its roots as a renewal movement and the emphasis placed on doctrine.[3] Albert Outler's question mentioned in the introduction, "Do Methodists have a doctrine of the Church?" echoes and sometimes haunts conversations regarding Methodist ecclesiology. Outler offers an accurate, but ambiguous, response, "The answer 'yes' says too much; 'no' says too little. 'In a manner of speaking,' which is more nearly accurate than the other two, seems nevertheless equivocal."[4] John Wesley's passion and commitment for church renewal as well as his imperative to "spread scriptural holiness" offer a complementing refrain, if not a direct response, to questions like Outler's. Jones explains this creative tension and characterizes United Methodist ecclesiology as a "means of grace": "United Methodist ecclesiology and understanding of the means of grace is practical. From a firm base in a traditional Anglican approach, the Church makes adaptations to enhance its mission."[5]

Richard Heitzenrater also responds to Outler's question by describing the church as a means of grace in an effort to align the being of the church, or what it "is," and the practices of the church, or what it "does."[6] The means of grace in Wesleyan tradition acknowledge the presence and accessibility of God's grace for those participating in individual or communal practices.[7] The church is the primary location in which one lives out one's faith, as a participant in a community of faith and member of the body of Christ. Jones explains that the church may be best understood "as both a means of grace in itself and as the locus where God's grace is most consistently found."[8] As Jones describes, the church is the place where, through worship, prayer and the sacraments, one's understanding of Christian doctrine and its embodiment is formed and challenged.[9] From the proclamation of the gospel to its demonstration in words and actions with other members of the body of Christ and those outside the church God seeks to include in God's reign, the church at its best functions as a, though not the only, means of God's grace.[10] The United Methodist Church's character as a means of grace includes much, if not all, of its organization and polity. While these may falter in specific circumstances, throughout history the formation of the denomination's structure has kept its missional purpose at the center. For example, the structure of annual conferences, the episcopacy, the itineracy, ordination, and general boards may be understood as prudential means of grace.[11] As Jones points out, "No church is required to have any of these [structures],"[12] yet these have largely served to facilitate United Methodism's, and its predecessors', participation in the reign of God.

For United Methodists, there are a number of doctrinal materials that lend texture and depth to our understanding of the nature of The United Methodist Church. Among The United Methodist Church's doctrinal standards are two historic documents in which the nature of the church is described—"The Articles of Religion" and "The Confession of Faith of The Evangelical United Brethren Church." These documents, both among United Methodism's constitutionally protected doctrinal standards, will be discussed in more detail in the next chapter. The specific descriptions of church from these documents and our doctrinal heritage demonstrate the tension referred to earlier by Jones: "The first place where this tension shows up is in the different senses of the word 'church' used in the constitutional standards."[13] These references to the nature of the church provide a frame within which to consider biblical and practical theological components of the church's nature.

The earliest doctrinal resource describing the church for United Methodists, with the exception of scripture and the creeds of the early church, are "The Articles of Religion of The Methodist Church." "The Articles of Religion" date to medieval England during the reigns of Henry VIII and Elizabeth I and the establishment of the Church of England. In Article XIII, "Of the Church," the definition of church emphasizes the "visible" church.[14]

Article XIII—Of the Church

The visible church of Christ is a congregation of faithful men in which the pure Word of God is preached, and the Sacraments duly administered according to Christ's ordinance, in all those things that of necessity are requisite of the same.[15]

In addition to acknowledging the visible church as a means of grace, this description highlights three marks: (1) a body of faithful

15

persons, (2) where the word of God is preached, and (3) the sacraments administered.[16] As discussed earlier, these "marks" indicate ways in which the community of faith, or local church, functions as a means of grace through its gathering in worship to hear the scriptures preached and to participate in the sacraments of baptism and the Lord's Supper.

The Evangelical United Brethren "Confession of Faith" dates to the early nineteenth century with the leadership of Jacob Albright (1759–1808) and George Miller of The Evangelical Association and Philip William Otterbein (1726–1813) as well as Christian Newcomer and Christopher Grosch of the United Brethren in Christ.[17] In Article V, "The Church," similar themes occur to Article XIII above, but with additional components including the Nicene Creed's reference to the four marks of the church and the role of the Holy Spirit.

Article V—The Church

We believe the Christian Church is the community of all true believers under the Lordship of Christ. We believe it is one, holy, apostolic and catholic. It is the redemptive fellowship in which the Word of God is preached by men divinely called, and the sacraments are duly administered according to Christ's own appointment. Under the discipline of the Holy Spirit the Church exists for the maintenance of worship, the edification of believers and the redemption of the world.[18]

This article from "The Confession of Faith" does not mention the qualification of "visible" in relation to the church. However, it does echo the marks of a community of believers, the importance of the preaching of the word of God, and the administration of the sacraments similar to Article XIII.[19] The article from "The Confession of Faith" includes the four marks of the church from the Nicene Creed informed by the New Testament: "We believe it is one, holy, apostolic and catholic."[20] This article also articulates the role of the Holy Spirit "for the maintenance of worship, the edification of believers and the redemption of the world," demonstrating a distinctiveness of the Wesleyan and Evangelical United Brethren traditions of practical divinity or the integration of belief and practice.

Taken together, according to Jones, "Article XIII and Confession V are best understood to be speaking of the 'Church universal, which is one Body in Christ' of which the United Methodist Church understands itself to be a part."[21] United Methodism declares a number of basic Christian affirmations in the *Book of Discipline* that link its identity as church in communion with other Christians.[22] These include belief in the triune God—Father, Son, and Holy Spirit—as well as the biblical witness to God's activity and the church universal.[23] The *Discipline* highlights the following affirmations:

- "We hold in common with all Christians a faith in the mystery of salvation in and through Jesus Christ."

- "We share the Christian belief that God's redemptive love is realized in human life by the activity of the Holy Spirit, both in personal experience and in the community of believers."

- "We understand ourselves to be part of Christ's universal church when by adoration, proclamation, and service we become conformed to Christ."

- "With other Christians we recognize that the reign of God is both a present and future reality."

- "We share with many Christian communions a recognition of the authority of Scripture in matters of faith, the confession that our justification as sinners is by grace through faith, and the sober realization that the church is in need of continual reformation and renewal."[24]

In both Article XIII and Article V the administration of the sacraments are mentioned as a constitutive part of the church's identity. Though discussing in detail the administration and theology of the sacraments of baptism and the Lord's Supper is not in the purview of this project, it is important to acknowledge their role in vital communities of faith. Among the means of grace, both sacraments are outward and visible signs of inward and spiritual grace.[25] Indeed, the liturgies of the sacraments give voice to the missional themes of Wesley's early Methodist renewal movement within the Church of England. From *The United Methodist Hymnal,* we are commissioned into this missional imperative in the baptismal liturgies, "With God's help we will proclaim the good news and live according to the example of Christ."[26]

United Methodist ecclesiology may initially seem elusive. However, it is deeply rooted in the soil of Christian doctrine and practice. A distinctive characteristic of United Methodism and its predecessors, Wesleyan traditions agilely hold together an integration of belief and practices that consistently reflects upon both in light of its identity and mission in the midst of a broken world longing for hope, which the gospel of Jesus Christ can bring. According to Jones, "with mission at the heart of its life, the United Methodist Church understands the church to be sent into the world to bear witness to the reign of God there."[27]

Mission of the Church

The mission of the Church is to make disciples of Jesus Christ for the transformation of the world. Local churches and extension ministries provide the most significant arena through which disciple-making occurs.

—*2016 Discipline,* ¶120

The mission of The UMC appears in the *Discipline* at the opening of part IV, "The Ministry of All Christians." Its mention of the local churches' and extension ministries' roles in the mission of the church offers an example of United Methodism's distinctive ecclesiology and implicitly acknowledges our connectional character. Similar to John Wesley's renewal movement within the Church of England, while thousands attended occasions for Methodist field preaching, the vast majority of those converted into Christian faith and discipleship participated in religious societies, or small groups called class and band meetings.[28] The mission statement does not explicitly mention the place of local churches within the connectional structure of the denomination, though this too has been a distinctive characteristic of Wesleyan/Methodist traditions about which it may be argued, facilitates access to broader and deeper resources than a congregational polity.

In the following paragraph, a "Rationale for Our Mission" immediately follows "The Mission" providing a frame, with allusions to scripture, within which to better understand "The Mission." For example, the "Rationale for Our Mission" begins,

> The mission of the Church is to make disciples of Jesus Christ for the transformation of the world by proclaiming the good news of God's grace and by exemplifying Jesus' command to love God and neighbor, thus seeking the fulfillment of God's reign and realm in the world.[29]

This statement expands upon the scriptural reference from Matthew 28:16-20 in "The Mission," adding another reference to Matthew 22:37 and 39 as well as scriptural themes of God's grace and the fulfillment of God's reign. The following statement in the "Rationale" also includes a direct reference to scripture: "The fulfillment of God's reign and realm in the world is the vision Scripture holds before us."[30] In the next several pages we will explore a few key themes from scripture found in "The Mission."

As mentioned previously, "The Mission" is most directly informed by the scripture text of Matthew 28:16-20, also known as the "The Great Commission":

> Now the eleven disciples went to Galilee, to the mountain where Jesus told them to go. When they saw him, they worshipped him, but some doubted. Jesus came near and spoke to them, "I've received all authority in heaven and on earth. Therefore, go and make disciples of all nations, baptizing them in the name of the Father and of the Son and of the Holy Spirit, teaching them to obey everything that I've commanded you. Look, I myself will be with you every day until the end of this present age.

Though Matthew's commission text is the most well known of the gospel commissions, each of the four gospels, as well as Acts, includes a commission text.[31] Each of these texts fulfills a similar purpose, to commission Jesus's disciples to continue the Christian mission and participate in God's reign, while featuring distinctive themes. A number of key themes appear in Matthew's commission including: (1) discipling, (2) the nations (or Gentiles), by (3) baptizing and teaching all Jesus commanded.

Discipling in Matthew 28

The language of discipling often seems to indicate the role current Christian disciples are called to play in discipling new Christians. This is not an inaccurate understanding of the term as it is often used. However, such an interpretation does sometimes overlook or misunderstand the role God plays in Christian discipling. Sarah Lancaster provides an insightful perspective on God's role in Christian discipling in her reflections upon John Wesley's commentary on Matthew 28:19 in his *Explanatory Notes upon the New Testament*.[32] According to Lancaster, the Greek verb, *mathēteuein*, which is often translated into English "to make disciples" or literally "to disciple," indicates an integrative practice performed by God with those responding to God's call.[33] Those responding to God's call are invited by God to share the message of salvation in Jesus Christ through the Holy Spirit with God, the primary actor in salvation.

"Nations" or "Gentiles"?

A second theme from Matthew's commission echoes a concern articulated in the "Rationale for Our Mission": respectful ministry practices among those of other religious faiths. The "Rationale for Our Mission," quoted above, continues with the following statements: "The United Methodist Church affirms that Jesus Christ is the Son of God, the Savior of the world, and the Lord of all. As we make disciples, we respect persons of all religious faiths and we defend religious freedom for all persons."[34] Respect for persons of all religious faiths and no faith is an important component of our ministry practices. Indeed, even an unintentional lack of respect can undermine one's intended message and gestures of hospitality to the Christian faith. In the following paragraphs we will explore the implications of the language in Matthew 28:19a for faithful and respectful discipling practices.

Though the majority of exegetes translate the phrase *panta ta ethnē* as "all nations," there is no clear consensus on this point. A significant, and persuasive, minority translates the phrase as "all Gentiles." This seemingly slight shift leads to a number of interpretations, ranging from reading the commission in Matthew as a mandate to travel across geographic distances to evangelize nations and cultures different from our own, to signaling that the time for evangelizing Israel has past and the church's efforts must be to the Gentiles and no longer to the Jews.[35] Though the current discussions lack unanimity, the depth of exegetical and theological reflection offers some helpful guidance to encourage discipling practices that respect persons from other religious faiths as described in the *Discipline*.[36]

In Matthew's commission, those to be discipled are described as *panta to ethnē* (all the nations).[37] This use of *ethnē*, the plural of the singular *ethnos*, which in the Septuagint is the normal rendering of *gōyim* (nations), often indicates a sociological or ethnological description.[38] Therefore, most translations in Matthew of "all nations" take on the meaning of separate ethnic or cultural societies. However, some scholars have demonstrated that usage of the plural *gōyim* and *ethnē* in later Old Testament texts indicates instead an almost exclusive religo-ethical usage, not for nations, but for Gentiles in contrast to Jews.[39] In these later texts, *Jew* was understood primarily as religious rather than as a sociological or ethnic description.

According to David Bosch, an influential biblical scholar and missiologist of the later twentieth century, the ambiguity in translating *panta to ethnē* rests in the final term, which can mean "nations" or "Gentiles," so that the meaning may not be discerned through word-equivalency alone; reflection upon context and usage is also needed.[40] Some studies demonstrate that *ethnē* in Matthew 28:19 would most likely not describe separate ethnic units but rather all the Gentiles as distinct from the Jews on theological grounds. While it could indicate distinctive sociocultural entities, other Greek terms would more closely express this meaning, such as *phylē* (people as a national unit of common descent), *laos* (people as a political unit with a common history;

this is the Greek word most frequently used for the Jews as a people), and *glōssa* (people as a linguistic unit).[41]

Throughout Matthew's narrative there is a foreshadowing of the Gentile mission beginning with significant figures in the genealogy pericope: Abraham, Rahab, and Ruth.[42] The initial mission in Matthew 10:5b-6 restricts the disciples to Israel: "Don't go among the Gentiles [*ethnon*] or into a Samaritan city. Go instead to the lost sheep, the people of Israel." However, there is a hint that this restriction will be lifted in the narrative of the Canaanite woman who challenges the restriction with her faith.[43] As Amy-Jill Levine points out, "Matthew creates a harmonious narrative by matching the reference to 'Emmanuel,' which means 'God is with us' in chapter 1 to the final verse in chapter 28, 'I am with you always,' so the references to Gentiles prior to Jesus's birth in chapter 1 are matched with the mission to the Gentiles made explicit in the Gospel's penultimate verse."[44] The combination of *panta* and *ethnē* creates a nuanced meaning of "the entire world of humanity," indicating a mission, not "people by people" but one that reaches far beyond the confines of understanding.[45] An inclusivity, similarly, qualifies the Jews as no longer the primary target of mission with the commission in Matthew 28.[46]

Many working in postcolonial theory and historical studies perceive the Great Commission and its standard interpretations in the contemporary context as contributing factors to the complexities, and often evils, of colonialism.[47] Arguably, since the Middle Ages, "mission" was largely accomplished through the expansion and acquisition of territory by Christian nations, though historically Matthew 28:19a did not directly inform such strategies. Musa Dube, criticizing such an interpretation and use of the commission in Matthew to condone less than faithful practices of discipleship, asserts that it has wrongly

> give[n] Christians an unrestricted passport to enter all nations . . . without any consultation whatsoever with the nations in question . . . without any suggestion that they must also in turn *learn* from all nations. . . . Ultimately, the Great Commission dismisses any relationship of reciprocity between Christian disciples and those nations being entered and discipled.[48]

22

The commission in Matthew when read exegetically and theologically in light of the gospel as a whole provides a frame for faithful, and respectful, Christian practices in sharp contrast to those destructive practices perpetrated by some in the name of Jesus Christ and the mission of the church.

Jesus's Commandments

The two activities named by Jesus in Matthew's commission are baptizing (in the name of the Trinity) and teaching (everything Jesus commanded the disciples). Although baptism is a sacrament and with its remembrance an essential practice within the life of the Church that will be discussed further in chapter 4, Jesus's instructions to teach provide a helpful context within which to reflect upon his commandments and are the focus of this section. In addition to its prescription in the commission text, the practice of teaching is central to the gospel of Matthew.[49] Jesus is described in Matthew 7:29 as the teacher with authority. He is often referred to as rabbi, or teacher. In addition to Jesus's role as teacher, the gospel of Matthew is organized into five teaching lessons. In Matthew, these teaching lessons alternate Jesus's teachings on the reign of God with Jesus's actions and ministry in the reign, demonstrating "kingdom" living. For example, in Matthew 5–7 Jesus gives the Sermon on the Mount, including the Beatitudes. In Matthew 8–9 Jesus comes down from the mountain with the crowds following him. He is then confronted by many in need of healing. Jesus responds to these needs with numerous miracles.[50]

To what is Jesus referring when he commands the disciples to teach "them to obey everything that I've commanded you?" Jesus offers a summary. In Matthew, a Pharisee poses the (trick) question to Jesus, "What is the greatest commandment in the Law?" To which Jesus replies, "*You must love the Lord your God with all your heart, and with all your being, and with all your mind.* This is the first and greatest commandment. And the second is like it: *You must love your neighbor as you love yourself.* All the Law and the Prophets depend on these two commands" (Matthew 22:34-40). Jesus's commission in Matthew to make disciples has a didactic or catechetical emphasis, encouraging persons to love God and neighbor.[51]

Matthew begins with a presupposition: Disciples are not born; they are made—and even more disciples are not made in a week, or month, or even a year—disciples are cultivated over a lifetime.[52] Additionally, disciples are not made merely by human efforts. Disciples are made by God, and often we are invited to participate. Discipleship according to Matthew is more than intellectual knowledge of orthodoxy—right doctrines.[53] For the ancient Greeks and us, teaching tends to concentrate on knowledge, what we know with our minds. For Matthew, teaching is an appeal to a person's will for a concrete decision to follow God. Jesus commissions the disciples to teach all that he commanded. For Matthew, this included orthodoxy, or right beliefs/belief in God. However, it also included orthopraxis, or right living/practices. Indeed, faithful orthodoxy is orthopraxis.[54] Word and deed are integrated in Jesus's teaching on the reign of God in Matthew and in each of the Gospels.[55]

The Process for Carrying Out Our Mission

The mission statement of The United Methodist Church and its rationale are followed by a paragraph describing the process for carrying out our mission, in which specific practices are outlined. These practices include proclaiming the gospel and gathering persons into the body of Christ to lead persons to commit their lives to God through baptism and profession of faith in Jesus Christ, nurturing them through worship, the sacraments, and other means of grace.[56]

> We make disciples as we:
> —proclaim the gospel, seek, welcome and gather persons into the body of Christ;
> —lead persons to commit their lives to God through baptism by water and the spirit and profession of faith in Jesus Christ;
> —nurture persons in Christian living through worship, the sacraments, spiritual disciplines, and other means of grace, such as Wesley's Christian conferencing;
> —send persons into the world to live lovingly and justly as servants of Christ by healing the sick, feeding the hungry, caring for the stranger, freeing the oppressed, being and becoming a compassionate, caring

presence, and working to develop social structures that are consistent with the gospel; and

—continue the mission of seeking, welcoming and gathering persons into the community of the body of Christ.[57]

This process not only outlines specific practices, it also outlines a dynamic that may be described as "gathering, going, and gathering again." At times the tendency within the study of mission and evangelism has focused on a traditional notion that evangelism, particularly in the New Testament, functions mainly as a centrifugal dynamic of "going out." While this is an important aspect, a merely centrifugal understanding of evangelism does not offer a comprehensive representation of biblical foundations or life in communities of faith in which disciple-making is a defining characteristic.

Mortimer Arias addresses this truncation when he argues for the biblical emphasis on hospitality as a paradigm for missional evangelism, particularly as a distinctive mark of Christians and their communities in the New Testament.[58] Arias explains, "Christian mission from its beginning has been centrifugal mission—going from the center to a periphery in the world. Mission cannot remain at any center, it has to move to new boundaries and frontiers: 'to all peoples everywhere;' 'to the whole world;' 'to the whole creation;' 'to the end of the earth;' and 'to the end of time.'"[59] When many think of God's mission and the church's participation in evangelism, the general dynamic is one of *going*. Yet the dynamic of *gathering* is also modeled, particularly in the Old Testament: "Israel is the missionary people of God, 'the light of the nations,' whose primary mission is not to *go* but to *be* the people of God."[60] However, even in the New Testament, the notion of centripetal mission remains—"by attraction, by incarnation, by being."[61] Indeed, Matthew's commission text, and the description of "The Process for Carrying Out Our Mission," describes the gathering of those participating in discipling, whether new or long standing, in worship, including baptism, and teaching.

A similar recognition of the dual dynamic of centripetal and centrifugal evangelistic practices appears in another recent study. Brad Kallenberg concludes, "Faithfulness in evangelism must simultaneously attend to both the group and the individual."[62] Evangelism informed by biblical foundations includes not just centrifugal proclamation to the individual but centripetal participation in the life of the gathered Christian community. Drawing on insights from postcritical philosophy as well as his campus ministry experience, Kallenberg argues for the essential role of communities in initiating and forming Christian disciples: "The first lesson for evangelism to be gleaned from postcritical philosophy, then, is the importance of embodying the story of Jesus in our communal life. Such a community provides the context that demystifies the gospel by making it concrete."[63] "Simply put," says Kallenberg, "when viewed through a postcritical lens, conversion can be understood as entailing the change of one's social identity, the acquisition of a new conceptual language, and the shifting of one's paradigm."[64]

At least two components foster the acquisition of this new conceptual Christian language. First, "fluency is gained by participation in the linguistic community's *form of life*—that weave of activity, relationships, and speech that gives the community its unique personality."[65] And second, "we learn a conceptual language . . . by means of our community's stockpile of interpretive stories."[66] Christian initiation and formation includes a changed social identity and a new conceptual language facilitated through narratives—the most significant found in biblical texts—as well as activities and relationships cultivated within the gathered community of faith.

Similarly, in the guidance offered in "The Process for Carrying Out Our Mission," United Methodists are encouraged to participate in similar practices of gathering, going, and gathering to gain fluency in a new language and form of life. We begin in worship, gathered to hear the gospel proclaimed, welcoming persons into the body of Christ. In the context of worship and the life of the local church, community of faith, we participate with God to lead persons to commit their lives in faith to God in Jesus Christ through the Holy Spirit. Nurtured in Christian discipleship, through worship, the sacraments, and other means of grace, including spiritual disciplines, we grow in faith together guided by the Holy Spirit. Then, in response to receiving God's grace through worship, sacraments and means of grace, God sends us "into the world to live lovingly and justly as servants of Christ by healing the sick, feeding the hungry, caring for the stranger, freeing the oppressed, being and becoming a compassionate, caring presence, and working to develop social structures that are consistent with the gospel."[67] This dynamic is not necessarily completed, but is ongoing with the gathering of those awakened and initiated into God's reign through the ministries and practices described above to continue life in Christian faith and discipleship together.

A Global and Worldwide Mission

The section on "The Mission and Ministry of the Church" continues with paragraphs on the "The Global Nature of Our Mission" and "Our Mission in the World" as well as "A Companion Litany to Our Covenant for the Worldwide United Methodist Church." These paragraphs and litany emphasize the global nature of our ministry, including the expectation "that all ministries in the Church be shaped by the mission of making disciples of Jesus Christ."[68] Also included is an affirmation of the visible church of Christ for "the worth of all humanity and the value of interrelationship in all of God's creation."[69] Another significant theme in the concluding paragraphs of this section is the connectional nature of United Methodism. According to the *Discipline*,

> Only when we commit ourselves to the interdependent worldwide partnerships in prayer, mission, and worship can connectionalism as the Wesleyan ecclesial vision be fully embodied. Guided by the Holy Spirit, United Methodist churches throughout the world are called afresh into a covenant of mutual commitment based on shared mission, equity, and hospitality."[70]

Though separated by centuries and written for different contexts, the themes articulated in our mission statement, its rationale, process, and global nature in the world echo through the descriptions of church from our doctrinal statements, the Articles of Religion and Confession of Faith, discussed earlier in the chapter. Responding to God's grace, United Methodists seek to embody a Wesleyan integration of belief and practice in which disciple-making within a missional imperative informs our identity as a church in the world. Our connectional nature, originating in Britain and currently stretching across the globe, also continues to hold us accountable and inspire us by a network of witnesses to Jesus Christ in and through which the Holy Spirit enables us to participate in God's reign.

A Companion Litany to Our Covenant for the Worldwide United Methodist Church

Leader: In covenant with God and each other, we affirm our unity in Christ.

People: We will take faithful steps to live as a worldwide church in mission for the transformation of the world.

Leader: In covenant with God and each other, we commit ourselves to be in ministry with all people.

People: In faithfulness to the gospel, we will cross boundaries of language, culture, social or economic status as we grow in mutual love and trust.

Leader: In covenant with God and each other, we participate in God's mission as partners in ministry.

People: We share our God-given gifts, experiences, and resources recognizing that they are of equal value, whether spiritual, financial, or missional.

Leader: In covenant with God and each other, we commit ourselves to full equality.

People: We uphold equity and accountability in our relationships, structures, and responsibilities for the denomination.

Leader: In covenant with God and each other, we enter afresh into a relationship of mutuality.

People: With God's grace, we joyfully live out our worldwide connection in mission for the transformation of the world.[71]

– Chapter Two –

Defining Documents:
Doctrinal Standards

The Wesleyan tradition and The United Methodist Church emerge from a missional imperative.[1] This is distinctive for United Methodism, since other denominational traditions often trace their roots to disagreements regarding confessional or doctrinal matters. In the "Large" *Minutes*, John Wesley summarized his understanding of Methodism's purpose: "What may we reasonably believe to be God's design in raising up the Preachers called 'Methodists'? A. To reform the nation, and in particular the Church, to spread scriptural holiness over the land."[2] This means United Methodism, and the Wesleyan tradition more broadly, affirms basic traditional Christian commitments proceeding from the Church of England of Wesley's day, rather than pursuing a doctrinal distinctiveness from other Christian traditions. In addition to the importance of basic Christian doctrine, this commitment to foundational Christian beliefs deeply informed the practices of the early Methodist movement leading to its impact of renewal.

Wesleyan Roots

Despite their considerable social status, privileged education, and theological formation, the Wesleys did not emphasize a sophisticated set of doctrines for the Methodist movement. Instead, John described a shared desire with his brother Charles in his "A Plain Account of the People Called Methodists," to preach and "to convince those who would hear what true Christianity was and to persuade them to embrace it."[3] John Wesley urged early Methodists to follow "only *common sense* and *Scripture*" but added that in "looking back, [there was generally] something in *Christian antiquity*."[4] This commitment to basic Christian doctrines rooted in scripture and early Christian tradition, in their depth and focus, fed the vitality of the Methodist renewal movement.

The Wesleys "chiefly insisted upon" the following four points:

> First, that orthodoxy, or right opinions, is at best but a very slender part of religion, if it can be allowed to be any part of it at all; that neither does religion consist in negatives, in bare harmlessness of any kind; nor merely in externals, in doing good, or using the means of grace, in works of piety (so called) or of charity: that it is nothing short of or different from the 'mind that was in Christ'; the image of God stamped upon the heart; inward righteousness, attended with the peace of God and 'joy in the Holy Ghost.'
>
> Secondly, that the only way under heaven to this religion is to 'repent and believe the gospel'; or (as the Apostle words it) 'repentance towards God and faith in our Lord Jesus Christ.'
>
> Thirdly, that by this faith, 'he that worketh not, but believeth on Him that justifieth the ungodly, is justified freely by His grace, through the redemption which is in Jesus Christ.'
>
> And, lastly, that 'being justified by faith,' we taste of the heaven to which we are going, we are holy and happy, we tread down sin and fear, and 'sit in heavenly places with Christ Jesus.'[5]

In this way, John Wesley, with Charles, emphasized basic Christian doctrinal foundations as mentioned above—all are made in the image of God and, if they choose to receive it, may have the mind of Christ, repentance, justification, and sanctification, respectively. These doctrines, as described by the Wesleys, resonated with a person's spiritual journey. Similar to the Wesleys' concern for their time and context, contemporary United Methodism would arguably also benefit from prioritizing a deep simplicity of belief accessible to all, rather than complex theological claims.[6]

John Wesley reflects near the end of his ministry in his sermon "Causes of the Inefficacies of Christianity." The sermon opens with the assertion that Christian communities worldwide had done so little good because they produced so few *real* Christians.[7] The sermon continues by outlining three characteristics Christians often lacked: (1) a sufficient understanding of doctrine, (2) adequate discipline, and (3) self-denial. Thus, according to Wesley, an inadequate view of salvation that was confined only to forgiveness of sins, in an antinomian posture, led Christian communities to nurture few real Christians.[8] Similar concerns for how we appropriate belief persist in the contemporary context. Our ability as United Methodist clergy and laity to comprehend and communicate salvation, integrating this understanding with our Christian practices, has a direct impact on our participation in God's reign and the renewal of the church.

From this perspective, and with deep concern for the spiritual well-being of others, John Wesley drew from the standard doctrinal resources of the Church of England—the *Book of Common Prayer*, Catechism, Thirty-Nine Articles of Religion, and the *Book of Homilies*. These materials also informed those he compiled for the Methodists in North America. In Wesley's concern to share and shape doctrinal materials for Methodists in North America, later to become The Methodist Episcopal Church, the materials Wesley sent to America reflected, though with his revisions, the doctrinal materials of the Church of England. For example, Wesley sent the following with Thomas Coke in 1784: "The Sunday Service," *Hymnal*, the Articles of Religion (revised), Catechism, the General Rules, and a selection of John Wesley's *Sermons* as well as his *Explanatory Notes upon the New Testament*.

The following sections describe defining doctrinal documents, specifically constitutional standards, of The United Methodist Church. These documents give a perspective on who we are as a Christian community of faith. Our doctrines provide the primary framework through which we appropriate scripture and the great texts of Christian tradition into a living faith as a church sent in mission to the world.

The Constitution and Restrictive Rules

The Constitution and Restrictive Rules provide a framework from early American Methodism within which to understand those materials they protect and restrict, respectively. The Constitution, though with early American Methodist roots, is a relatively contemporary document that has been revised frequently, almost every four years since 1968, the time of union between The Methodist Church and The Evangelical United Brethren Church to form The United Methodist Church. The Constitution protects key components of the denomination such as the General Conference and other conferences, the episcopacy, itineracy, and clergy members' right to trial. The Restrictive Rules, dating to early American Methodism in their present form, "restrict" the powers granted by the Constitution to the General Conference as well as other denominational bodies, and so on. The Articles of Religion are the oldest of the doctrinal materials, representing a connection with the earliest Church of England and its founders, Henry VIII and Elizabeth I. The Articles of Religion offer a broad map of Christian doctrine rooted in Christian tradition, while the Confession of Faith, from The Evangelical United Brethren Church—a predecessor denomination to United Methodism—gives a description of doctrinal commitments in creedal form. The General Rules, prepared for the united societies of the early Methodist renewal movement in eighteenth-century Britain, demonstrate the importance placed by the Wesleys on the integration of practices and belief. Select sermons of John Wesley and his *Notes upon the New Testament*, though controversial with regard to their doctrinal authority, also serve as doctrinal foundations for United Methodism.

The current Constitution of The United Methodist Church was adopted in 1966 in preparation for the establishment of the formation of one church, resulting from the amalgamation of The Methodist Church and The Evangelical United Brethren Church.[9] The Constitution begins with a preamble describing the church in doctrinal terminology that states: "The church is a community of all true believers under the Lordship of Christ."[10] The preamble also affirms "The church of Jesus Christ exists in and for the world, and its very dividedness is a hindrance to its mission in that world."[11] In this way

32

the Constitution demonstrates the nature and mission of the church in its doctrine and practice.

The Constitution is comprised of five divisions. Division one is "General," establishing the union of the predecessor denominations in The United Methodist Church with mention of the Articles of Religion and Confession of Faith as well as demonstrating the significance of inclusiveness, racial justice, ecumenical relations, and titles to properties held.[12] The following divisions are "Organization"—within which the Restrictive Rules are included following the subsection on the General Conference—"Episcopal Supervision," "The Judiciary," and "Amendments" respectively. The subject of each of these divisions is expanded upon in the parts of the *Discipline* that follow. The Constitution demonstrates the practical embodiment of our doctrinal commitments in the organization and policies of the denomination contained in the *Discipline* as a whole.

One way to understand the level of authority granted to specific doctrinal standards within United Methodism is the difficulty and complexity of the process required to alter them.[13] As the Constitution of The United Methodist Church establishes, and upon which the *Discipline* expands in more detail, the General Conference is the only authoritative body empowered to speak for the denomination. In balance, the Restrictive Rules, first implemented in 1808 with the first Constitution by The Methodist Episcopal Church, restrict the activity of the General Conference through constraints on that power. With regard to doctrinal authority, the Restrictive Rules, specifically the first, second, and fifth, prevent the General Conference from revising, adding, or deleting doctrinal standards "without a three-fourths approving vote of the aggregate number of annual conference members."[14]

The doctrinal standards possessing the highest level of authority may be referred to as "constitutional standards."[15] These include the Articles of Religion (protected by the first Restrictive Rule), Confession of Faith (protected by the second Restrictive Rule), General Rules (protected by the fifth Restrictive Rule), and the Constitution. Additionally, the Constitution and General Rules may only be changed with a two-thirds approving vote of the annual conference members.[16] Notably, there has been no vote or action within The Methodist Episcopal

Church or traditions stemming from it to revise the constitutionally protected doctrinal standards including the General Rules.[17] Though our constitutional standards are clearly distinct from one another in substance, they share authority both in their protection by the Constitution as well as their significance for the constancy of teaching within the Methodist tradition.

The Articles of Religion are formally recognized as doctrine of The United Methodist Church, protected by the Constitution, and they serve as one of our doctrinal foundations. The Constitution also protects the Evangelical United Brethren Confession of Faith and John Wesley's General Rules for the United Societies, which will be discussed in the following pages. Each of these foundational resources emerges from a particular chapter in the story leading to the formation of The United Methodist Church.

"A Sufficient Understanding of Doctrine": Articles of Religion

Most of the Articles of Religion were initially composed during the sixteenth-century English Reformation when Henry VIII (1491–1547) took the first major step in separating the Church in England from the Church of Rome and establishing it under the English monarch. With the Act of Supremacy in 1534, Henry was declared head of both the church and the state, and the Church of England was proclaimed the official religion of the country and an integral part of the political structure. Matters concerning the church—including doctrine, structure, and policy—had to pass through parliament,[18] and so church and state affairs were closely intertwined. Even today, bishops from the Church of England serve as "Lords Spiritual" in the House of Lords, the upper house of the British parliament.

Theologically the Henrician church was not typically "Protestant" in the Lutheran or Calvinist sense. The first official statement of the English faith, the Ten Articles of Religion (1536), was relatively brief and did not include the familiar Protestant bias against transubstantiation and celibacy of the clergy. The two most notable changes in the transition from the Church *in* England to the Church *of* England were in polity and liturgy—the monarch not the pope was head of the church, and the service was to be read in English not Latin. Also during Henry's reign, the composition of the Six Articles in 1539, a revision of an earlier doctrinal statement, reflects the proximity of the Henrician church to the Roman Catholic traditional doctrines, reaffirming transubstantiation and the need for a celibate clergy.[19]

In 1559, Elizabeth I achieved, with remarkable savvy, the Elizabethan Settlement, which consisted of a series of parliamentary acts defining the relationship between the English crown and the church. Through this settlement, Elizabeth sought to protect the established church from the traditional claims of Roman Catholicism on the one side as well as from the radical reform, and often Calvinist Protestant, tendencies of the Puritans on the other. This stance is referred to as the *via media* or "middle way" between Rome and Geneva. Elizabeth was above all politically astute realizing that a unified country would be a more stable country and a stronger country in diplomatic and military affairs.[20]

Elizabeth procured a new Act of Supremacy in 1559 that established her as the head of state and "supreme governor," not head, of the church, learning from her father's difficulties. The Act of Uniformity (1559) defined the standards for liturgy and doctrine requiring the church to use the *Book of Common Prayer* and the clergy and other officials to subscribe to the Thirty-Nine Articles of Religion as well as providing a standard exposition of accepted teachings in an enlarged *Book of Homilies*.[21]

The Thirty-Nine Articles developed during Elizabeth's reign informed the Church of England in John Wesley's day and were the immediate predecessors to the Articles of Religion of United Methodism. Moving to their role in American Methodism, to equip the emerging church in North America, John Wesley drew from the Thirty-Nine Articles and sent a revised version, along with the "Sunday Service" (Wesley's abridgment of the *Book of Common Prayer*),[22] to the American colonies in 1784. John Wesley revised the Thirty-Nine Articles of the Church of England, deleting fifteen articles[23] and altering the text of nine.[24] An article was later added by the 1784 Conference and another was revised prior to 1808 by The Methodist Episcopal Church; however, fourteen remain unchanged from the original text.[25] According to Bishop Scott Jones it is not easy to determine the reasons or motivations for Wesley's editorial decisions, though his revisions frequently followed three possibilities: "On some occasions, he did not agree with the author's views and excised statements that he did not want to reprint. In other cases, he regarded the content as important but thought it could be said more cogently. In still other cases, he regarded the material as superfluous and thought it did not need to be reprinted for the intended audience, even though he did not object to it."[26]

As we have noted, Wesley based the teaching of the early Methodist revival in an uncomplicated Christianity grounded in "scriptural doctrines contained in the Thirty-Nine Articles, the Homilies, and the *Book of Common Prayer*" of the Church of England. Wesley continued to embody a "middle way." Many scholars, including Albert Outler, have described Methodism as an "evangelical Catholicism."

American Methodism contains its own distinctive emphases that also reflect the contribution of the Evangelical United Brethren strand of the tradition. These are particularly expressed by Philip William Otterbein of the Church of the United Brethren in Christ and Jacob Albright of The Evangelical Association tradition.[27] The Wesleyan movement, United Brethren in Christ, and Evangelical Association emphasize Christian life—faith put into practice.[28] This distinctiveness may offer a frame through which to view and better understand the Articles of Religion and Confession of Faith. United Methodism emphasizes a combination of doctrines—grace, justification, and sanctification as well as the creating, redeeming, and sanctifying activity of God.[29] The distinctiveness of Methodist doctrine may be described in three categories: saving doctrine, biblical doctrine, and practical doctrine.[30] In faith, individuals and the church respond to God's activity participating in God's mission in service to the world.

The Confession of Faith of The Evangelical United Brethren Church

The Confession of Faith adopted in 1962 is an integration of the United Brethren in Christ Confession of Faith, dating to its earliest form composed by Philip William Otterbein in 1789, and the Articles of Religion of The Evangelical Association, initially led by Jacob Albright, dating from 1809.[31] The Conference of 1807 charged Albright with preparing doctrinal articles. However, he died prior to their completion.[32] George Miller assumed the task, recommending the 1809 Conference adopt a German translation of the Methodist Articles of Religion with the addition of an article "Of the Last Judgment" borrowed from the Augsburg Confession.[33] A number of other revisions occurred throughout the nineteenth century resulting in nineteen articles.[34] The Evangelical United Brethren Confession of Faith, brought without revision to the union with The Methodist Church in 1968, is a revision of the Confession of Faith adopted in 1962 by the newly amalgamated church formed by the union of The Evangelical Association and the United Brethren in Christ in 1946.[35]

The most recent revision process culminating in 1962 was initiated by the 1958 General Conference and led by the Board of Bishops, who invited input initially from four respected theologians within the denomination. Feedback from a fifth theologian, Professor L. Harold DeWolf of Boston University School of Theology, was also invited. DeWolf's input represented a respected theological voice from The Methodist Church with whom The Evangelical United Brethren Church was in discernment regarding a future union.[36] Those invited to offer input then expanded to a select group of ecclesial leaders from which fifty responded.[37] The new Confession was adopted by General Conference in 1962 with discussion on the floor and relatively friendly amendments submitted in writing to the bishops for consideration and inclusion.[38]

The Evangelical United Brethren Confession of Faith continues to use the language of "We believe . . . ," providing a "terse, less technical, and earthy" expression as compared with the Articles of Religion, which are "formal, more reflective of technical language . . . and less capable of being understood by the lay folk."[39] The Confession of Faith's language, for some, falls within the genre of creed. United Methodism, based on its doctrinal standards, is technically a *creedal* church since included in constitutionally protected doctrinal materials is the Confession of Faith from The Evangelical United Brethren Church. However, according to the *Discipline*, within the Wesleyan and related traditions such creeds were not employed as a reductionistic confessional formula and therefore a doctrinal test.[40] There are layers to our doctrinal expressions that allow for connection to Christian tradition and ongoing discernment and deliberation of theological concepts and commitments, as will be discussed in the following chapter.

Though distinct in a number of ways, "both the Confession of Faith and the Articles of Religion provided a link with the apostolic, universal church. Both were received as summations of Scripture and as guidelines to its use."[41] Both documents describe the basic and essential loci of Christian doctrine. According to Jason Vickers, three key theological differences exist: (1) The Confession of Faith's article on the Holy Spirit (Article III) represents a significant expansion from the description of its parallel in the Articles of Religion (Article IV). In the former, the Article moves beyond the intratrinitarian relationships to include implications for relationship with humanity.[42] (2) As discussed in the previous chapter, the Confession of Faith's article on the church (Article V) is substantially longer than the same material in the Articles of Religion. The Confession of Faith adds the Nicene marks, "one, holy, apostolic and catholic" and stresses the Holy Spirit's relationship to the church.[43] (3) The Confession of Faith, unlike the Articles of Religion, includes an article on sanctification and Christian perfection.[44] Interestingly, Article XI represents "the most explicit discussion of the historic doctrine of sanctification" in the current United Methodist *Discipline*.[45]

There is an unfortunate tendency among United Methodists to ignore the theological heritage of the Evangelical United Brethren among our doctrinal materials. As Steven O'Malley, a historian of the Evangelical United Brethren, points out, this is shortsighted for at least two reasons: (1) It does not recognize the broader (that is, continental Reformation and Pietist) roots of the movements, and (2) it misses the opportunity to draw on the more distinctive Wesleyan themes present in the Confession of Faith (that is, sanctification and Christian perfection) in contrast to the revised Articles of Religion.[46]

"To Watch Over One Another in Love": The General Rules

In his "Causes of the Inefficacies of Christianity," John Wesley laments the lack of discipline and sustained Christian practice on the part of congregants, deficiencies that contemporary congregations also demonstrate, preferring instead techniques promising immediate results. John, with Charles, facilitated connection within the early Methodist movement, not merely to one another for mutual support and accountability but also to the movement's aim to form believers in holiness of heart and life.[47] John tirelessly claimed that earnest Christian formation would not occur, "without society, without living and conversing with [others]."[48] The distinctiveness of the early Methodist movement was not in its innovation, but in a simple integration of doctrine and practice toward a faithful embodiment of Christianity. This was embodied through an intentionally comprehensive program of preaching and small groups to encourage the bearing of fruit within the lives of Christians (Luke 13:8).

In "A Plain Account of the People Called Methodists," Wesley described and offered a rationale for the organization and practices of the movement, particularly small-group gatherings for Christian formation and nurture.[49] In response to requests for pastoral mentoring, John facilitated regular gatherings of interested persons. These gatherings resembled religious societies common among the Church of England, as well as Pietism, and grew into networks of Methodist communities of faith, called circuits, across Britain.[50] Sometimes referred to broadly as united societies, these gatherings arising initially in Bristol, included class meetings with a further breakdown into penitent, select, and other bands. Class meetings usually consisted of ten to twelve members and were organized geographically. Participants most often adhered to a class meeting as a basic unit for spiritual formation and nurture, then, if inclined, also participated in a band. Bands were smaller gatherings organized around an interest or demographic (for example, young married women, single men, and so on) and provided additional guidance and nurture beyond the class meetings. These small groups, both classes and bands, provided opportunities for early

Methodist laypersons, particularly women and young adults, to assume leadership roles such as leaders, lay assistants, stewards, and visitors of the sick.[51] These small groups provided a context in which most early Methodists experienced conversion to the Christian faith and personally encountered the doctrines of justification and sanctification, facilitated by consistent practices of the means of grace.

In the early Methodist renewal movement led by the Wesleys, laypeople were more influential than preachers or clergy in facilitating significant spiritual experiences such as conviction or awakening, new birth, and sanctification.[52] The most frequent social context for early Methodist conversions was solitude, followed by small groups, not larger preaching occasions.[53] Most individuals began participating in Methodist societies prior to their experience of the new birth. More than half received a spiritual experience (ranging from the subtle to the very dramatic) within the first year.[54]

The General Rules, written by Wesley in 1743 for the united societies, describe the gatherings as "a company of men [and women] having the form and seeking the power of godliness, united in order to pray together, receive words of exhortation, and to watch over one another in love, that they may help each other to work out their salvation."[55] The one condition for admission remained, "a desire to flee from the wrath to come, and to be saved from their sins."[56] Continuance in the societies then required a bearing of fruits facilitated by the following three general rules: (1) by doing no harm and avoiding evil of every kind; (2) by doing good, and (3) by attending upon the ordinances of God.[57]

The "ordinances of God" consisted of what Wesley often referred to as the means of grace. In the context of bands and classes, individuals encouraged one another in their Christian journeys through practices of piety and mercy. Through these practices individuals might come to know faith in the triune God. Works of piety emphasized individual spiritual growth through public and private prayer, scripture study, confession, fasting, and worship. Works of mercy included feeding the hungry, clothing the naked, and visiting the imprisoned, sick, and afflicted. Interestingly, at times Wesley prioritized works of mercy over works of piety.[58] This emphasis was an intentional correction to a tendency in Anglican theology and practice at the time to focus upon works of piety to the exclusion, or minimization, of works of mercy.[59]

The inclusion of the General Rules as doctrine protected by the Constitution is significant and contributes to the distinctiveness of United Methodism. The General Rules and their description as means of grace provide a guide to encourage Christians within The United Methodist Church to practice their faith against the backdrop of their deep doctrinal commitments. Individuals in covenant with their brothers and sisters in Christ nurture their faith in the triune God together through practices of piety, while also serving their neighbors through practices of mercy. The General Rules, while distinct, if not unusual as formally protected by the Constitution, demonstrate the significance of living out one's belief for United Methodists.

Wesley's *Sermons* and *Notes upon the New Testament*

The doctrinal standards previously discussed in this chapter—the Articles of Religion, the Confession of Faith, and the General Rules—are explicitly named as doctrine in the Constitution and its Restrictive Rules. However, there is an area of some discussion. The first Restrictive Rule also refers to "our present existing and established standards of doctrine."[60] The interpretation of this latter clause is disputed, and its meaning continues to provoke debate. A rationale based on the *Discipline*, specifically "Our Doctrinal Heritage," claims this clause includes Wesley's *Standard Sermons* and his *Explanatory Notes upon the New Testament*.[61] Richard Heitzenrater argues that the phrase covers only the Articles of Religion.[62] Bishop Jones argues that the General Conference is the only authoritative arbiter of this discussion, and the General Conference has decided the *Sermons* and *Notes* are included as doctrinal standards. According to the *Discipline*, "Within the Wesleyan tradition, then as now, the *Sermons* and *Notes* furnish models of doctrinal exposition."[63] According to this statement, these texts, with those explicitly named, carry the weight of tradition. An additional premise for the inclusion of Wesley's *Sermons* and *Notes* among the constitutional standards may be acknowledged in the *Discipline* under "Our Doctrinal Heritage":

> In the Plan of Union for The United Methodist Church, the preface to the Methodist Articles of Religion and the Evangelical United Brethren Confession of Faith explains that both were accepted as doctrinal standards for the new church. Additionally, it stated that although the language of the first Restrictive Rule never has been formally defined, Wesley's *Sermons* and *Notes* were understood specifically to be included in our present existing and established standards of doctrine. It also stated that the Articles, the Confession, and the Wesleyan "standards" were "thus deemed congruent if not identical in their doctrinal perspectives and not in conflict." This declaration was accepted by subsequent rulings of the Judicial Council.[64]

The inclusion of Wesley's *Sermons* and *Notes* adds to the complexity of materials among our constitutionally protected doctrinal standards as well as their depth and meaning for Methodist teaching including "Our Theological Task."

While there is merit to including Wesley's *Sermons* and *Notes* among authoritative materials, questions remain. For example, what sermons are to be included? And how to relate select sermons and *Notes* to the constitutional standards when they are not in alignment? "Our Doctrinal History" refers to the origin of using Wesley's *Sermons* as doctrinal standards in the Model Deed of 1763: "preach no other doctrine than is contained in Mr. Wesley's *Notes Upon the New Testament* and four volumes of *Sermons*."[65] Navigating the historical questions surrounding this issue names the difficulty of resolving the ambiguity, arguing the most reliable interpretation is "based on the status of the 'four volumes of sermons' in 1784" that leads to relying upon "the first fifty-three in the *Bicentennial Edition of the Works*."[66]

In any case, and most important, the substance of Wesley's *Sermons* and *Notes* provides explication and interpretation of doctrinal concepts described in the constitutionally protected standards. However, the *Sermons* and *Notes* are not meant to replace, but complement, the current constitutional standards.

42

Conclusion

This chapter outlines those doctrinal materials protected by the Constitution, often referred to as constitutional standards. By placing these, the Articles of Religion, Confession of Faith, General Rules, and Wesley's *Sermons* and *Notes*, in historical context within the Wesleyan tradition as well as reflecting on their content and purpose, the doctrinal standards of United Methodism demonstrate the importance of integrating Christian belief with Christian practice. In United Methodism and its predecessor traditions and denominations, beliefs shape practice, informing our polity and facilitating our mission. The chapter that follows discusses additional documents also carrying doctrinal authority as contemporary statements, including the significance of liturgy through *The Book of Worship* and *Hymnal*. The materials discussed in the next chapter further demonstrate the role of belief in shaping United Methodist practice.

– Chapter Three –

Contemporary Statements: Operational Doctrine

The United Methodist Church is an amalgamation of several traditions and Protestant denominations bringing together a number of doctrinal and other formative documents. Chapter 2 explores documents dating to earlier generations of the Wesleyan and Methodist movement—the Constitution and Restrictive Rules, Articles of Religion, Confession of Faith, General Rules, and John Wesley's *Sermons* and *Notes*—documents that provide an important framework for our doctrinal identity and shape the constitutional standards of our most formal and protected categories. This chapter explores contemporary statements that also shape and inform our theological reflection, life together, and witness in the world.

Contemporary statements are less formal, yet not necessarily less influential. Indeed, the influence of these materials may result in a tendency to treat them as formal doctrine, for example: the Social Principles (all or select) can function in some circumstances as equal in authority to constitutional standards. At times, this can challenge the integrity of our Wesleyan identity and even undermine the vitality of a shared Christian witness. Contemporary statements are intended to be consistent with constitutional standards, building on and appropriating doctrinal foundations toward a faithful witness of the church in the world. Contemporary statements are also protected in that there are processes, of less intensity than for formal materials, required to revise them. Similar to constitutional standards, and perhaps even more so, contemporary statements inform our theological reflection, spiritual formation, and responses to pressing issues. Indeed, these materials may have an even greater impact on our lives in communities of faith and in the world, though they speak most directly to a North American perspective. For example, the Social Principles tend to focus on concerns of more direct interest and impact upon those in the United States. The 2012 General Conference voted to sustain the current language and position on homosexuality, deciding not to add language describing the differences of opinions on the issue within the denomination. The 2016 General Conference invited the Council of Bishops to propose a plan for addressing the incongruities regarding human sexuality within the denomination. The 2016 General Conference voted to affirm the Council of Bishops' plan, which called for a hold on all legislation regarding the human sexuality debate. This decision was made in lieu of the plan that would call for the Council of Bishops to also appoint a study commission to reflect upon ecclesial unity in light of the debate and a possible special General Conference session to convene prior to 2020. Meanwhile, some in central conferences are more concerned with the practice of polygamy, which is not currently mentioned in the Social Principles. There is an ongoing effort to revise the Social Principles to enhance its representation of the worldwide church, which will be brought before a future General Conference. Another example is *The United Methodist Hymnal*, composed by an appointed body and approved by General Conference; it significantly affects the worship life of most, if not all, congregations, particularly in the United States. In this way, the *Hymnal*, as well as the other materials discussed below, operates as doctrine, even if at first glance a collection of hymns would not appear as constituting a doctrinal statement.

Additional sections of the *Discipline* beyond the Constitution and formal doctrinal standards are the focus of this chapter, including (1) "Our Doctrinal Heritage," "Our Doctrinal History," and "Our Theological Task"; (2) the Social Creed, Social Principles, and the *Book of Resolutions*; and (3) liturgical resources—*The United Methodist Hymnal* and *The United Methodist Book of Worship*. (Although the section "Ministry of All Christians" is technically a component of our contemporary statements, this material is discussed in chapters 1 and 4.) These materials also are intended to serve as doctrinal statements, though relatively more contemporary. However, unlike the constitutional standards, they are not placed in the *Discipline* with the same apparent rationale, but rather in a variety of locations.[1] In addition to these contemporary statements included in the *Discipline*, at least two documents also provide a similar function, though these will not be discussed in detail: (1) "This Holy Mystery," a document produced by a study commission, describes the denomination's understanding and practices of the Lord's Supper; and (2) "By Water and the Spirit," also produced by a study commission, describes the denomination's understanding and practices of baptism. A third study reflecting on ecclesiology has produced a document entitled "Wonder, Love, and Praise" to be considered at the 2020 General Conference.

Our Doctrinal Heritage, History, and Theological Task

These sections of the *Discipline*—"Our Doctrinal Heritage" and "Our Doctrinal History" followed by "Our Theological Task"—appear in close proximity in the *Discipline*. "Our Doctrinal Heritage"[2] appears before "Our Doctrinal History,"[3] and both come immediately before "Our Doctrinal Standards and General Rules,"[4] our constitutional standards or formal doctrine, discussed in chapter 1. "Our Doctrinal Heritage" and "Our Doctrinal History" introduce Part III, "Doctrinal Standards and Our Theological Task," providing a historical frame for understanding the constitutional standards or formal doctrine; "Our Theological Task"[5]— perhaps better known as the "quadrilateral"—concludes Part III, offering a description of the method for theological reflection and discernment. As previously mentioned, the constitutionally protected and most formal doctrinal standards require an extensive process in order to make revisions, although it is a process that has as yet not been pursued in the denomination's history. On the other hand, "Our Doctrinal Heritage," "Our Doctrinal History," and "Theological Task" have received minor revisions since their adoption, and it is likely that "Our Theological Task" will receive attention by study commission(s) in future quadrennia so as to incorporate further contributions to the topic.

Our Doctrinal Heritage

The opening statement of "Our Doctrinal Heritage" locates United Methodism within the Christian tradition and in relationship to the triune God: "United Methodists profess the historic Christian faith in God, incarnate in Jesus Christ for our salvation and ever at work in human history in the Holy Spirit."[6] Connecting our doctrinal heritage to our theological task, this particular section explains United Methodism's sharing in the common heritage of Christians. This section demonstrates United Methodism's connection to the larger Christian tradition by focusing on theological and doctrinal emphases of the Christian historical narrative: "This heritage is grounded in the apostolic witness to Jesus Christ as Savior and Lord, which is the source and measure of all valid Christian teaching."[7] That common heritage includes the major narratives of Christian history beginning with determination of the canon of scripture and the adoption of the ecumenical creeds such as Nicaea and Chalcedon along with the Apostles' Creed. United Methodism's sharing in a common Christian heritage includes the Protestant Reformers' recovery of biblical witness as well as other teachings featured in the Articles of Religion.[8]

As discussed in chapter one, our "Basic Christian Affirmations" demonstrate United Methodism's shared conviction with a broad orthodox and evangelical Christianity. Within these basic Christian affirmations exist particular themes drawing from our distinctive United Methodist and Wesleyan roots. According to the *Discipline*, "the underlying energy of the Wesleyan theological heritage stems from an emphasis upon *practical divinity*, the implementation of genuine Christianity in the lives of believers."[9] The Wesleyan movement, as well as the United Brethren in Christ and Evangelical Association, share a commitment "to reform the nation, particularly the Church, and to spread scriptural holiness over the land."[10] The embodiment of this Wesleyan emphasis, "faith and love put into practice,"[11] is explicated through distinctive Wesleyan theological emphases:

- prevenient grace

- justification and assurance

- sanctification and perfection

- faith and good works

- mission and service

- nurture and mission of the church[12]

These emphases, which punctuate our constitutionally protected doctrinal standards, are then connected to Christian life and discipleship. Within the Wesleyan tradition, arguably one of the most consistent and prominent themes is the interdependence between "Christian doctrine and Christian living."[13] This link is facilitated through Christian practices shaped by beliefs, or the means of grace. As the *Discipline* explains, and chapter 2 explored, the General Rules were formulated for early participants in the Wesleyan and Methodist renewal movement in Britain to encourage Christian formation and discipleship. This emphasis upon the link between Christian belief and practice continues in United Methodism, for example with the Social Principles, which will be discussed in more detail in a subsequent section.

Our Doctrinal History

"Our Doctrinal History" follows the section on "Our Doctrinal Heritage" and provides further historical context for our doctrinal and theological commitments within the Wesleyan and subsequent traditions. While the opening paragraphs echo information offered in the previous section, the section as a whole offers an additional framework within which to understand United Methodism's constitutionally protected doctrinal standards that follow. For example, each of the subsections—which include "The Wesleyan 'Standards' in Great Britain," "Doctrinal Standards in American Methodism," and "Doctrinal Traditions in The Evangelical Church and The United Brethren Church"—presents the historical context and theological landscape from which the various doctrinal materials emerged and the narrative leading to their role and impact. Thus, in "Doctrinal Traditions in The Evangelical Church and The United Brethren Church," we learn how Jacob Albright's Evangelical Association and Philip William Otterbein's United Brethren in Christ "considered evangelism more important than theological speculation," but that such positions were not far removed from central Methodist precepts.[14]

These pages (¶103) in the *Discipline* are a helpful and orienting summary to the doctrinal standards in the Wesleyan tradition. Following John Wesley's death and through much of the nineteenth century, undercurrents as well as debates persisted related to Wesley's theological commitments and their appropriateness in the American religious context. Despite Wesley's lifelong allegiance to the Church of England, his successors in American and British Methodism separated from the Church of England. This differentiation of American Methodists from the British Methodists and Church of England continued long after the institutional separations in the form of biographies and other theological and scholarly works to validate partisan agendas.[15] In the early twentieth century, another dynamic emerged that tended to skew accounts of and critical reflections upon Wesley's contributions, an emphasis upon experience as well as a critique of conversion as a model of Christian initiation.[16] After 1960, Wesley and his theological contributions began to be reclaimed, particularly by scholars Frank Baker and Albert Outler.[17]

Our Theological Task

The section entitled "Our Theological Task" follows the appearance of our doctrinal standards and offers a methodology for practicing our theological commitments. It includes what is often referred to as the "quadrilateral"—a fourfold set of components derived from the Christian and Wesleyan traditions. Albert Outler coined the term *quadrilateral* in this context during his role as chair of a Theological Study Commission, which, beginning in 1968, was charged with composing a doctrinal statement for the new denomination, adopted four years later at General Conference.[18] This term, often with the qualification of Wesleyan—"Wesleyan quadrilateral"—has become a familiar concept within and beyond United Methodism, although its widespread use has led to some confusion and even misappropriation of Wesley's theological commitments as well as Outler's intentions.[19] Interestingly, the term did not appear in the final report of the commission or in the current disciplinary paragraph. The debates that followed the introduction of the language *Wesleyan quadrilateral* facilitated the composition of revisions to the 1972 statement included in the 1988 *Discipline*.[20]

As Randy Maddox points out, "no scholar has claimed that the term 'quadrilateral' appears in John Wesley's writings."[21] However, a growing frequency occurs during the twentieth century of references to Wesley's drawing on various combinations of *four* components for support in his theological arguments.[22] These components are scripture, the early church and the Church of England (articulated as *tradition*), reason, and experience. According to Maddox, Wesley referred to two or three of these in an appeal, but there are no known examples of all four components receiving reference in one argument: "His most common conjunction in certifying a position as Christian is to argue that it is both scriptural and rational. Examples can also be found of joint appeals to Scripture and 'tradition,' or Scripture and experience. Finally, there are instances of appeals linking Scripture, reason, and 'tradition'; or Scripture, reason, and experience."[23]

The 2012 *Discipline* describes "The Nature of Our Theological Task" in four dialectic and complementary aspects drawing from Wesleyan and subsequent traditions toward a contemporary methodology. Our theological task is: (1) critical and constructive, (2) individual and communal, (3) contextual and incarnational, and (4) essentially practical.[24] These aspects are embodied in the "Theological Guidelines: Sources and Criteria" that follow: scripture, tradition, experience, and reason.[25]

When understanding—and practicing—"Our Theological Task" it is important to maintain scripture as primary. This is not to say that scripture is necessarily inerrant or infallible but that it is seen as inspired and authoritative, taking precedence over other theological sources. According to Bishop Jones, "when Wesley talked about the doctrine of the Methodist people, he understood that all of that doctrine was based on Scripture."[26] Therefore, like much of Christian tradition, United Methodism continues to hold scripture as inspired, authoritative, and primary, especially since it demonstrates a wholeness of narrative and purpose. As Wesley states, "the Bible is a unity that is internally coherent and consistent . . . the wholeness of Scripture is constituted by its doctrinal content, specifically soteriology."[27]

The second component of "Our Theological Task" is stated simply as "tradition." However, this term is best understood when we take into account Wesley's time and context. It could be argued that for Wesley there should be five chronological eras dividing Christian tradition to include Christian antiquity (as an initial era) as well as the early Church of England (as a latter one).[28] The earliest centuries of the Christian tradition provide sermons and treatises as well as ecumenical creeds despite the limited resources available beyond scripture from this period. John Wesley also held in high esteem the early chapters of the Church of England during the Elizabethan period, following its separation from the Roman Catholic Church—a period that produced the *Book of Homilies, Book of Common Prayer,* and the Articles of Religion.

When considering experience in particular it is important to remember each of these components, whether all four, or selections with scripture as primary, overlap in their roles as sources and criteria for theological reflection. As scripture is interpreted by Christians in particular eras of tradition, experience—both personal and communal—also informs this interpretation and theological reflection. Experience, in the Wesleyan tradition, most often refers to Christian experience and is multifaceted, offering an understanding—and experience—of God's grace as described in scripture as well as tradition.[29] According to Maddox, human experience is most often mediated: "As Immanuel Kant formulated it in an influential thesis: all human experience is *interpreted* experience, because it is *mediated* through our preexisting intellectual concepts."[30] Therefore, for Wesley, experience may be mediated, but ideally for Christian experience, through one's faith.

Reason, the fourth component articulated in our methodology for theological reflection, builds upon the previous three components. According to Rebekah Miles, for Wesley "reason could not serve as an independent source of knowledge [since] . . . reason was limited not only by sin, but also by its own nature and role."[31] Miles goes on to explain that reason, for Wesley, does not generate knowledge. Rather, reason "processes data and knowledge that originate in experience. It is a tool, not a source." As the *Discipline* explains, God's revelation and grace "continually surpass the scope of human language and reason." However, we continue to "believe that any disciplined theological work calls for the careful use of reason."[32] Reason enables our pursuit of the Christian faith and our living out of the same.

Each of these resources—tradition, experience, and reason—facilitates our study of scripture. While each makes a distinctive contribution, they work together to inform and shape our faithful Christian witness as United Methodists.[33]

However, it is not for individual Christian witnesses alone that theological reflection is important—it is also fundamental to address the challenges found collectively in ecclesial contexts. The issues confronted by the church in the world continue to present serious complexities and threaten the church's witness. As the following section describes in its discussion of the Social Creed, Social Principles, and *Book of Resolutions*, despite the complexity and at times seemingly insurmountable challenges, United Methodism continues to demonstrate strong commitments to justice and reconciliation participating in God's unfolding reign. However, these commitments are not made without attention to and consideration of ecumenical concerns as we share in God's mission within the body of Christ across denominational boundaries.

Social Creed, Social Principles, and the *Book of Resolutions*

The United Methodist Church provides contemporary statements, specifically the Social Creed, Social Principles, and the *Book of Resolutions*, describing the social responsibilities of Christians. The Social Creed, Social Principles, and the *Book of Resolutions* are different in genre and appeared over time, the subsequent materials helping to interpret earlier material. For example, the Social Creed was first composed in 1908. The Social Principles with the *Book of Resolutions* appeared at the time of The United Methodist Church's creation, the

Book of Resolutions in 1968 and the Social Principles in 1972 following a study commission.

The Social Creed is a statement of basic convictions emerging from ecumenical efforts among American denominations in the first decade of the twentieth century. It informs, but is still distinct from, the Social Principles, which provide a lengthier narrative and more contemporary statement growing from collaboration of partners in the newly formed United Methodist Church in 1968. The Social Principles represent a statement of basic convictions, moral principles, and applications or commitments drawing from the Wesleyan/Methodist traditions as well as those of the Evangelical United Brethren. The *Book of Resolutions* is a compilation of statements adopted by General Conference to represent the denomination's broad commitments—even if sometimes contradictory—to social concerns of the contemporary context.

Social Creed

Methodism is the only tradition among mainline and other Protestant denominations that has consistently used the term *Social Creed*. It is also the only tradition that continues to authorize the use of a social creed to the present time.[34] The Social Creed was a relatively late response among Methodists to the disadvantages and needs incurred by the industrial revolution. Methodists in particular did not assume such social responsibility until 1908 with the adoption of the Social Creed. The first church groups to respond to new social conditions were Unitarians, Congregationalists, and Episcopalians. The Methodists and Baptists awoke to their social duty later. It is argued that within all denominations clergymen and professors designed the social gospel response to the urban impact. However, these arguments tend to overlook the contribution of women to the formulation and practice of social outreach. Women often assumed the responsibility for practices that manifest the social awareness of Christian churches during this period.

In response to such social challenges, the Methodist Federation for Social Service (MFSS) was organized in Washington, DC, on December 3-4, 1907. Through this group and its leaders, the Social

Creed came to fruition.[35] Although the MFSS chose to remain unofficial in its relationship to General Conference and the denomination generally, strategies were employed to bring awareness of social and economic issues to the General Conference of The Methodist Episcopal Church in 1908.[36] Although Herbert Welch and Harry Ward, two MFSS officers, were not delegates to General Conference, they worked with the subcommittee on "The Church and Social Problems," writing much of the report (later acknowledged to be primarily the work of Ward) that was approved by the General Conference on May 30, 1908.[37] Within this three-page report was the list of affirmations that composed the original Social Creed[38]—affirmations that became recognized as a "Methodist platform on social problems" and moved the denomination into a leadership role among churches addressing such questions.

The Social Creed of The Methodist Episcopal Church (1908)

The Methodist Episcopal Church stands

For equal rights and complete justice for all men in all stations of life.

For the principle of conciliation and arbitration in industrial dissensions.

For the protection of the worker from dangerous machinery, occupational diseases, injuries, and mortality.

For the abolition of child labor.

For such regulation of the conditions of labor for women as shall safeguard the physical and moral health of the community.

For the suppression of the "sweating system."

For the gradual and reasonable reduction of the hours of labor to the lowest practical point, with work for all; and for the degree of leisure for all which is the condition of the highest human life.

For a release from employment one day in seven.

For a living wage in every industry.

> For the highest wage that each industry can afford, and
>> for the most equitable division of the products of
>> industry that can ultimately be devised.
> For the recognition of the Golden Rule and the mind of
>> Christ as the supreme law of society and the sure
>> remedy of all social ills.[39]

During the autumn of 1908, Frank Mason North, another Federation leader, created a second version of the Social Creed.[40] North was involved in both social activism and ecumenical efforts, and in December of 1908 he presented a report to the Federal Council of Churches of Christ in America that included the Methodist document and four additional affirmations regarding rights for workers and abatement of poverty.[41] North lacked any explicit authorization to share the Methodist Social Creed with other denominations, let alone transform the affirmations.[42] However, because of this act, both North and Ward have been designated as original authors of the Social Creed, most likely because of the close proximity of the developments; although during their lifetimes, North received most of the credit since his efforts were more public than Ward's unofficial work with the General Conference subcommittee.[43]

The Social Creed served as a symbol of both ecumenical and social commitment for the Federal Council of Churches.[44] As the revised affirmations were adopted by member denominations, additional changes were often made, threatening the common text. In response the Federal Council of Churches undertook a third revision in 1912 that acknowledged the growing interest in social and economic issues. Two additional declarations were included, and the document was expanded to mention the family, child development, health, liquor traffic, and property.[45]

One example of the many efforts by women is the Deaconess movement organized in the Women's Home Missionary Association of The Methodist Episcopal Church by Lucy Rider Meyer and Jane Bancroft Robinson.[46] While deaconesses visited the poor—for the purpose of ministering to their physical and spiritual brokenness—as nurses and domestic visitors, many also functioned in part as students and agents of the new field of quantitative sociology. Deaconesses began to realize that the causes of the depression, sickness, chemical dependency, and despair that they witnessed were not merely the fault of the impoverished themselves but also represented systemic oppression of the immigrant and poor. Their experience challenged older notions that poverty was solely the result of individual depravity. In its later years under the leadership of Isabelle Horton and Winifred Chappell, the Deaconess movement worked toward and offered social critique of various efforts addressing social reform in the area of child labor, employment advocacy, temperance, and prostitution.

The sixteen-point Social Creed adopted in 1912 served as the basic pronouncement of the Federal Council of Churches for twenty years, although there were tensions among the member denominations leading to revisions and additions.[47] Additional paragraphs were appended on topics such as community service, industrial conditions, and labor rights.[48] In the years following 1912, a controversy emerged with regard to the language of creed. Some construed the language as reserved for the ecumenical creeds of Christendom, and favored instead the language of social ideals. By 1928 the dominant term used among Federal Council of Churches members for the Social Creed was *social ideals*. By 1928 it was felt that the word *creed* in reference to social concerns suggested that a humanitarian platform was replacing religious convictions, while the word *ideals* conveyed the notion of goals yet to be achieved by institutions in which all members had not reached consensus.[49] With the growing radical platform of the Methodist Federation of Social Service and Ward's emphasis on actions rather than words, the Social Creed does not appear in the 1936 *Methodist Episcopal Discipline.*[50] In its place are statements on "The Spiritual Life of the Church" and "Social and Economic Questions." A majority of the laity within the denomination challenged the Methodist Federation of Social Service at General Conference, resulting in the loss of the Social Creed.

Thus, The Methodist Episcopal Church did not carry the Social Creed into the union of 1939 with The Methodist Episcopal Church, South, and Methodist Protestant Church. In 1916 the Methodist Protestant Church adopted the original Methodist Episcopal Social Creed composed by Ward, but in the 1920s the Social Creed dropped out of the *Methodist Protestant Discipline.* The Methodist Episcopal Church, South, embraced the Federal Council version in 1914, which was later revised in 1932. Since The Methodist Episcopal Church, South, continually included the Social Creed in its *Discipline*, it provided the thread of continuity.[51]

The Social Creed remained a regular part of The Methodist Church's *Discipline*, although the statements comprising it were subject to change—a practice that continues. The current *Discipline* includes a litany inspired by the Social Creed for use in worship services.[52] The Board of Christian Social Concerns was later formed in 1952 by an amalgamation of various groups to implement the denomination's official creed, reduce duplication of work, and provide a strategic and symbolic presence in Washington, DC, across from the Capitol Building.[53] This work continues based in the same location through the General Board of Church and Society.

Social Principles

The Social Principles are the result of a collaborative effort of representative members from the Methodist and Evangelical United Brethren of the newly amalgamated United Methodist Church. The social declarations of these groups were not in conflict and initially both were printed as the new denomination's Social Principles from 1968. A commission to study the Social Principles was appointed later in 1968 guided by Bishop James Thomas.[54] Instead of selecting one or merging the two, a new document was drafted resulting in Social Principles that restate and build upon the denomination's Social Creed. Moreover, the commission set out to prepare Social Principles that could be used in congregational worship as well as in planned social action.[55]

The study commission invited input from individuals and congregations as well as papers from scholars and practitioners to compose a form of the Social Principles closely resembling the text adopted by the 1972 General Conference. The document opens with a theological preamble and concludes with the Social Creed. The Social Principles continue to be organized into the current six sections: "The Natural World," "The Nurturing Community," "The Social Community," "The

Economic Community," "The Political Community," and "The World Community." The Social Principles demonstrate influence from a number of theological perspectives including Wesleyan sanctification, social gospel, Boston Personalism, and ecumenism.[56] An instructive diagram in the opening pages of the *Book of Resolutions* demonstrates the relationship of both resolutions to Social Principles as well as the relationship of these to scriptural foundations.

Succeeding General Conferences have modified the document adding concerns about gender, ethnicity, age groups, inclusive language, and other contemporary issues. The Social Principles are designed for ongoing revision. For example, over forty years ago The United Methodist Church did not condone divorce with the exception of situations involving adultery, declining to preside at weddings of divorced persons in most circumstances.[57] More recently, the United Methodist Social Principles state "divorce is a regrettable alternative in the midst of brokenness" and "divorce does not preclude a new marriage."[58] The 2012 General Conference made numerous additions and revisions including "Natural World" statements—such as those addressing energy resource utilization, animal life, and food justice. In addition, statements addressing genetic technology, media violence, health care, and mental health appear in "The Social Community" section, with statements on graft, corruption, and finance appearing in "The Economic Community" category.[59] According to the *Discipline*, "the Social Principles . . . are a prayerful and thoughtful effort on the part of the General Conference to speak to the human issues in the contemporary world from a sound biblical and theological foundation as historically demonstrated in the United Methodist traditions."[60]

While the Social Principles reflect an American, particularly United States, set of interests and commitments, they are meant to be culturally adaptable including the permission for central conferences to make revisions.[61] A recent development related to the Social Principles occurred at the 2012 General Conference. A growing number of General Conference delegates represent a vital and growing United Methodism outside the United States. Though the Social Principles are translated by the General Board of Church and Society into at least ten languages,[62] there is a growing sense that the Social Principles and the *Book of Resolutions* reflect mainly American United Methodist perspectives.

The 2012 General Conference approved legislation proposed in a petition from three European central conferences to implement a process of revision for the Social Principles with the purpose of making them "more succinct, theologically founded and globally relevant."[63] For those in United Methodism within the United States, one of the most familiar—and provocative—Social Principles comments upon human sexuality. To a United Methodist in Mozambique and other regions of Africa, for example, a more prominent debate is polygamy, a topic the Social Principles do not directly address.[64] The Connectional Table, an appointed body with global representation that coordinates mission, ministries, and resources to implement denomination-wide initiatives, recently developed a plan to facilitate revisions to the Social Principles. The plan includes the convening of conversations across the denomination including Africa, Europe, the Philippines, and the United States. Each conversation will be led by a panel composed of international representatives from the denomination.[65] These conversations are expected to give suggestions to the Connectional Table for a proposal from the Connectional Table to a future General Conference to revise the Social Principles for a more comprehensive representation of global United Methodism.

The Book of Resolutions

The *Book of Resolutions*, published every four years alongside the *Discipline*, is a collection of statements adopted by General Conference articulating the denomination's commitments to social issues. All legislation and resolutions approved by the General Conference are found in either the *Discipline* or the *Book of Resolutions*. The *Book of Resolutions*, totaling almost 1,100 pages in 2012, in many ways serves as an appendix to the *Discipline*. Prior to initial publication of the *Book of Resolutions* at the creation of The United Methodist Church in 1968, the *Discipline of the Methodist Church* printed all resolutions of any kind in an appendix.[66] The *Book of Resolutions* seeks to expand the Social Principles, which, like the *Discipline*, it also includes, into a contemporary and living document of social commitments for the denomination. Each resolution is presented to and must be approved by at least 60 percent of that General Conference for inclusion in the *Book of Resolutions*. The *Book of Resolutions* represents the compilation of adopted statements from the previous eight years—or three General Conferences. According to the *Discipline*, "resolutions are official expressions of The United Methodist Church for eight years following their adoption, after which time they shall be deemed to have expired unless readopted."[67] Program boards and agencies carry the responsibility to review resolutions and recommend revisions to the General Conference, though resolutions may be received by any delegates to General Conference. Numerous resolutions, particularly those related to our doctrines, have received continuous renewal since their initial approval and appearance in the *Book of Resolutions*.[68] Resolutions are organized according to their relatedness to the categories of the Social Principles. In addition to a searchable index of key words, scripture references are also included.

Liturgical Resources

The United Methodist Hymnal and *The United Methodist Book of Worship*, the most recent editions of which were published in 1988 and 1992 respectively, demonstrate operational doctrine through their pervasive use in worship and Christian formation in United Methodist congregations and gatherings of other bodies. The *Hymnal* and *Book of Worship* receive their authority as doctrinal sources through their adoption and approval by General Conference. According to the Constitution, the General Conference possesses the power "to provide and revise the hymnal and ritual of the Church and to regulate all matters relating to the form and mode of worship, subject to the limitations of the first and second Restrictive Rule."[69] The doctrinal themes contained within *The United Methodist Hymnal* are grounded in scripture. Some argue as much as 85 percent of the Bible may be present in the hymnody texts composed by Charles Wesley. Indeed, the *Hymnal* is organized around themes emphasized by John Wesley and often described as the "via salutis."[70] The 2016 General Conference approved the development of a new hymnal. *The Book of Worship* provides liturgies for services and acts of worship informed by the substance of the

Hymnal and our constitutional doctrinal standards as well as contemporary statements.

Hymnals in the Wesleyan Tradition to the Present

While John often receives more attention than his brother Charles, the theological integration and foundation of the early Methodist movement and its informal and operational theological frame is most clearly demonstrated in the composition and use of Charles's hymns. Hymn-singing in the early Methodist movement served primarily as catechesis for Christian discipleship.[71] Despite the scriptural doctrinal substance and significant influence of the hymns composed largely by Charles, the hymnbooks of the early Methodist movement did not receive doctrinal status.[72] In 1784, the Deed of Declaration granted doctrinal status to John's *Notes upon the New Testament* and the first four volumes of *Sermons*. No doctrinal status was given to a hymnbook during this period. According to Brian Beck:

> We deceive ourselves, I believe, if we imagine that John Wesley's extensive theological writings were the decisive influence in the formation of the Methodist preachers or their hearers. Their importance in the controversies of the time and their influence on the preachers who read them cannot be denied, but the words that lingered in the minds of the society members . . . were not snatches from [*Sermons* or *Notes*] . . . but [hymns].[73]

John compiled the first Methodist hymnbook during his time in Georgia in 1737. A dozen hymnbooks were published throughout John's and Charles's lifetimes, with the most definitive—the large hymnbook, entitled *A Collection of Hymns, for the use of the people called Methodists*, or simply *Wesley's Hymns*—appearing in 1780.[74]

In his hymns, Charles drew heavily from scripture.[75] John's arrangement of hymns in the 1780 hymnbook is helpful to those not familiar with Christian scripture. In spite of their lack of doctrinal status, some argue John considered and used the hymns as doctrinal materials.[76] The hymns consistently focus upon soteriological themes central to the gospel and Christian scripture.[77] According to Thomas Langford:

Charles Wesley is important not because he added new thoughts or insights to theological discourse, but because he creatively provided for the Methodist revival a theological character suited to its self-understanding. He added a distinctive theological dimension; or, perhaps better, he helped provide a new dimension to theological expression for the Methodist revival; that is, he kept theology immediately and ineluctibly [*sic*] related to the worship and service of God.[78]

Through the movement's hymns, Charles, with John, provided a doctrinal frame for the early Methodist movement—connecting belief with practices.[79]

The heritage of hymnody in American Methodism and its predecessor traditions begins in 1784 when Wesley's *Collection of Psalms and Hymns for the Lord's Day* and his revision of the *Book of Common Prayer*, or "Sunday Service," were adopted for standard use in the emerging denomination.[80] The United Brethren in Christ and Evangelical Association began producing hymnals in 1795 and 1810 respectively.[81]

Scholars describe Wesley's resources falling into disuse relatively soon after the establishment of the new movement. The main reason seems to be these resources had little resonance with the more informal worship style fostered in small gatherings, often in chapels as well as camp meetings on the frontier.[82] In 1790, Bishops Asbury and Coke recommended *A Pocket Hymn-Book Designed as a Constant Companion for the Pious, Collected from Various Authors*, which served the church until 1821.[83] Participants were expected to purchase and carry a hymnal for personal use, lending to the popularity of small pocket-sized resources. Hymnals, particularly those small in size, consisted mainly of hymn lyrics, absent of tunes, as well as absent of orders of worship services. This trend later shifted with the expansion and establishment of Methodism as a denomination. The Methodist hymnals published in 1849 and 1878 were the largest, both including almost 1,200 hymns, twice the number of the current (1989) edition, and the latter was the first to find its way in significant numbers into pews for use in worship.[84] Methodists began to publish separate hymn tunes as early as 1821 with *The Methodist Harmonist*, while the integration of hymn tunes within the official hymnbook began in 1857 in The Methodist

Episcopal Church. The 1964 *Methodist Hymnal* preceded the union of Evangelical United Brethren and Methodists by four years.[85] This resource included a range of traditional hymnody with only two liturgical services that occupied fewer than four pages.[86]

Hymnals can be a symbol and practice of reconciliation and union, such as the jointly produced hymnal of 1905 by The Methodist Episcopal and Methodist Episcopal Church, South, as well as a 1935 endeavor including the Methodist Protestants with the former two bodies. However, they can also be sites of division when the publication of hymnals follows schism and demonstrates differentiation by omission, inclusion, or reordering of hymns.

The 1989 *United Methodist Hymnal*, by contrast, consists of a wider range of hymnody from a variety of traditions. While not thoroughly inclusive, the 1989 *Hymnal* goes a long way toward attempting to represent a more multiethnic and diverse church.[87] It includes 678 selections within its major section, "Hymns, Canticles & Acts of Worship," organized within categories that indicate their significance related to theological and doctrinal foundations.[88] According to Carol Doran and Thomas Troeger, "the effect of interweaving hymns with poems and prayers from various centuries, traditions and cultures is to strengthen our sense of connectedness to the cloud of witnesses from the past to the larger church."[89]

Additionally, the 1989 *Hymnal* differs from earlier hymnals in that it includes at least four liturgical services with commentary and musical settings numbering over fifty pages. The fourth service is drawn from texts of the former Methodist and Evangelical United Brethren churches. Doran and Troeger remark, "The prominent placement of these services and the emphasis on the unity of word and table demonstrate the impact of the ecumenical liturgical movement upon the United Methodists, and they remind users of the book that the hymns they sing are part of a larger integrated act of corporate prayer."[90] As will be discussed below, liturgical services most often appeared in the *Discipline* or separate publications in early American Methodism prior to the publications of *The Book of Worship* in the twentieth century. Another twentieth-century innovation is the appearance of companion volumes to hymnals for the purpose of providing guidance to worship and music leaders.[91]

The Book of Worship *and Its Predecessors*

The early Methodist renewal movement within the Church of England did not produce distinctive liturgical resources beyond the Wesleys' hymns. The presumption here was that those participating in Methodist classes and bands, preaching events, and other missional enterprises also participated in weekly public worship in churches drawing on traditional Anglican resources. In preparation for the emergence of the new church in America, Wesley modeled the materials he compiled on those relied upon by the Church of England: hymns, sermons (similar to the *Book of Homilies*), and the "Sunday Service" (similar to the *Book of Common Prayer*), among others. The service book, officially approved as the "prayer book" of The Methodist Episcopal Church at the constituting Christmas Conference of 1784 in Baltimore, included services for baptism, marriage, communion of the sick, burial, and ordination, while taking its name from the services for Sunday worship.[92]

Though the "Sunday Service" composed by Wesley for American Methodism went through five London-published editions during the years 1784–1790, the service was not widely implemented. There is evidence of its use by Francis Asbury, who was set apart as "superintendent" in 1784 (later renamed bishop in 1787), and Richard Whatcoat, who was elected bishop in 1800.[93] However, although admired, others conceded it was not of much use possibly implicating the excessive cost, low literacy rates, and misalignment with emerging worship styles.[94] Following the death of John Wesley in 1791, many, if not all, references to the Methodist "liturgy" or "prayer book" were omitted from the 1792 *Discipline*.[95] In 1932, an effort was made to recover Wesley's resources for worship, particularly aspects of the "Sunday Service."[96]

The 1932 *Methodist Episcopal Discipline* included two orders of worship for Sunday as well as a third for morning or evening prayer.[97] From 1932 to 1939, orders of worship for Sunday multiplied and culminated in 1945 with the publication of the first official Methodist book of worship.[98] The 1945 *Book of Worship* provided multiple services for Sunday, while the 1965 *Book of Worship* eliminated all but two.[99] Both books recover early Wesleyan texts, including aspects of the "Sunday Service." The 1965 *Book of Worship* also offers a one-year Christian-calendar lectionary with three scripture readings—most often Old Testament, epistle, and gospel passages—as well as a psalm and other act of praise.[100] Ecumenical conversations during the 1970s and 1980s informed the three-year and three-lesson-plus-psalm lectionaries later appearing in the 1992 *Book of Worship*.[101]

Conclusion

Though contemporary statements may not receive the same level of authoritative protection as constitutional standards and most often speak from and to a North American perspective, their role in the life of the denomination is considerable. Contemporary statements, such as the Social Principles, and other resources, among those *The United Methodist Hymnal* and *Book of Worship*, inform the Christian witness of individuals and communities. Additionally, these contemporary statements further demonstrate the significance of integrating belief and practice among United Methodists. Through the influential character of these familiar materials, United Methodism has an opportunity to ground its practices, from worship to prophetic witness, in a deep Christian witness framed by our Christian doctrine and Wesleyan heritage. In the following chapters we will continue to explore this dynamic in relation to ministry roles and organizational structures.

PART II

UNITED METHODIST MISSION: CALLED AND FORMED FOR MINISTRY

– Chapter Four –

Pastoral Roles and Ordained Ministry

In the early Methodist movement, numerous roles filled by pastoral leaders, both lay and ordained, sustained ministries of renewal and participation in the reign of God. John Wesley did not ordain leaders for the Methodist renewal movement in Great Britain, though late in his life and ministry he eventually, if not reluctantly, set apart Thomas Coke and ordained and set apart Richard Whatcoat and Thomas Vassey, sending them to encourage and lead the Methodist movement in America. In the United States, ordained ministers most often itinerated to bring the sacrament of the Lord's Supper to the unfolding movement in an emerging nation. In Britain the ordained ministers within the Methodist movement were priests of the Church of England, ordained initially as deacons, similar to provisional members in contemporary United Methodism, before becoming priests or elders in full connection. Also in Britain, John Wesley established a number of lay and other set-apart roles, such as class leaders, stewards, and visitors of the sick, to oversee and nurture the ministry of religious societies or bands and classes as well as local preachers to minister across the connection.

Reflecting on the roles established to nurture the early Methodist renewal movement helps frame the varied leadership roles now existing within United Methodism and place them in a larger context. The varied roles deployed within United Methodism often receive attention

69

from study commissions charged by General Conference for clarification and possible revisions to facilitate alignment and participation in our shared mission. For this reason some of the roles mentioned in this chapter are relatively new or may continue to receive attention for ongoing clarification and revisions. In the following pages, several categories of pastoral roles, including those receiving ordination and full membership, will be explored.

Ministry of All Christians

Chapter 1 unpacks the nature and mission of the church, including ¶120 and following, reflecting upon key themes in the commission text in Matthew's Gospel, which features baptism as a prominent practice of disciple-making. Not only is baptism significant to the ministry and purpose of the church, but also through our baptisms all are called to ministries of sharing the gospel. According to the *Discipline*,

> Very early in its history, the church came to understand that all of its members were commissioned in baptism to ministries of love, justice, and service within local congregations and the larger communities in which they lived; all who follow Jesus have a share in the ministry of Jesus, who came not to be served, but to serve. There is thus a general ministry of all baptized Christians.[1]

While each baptized Christian, lay and ordained, is equipped with unique gifts and distinctive vocations, all are called to share the love of God in Jesus Christ through the power of the Holy Spirit. According to the *Discipline*, "the ministry of the laity flows from a commitment to Christ's outreaching love. Lay members of The United Methodist Church are, by history and calling, active advocates of the gospel of Jesus Christ. Every layperson is called to carry out the Great Commission (Matthew 28:18-20); every layperson is called to be missional."[2]

The ministry of all Christians is practiced by individuals as well as in and by communities. Individually, we minister to and with one another, sharing our gifts and fulfilling God's vocation for our lives: "The witness of the laity, their Christ-like examples of everyday living as well as the sharing of their own faith experiences of the gospel, is the primary evangelistic ministry through which all people will come to know Christ and The United Methodist Church will fulfill its mission."[3] The *Discipline* also describes the ministry of the community. Christians, as the body of Christ, the church, minister through their communal witness, both presently, across time, and in numerous locations around the world. In this way, the church demonstrates an eschatological character of already and not yet in its participation in the reign of God sent in ministry to the world:[4] "[The church] stretches out to human needs whenever love and service may convey God's love and ours. The outreach of such ministries knows no limits."[5]

Lay Ministry Roles

In the spirit of the early Methodist renewal movement, United Methodism continues to encourage ministry roles for all baptized members. Many of these roles are described in the *Discipline* at the conclusion of the chapter on "The Local Church" in the section "Lay Servant Ministries" and include the following: *local church* or *certified lay servant, lay speaker (certified), lay missioner,* and *lay minister.* The local church and certified lay servant as well as the lay speaker, often certified, are recognized and supported by a district or conference committee on Lay Servant Ministries.[6] The lay missioner follows the guidelines composed by the National Committee on Hispanic Ministries of the National Plan for Hispanic Ministries and may be certified by their annual conference.[7] Certified lay ministers may be certified by the district committee on ordained ministry.[8] There exist at least two additional ministry roles for laity, the *deaconess* and *home missioner,* supported through the United Methodist Women and an office of the same name.[9] Each of these roles is held by professing members of local churches and complements the roles of the ordained elder and deacon and is not intended to replace them.[10]

Local church or *certified lay servants* are called to serve the local church by leading meetings, conducting or assisting in conducting worship (including preaching), relating to appropriate committees and ministry areas, and assisting in the distribution of the Lord's Supper.[11] Lay servants assume these responsibilities when requested by the pastor, district superintendent, or committee on Lay Servant Ministries.[12] A local church lay servant may be recognized for service in the lay servant's charge after completing a basic training course providing background in United Methodist studies and basic pastoral skills.[13] To continue in service a local church lay servant may reapply once in every three years.[14] The certified lay servant completes both a basic and advanced course and may apply for reaffirmation annually. The certified lay servant may serve within one's charge or beyond the charge in local churches, the district, or the conference.[15]

The *lay speaker (certified)* is most directly related to the lay ministry facilitated by John Wesley in the early Methodist renewal movement in Great Britain.[16] Lay speakers are "called and equipped to serve the church in pulpit supply."[17] In order to qualify for their office, they must complete a number of courses—including the lay servant basic course, worship, preaching, and United Methodist studies[18]—be recommended by the local pastor in the church in which they hold membership, and then be voted upon by the charge conference prior to approval and certification by the Lay Servant Ministries district committee. To continue in service, lay speakers apply for recertification every three years.[19] Certified lay servants may transfer their certification to a new district.[20]

Lay missioners also receive training and may be certified by their annual conferences according to the guidelines of the National Committee on Hispanic Ministries.[21] Lay missioners serve on teams with a pastor-mentor to whom they are accountable; they also work "to develop faith communities, establish community ministries, develop church school extension programs, and engage in congregational development."[22]

Lay ministers are called "to enhance the quality of ministry to small membership churches, [and] expand team ministry in churches."[23] According to the *Discipline*, a certified lay servant, or person with equivalent training, may be certified as a lay minister by the district committee on ordained ministry.[24] Certified lay ministers complete additional training relevant to their assignment including preaching and exegesis, the care of the congregation, and other courses recommended by the General Board of Discipleship and General Board of

Higher Education and Ministry.[25] To continue in service, and receive recertification, the certified lay minister may apply or appear biannually before the district committee on ordained ministry.[26] Certified lay ministers may transfer their certification to a new district.[27]

Deaconesses and *home missioners* are called to minister "through diverse forms of service directed toward the world to make Jesus Christ known in the fullness of his ministry and mission."[28] Deaconesses, who are laywomen, and home missioners, who are laymen, are trained and serve full-time to alleviate suffering, eradicate injustice, facilitate full human potential, and share in the building of a global community through the church universal.[29] The 2016 General Conference affirmed deaconesses/home missioners as a lay order within The United Methodist Church. The appointments of deaconesses and home missioners are fixed by the bishop of the annual conference in which they serve[30] and in which they must hold local church membership.[31] Distinct from other lay ministry roles, "deaconesses and home missioners shall be seated at the sessions of the annual conference with voice and vote as lay members of the annual conference."[32] The United Methodist Women's national organization convenes the Committee on Deaconess and Home Missioner Service and retains staff to support their work.[33]

Ordination in The United Methodist Church

In The United Methodist Church, ordination is a gift, affirmation, and continuation of the apostolic ministry "through persons empowered by the Holy Spirit."[34] In ordination individuals are set apart for ministry, though as demonstrated by the roles already discussed and some that follow an individual may be called to pastoral ministry but not called to ordination, for example, licensed local pastors. Since the earliest days of American Methodism, traditional ordination has been marked by the election of candidates for ordination by the annual conference and ordination by the bishop laying hands. The 1787 *Book of Discipline* describes these marks as the constitution of elders. They are "constituted" by "the Election of the Majority in the Conference, and by the laying on of Hands of Bishop, and the Elders present."[35] These practices continue today in The United Methodist Church, though with support from additional bodies such as the board of ordained ministry in relation to both elder and deacon.

According to the 2012 *Discipline*, "ordination is fulfilled in leadership of the people of God through ministries of Service, Word, Sacrament, Order, Compassion, and Justice."[36] Ordained ministers are often referred to as *pastors*—a term that seems initially to appear among American Methodism in the 1892 *Discipline*[37] and that defines a pastor as "an ordained elder, provisional deacon, or licensed person approved by vote of the clergy members in full connection and may be appointed by the bishop to be in charge of a station, circuit, cooperative parish, extension ministry, ecumenical shared ministry, or to a church of another denomination, or on the staff of one such appointment."[38] Though there are a number of pastoral roles, there are two orders of ordained ministry in United Methodism: the deacon and the elder:

> Those who respond to God's call to lead in service, word, compassion, and justice and equip others for this ministry through teaching, proclamation, and worship and who assist elders in the administration of the sacraments are ordained as *deacons*. Those whose leadership in service includes preaching and teaching the Word of God, administration of the sacraments, ordering the Church for its mission and service and administration of the discipline of the Church are ordained as *elders*.[39]

The *Discipline* goes on to point out that ordained ministers practice their ministry in covenant with all Christians, "especially with those whom they lead and serve in ministry."[40] It is important that all practice faithful and effective ministries together participating and realizing God's reign. Through such ministry it is hoped and expected that local churches will intentionally nurture candidates for ordained ministry.[41]

Ordination is described as a complete dedication to the highest ideals of the Christian life for the sake of the mission of Jesus Christ in the world and the most effective witness to the Christian gospel.[42] Among the first qualifications for ordination is a person's conscious call from God to this ministry and the acknowledgment and authentication of that call by the church.[43] The United Methodist Church identifies the following qualifications for those presenting themselves as candidates for ordained ministry to discern God's call upon their lives:

a) Have a personal faith in Christ and be committed to Christ as Savior and Lord.

b) Nurture and cultivate spiritual disciplines and patterns of holiness.

c) Teach and model generous Christian giving with a focus on tithing as God's standard of giving.

d) Acknowledge a call by God to give themselves completely to ordained ministry following Jesus' pattern of love and service.

e) Communicate persuasively the Christian faith in both oral and written form.

f) Make a commitment to lead the whole church in loving service to humankind.

g) Give evidence of God's gifts for ordained ministry, evidence of God's grace in their lives, and promise of future usefulness in the mission of the Church.

h) Be persons in whom the community can place trust and confidence.

i) Accept that Scripture contains all things necessary for salvation through faith in God through Jesus Christ; be competent in the disciplines of Scripture, theology, church history, and Church polity; possess the skills essential to the practice of ordained ministry; and lead in making disciples of Jesus Christ.

j) Be accountable to The United Methodist Church, accept its Doctrinal Standards and *Discipline* and authority, accept the supervision of those appointed to this ministry, and be prepared to live in the covenant of its ordained ministers.[44]

Ordained ministers as well as licensed local pastors are required to have the highest commitment to Christian faith and life, which is demonstrated in the qualifications above. This does not assume perfection or achievement of holiness by one's own efforts but rather commitment to spiritual nurture and discipline through which the Holy Spirit works in us (or sanctification).

When individuals sense a call to pastoral or set-apart ministry, whether as ordained in full membership as an elder or deacon or as a licensed local pastor or associate member, they may present themselves as candidates. A useful resource in discerning one's call to ministry, whether lay or ordained, is *The Christian as Minister* published by the General Board of Higher Education and Ministry.[45] This text offers a helpful explanation of and guide to the process and requirements outlined in the *Discipline*. There are additional resources demonstrating processes for discernment of ministry roles in the appendix of *The Christian as Minister*.

License for Pastoral Ministry

In The United Methodist Church when persons sense a call to pastoral ministry and choose to pursue that call, they become candidates for licensed or ordained ministry. According to the *Discipline*, "the licensed or ordained ministry is recognized by The United Methodist Church as a called-out and set-apart ministry. Therefore, it is appropriate that those persons who present themselves as candidates for licensed or ordained ministry be examined regarding the authenticity of their call by God to set-apart ministry."[46] If a person not yet ordained as elder receives an appointment "to preach and conduct divine worship and perform the duties of a pastor" they also receive a license for pastoral ministry.[47]

The board of ordained ministry, after sufficient examination, may recommend to the clergy session of the annual conference the following persons eligible to receive license for pastoral ministry: (1) provisional elders, (2) local pastors having completed candidacy certification, orientation to ministry, studies for the license as a local pastor, or been recommended by the district committee on ordained ministry, (3) associate members, (4) deacons in full connection, and (5) licensed or ordained clergy from other denominations.[48]

From the earliest descriptions of pastoral ministry in American and British Methodism, the duties of the preachers, specifically local pastors, have included: "1. To Preach. 2. To meet the Societies of Classes, and Bands. 3. To visit the Sick. 4. To meet the Leaders. 5. To preach in the morning."[49] The directions go on to state, "11. You have nothing to do but to save Souls. Therefore spend and be spent in this Work. And go always not only to those that want, but to those that want you most."[50]

And, "12. Act in all Things, not according to your own Will, but as a Son [or Daughter] in the Gospel."[51] In the contemporary context, provisional elders and local pastors approved annually (by the board of ordained ministry and district committee on ordained ministry) may be licensed by the bishop to perform all the duties of a pastor.[52] Such duties include "the sacraments of baptism and Holy Communion as well as the service of marriage (where state laws allow), burial, confirmation, and membership reception, within and while appointed to a particular charge or extension ministry."[53] In other words, a licensed local pastor or provisional elder may perform the above duties within the specific local church or charge to which they are appointed.

There are three categories for those serving as local pastors: full-time, part-time, and student. *Full-time local pastors* "devote their entire time to the church in the charge to which they are appointed and its outreach in ministry and mission to the community."[54] Full-time local pastors are required to pursue theological education through the Course of Study (five years) or other curriculum approved by the General Board of Higher Education and Ministry but are not enrolled as full-time students in any school.[55] *Part-time local pastors* "do not devote their entire time to the charge to which they are appointed."[56] Part-time local pastors also pursue theological education but sometimes at a reduced number of courses (depending on residency), usually half, compared with full-time local pastors.[57] *Students* appointed as local pastors also pursue theological education as determined by the board of ordained ministry.[58] They may be appointed as full or part-time local pastors. Students appointed as local pastors may be appointed in an annual conference other than their home annual conference.[59] According to the *Discipline*, "students who are appointed as local pastors continue to relate to the district committee on ordained ministry in the conference in which they are certified candidates."[60] Local pastors within each of these categories "may serve on any board, commission, or committee with voice and vote, except on matters of clergy character, qualifications, status, and ordination."[61] One exception to this disciplinary rule applies to full-time local pastors who have completed the Course of Study: they may serve on the board of ordained ministry with voice and vote.[62]

Membership as Ministry

Alongside the roles assumed by those described above, there are additional categories of membership within which we may practice ministry in The United Methodist Church.[63] As previously discussed, one may practice pastoral ministry in a formally recognized role, receiving the title of "Reverend," without leading a local church, holding full membership in the annual conference, or ordination. The three main categories of membership for those ordained or practicing pastoral roles are *associate, provisional,* and *full.* Dating back to John Wesley's leadership of the early Methodist movement, the roles and membership have represented more complexity than simplicity. Additionally, while the following pages discuss the requirements and processes described in the *Discipline,* each annual conference possesses the authority to further modify requirements and processes for receiving annual conference membership.

Associate membership is most often held by licensed local pastors or ordained pastoral members of other denominations. Full and part-time local pastors may be elected to associate membership by vote of the clergy members in full connection, upon recommendation of the board of ordained ministry when they meet the following conditions: (1) being at least age forty, (2) having four years of service as full-time local pastors, (3) having completed five years of Course of Study and training for license as a local pastor, (4) having completed at least sixty semester hours toward the bachelor of arts in a University Senate–approved institution, (5) having been recommended by the district committee on ordained ministry and the board of ordained ministry, (6) declaring willingness to accept continuous appointment, and (7) satisfying the board of ordained ministry's expectations for wellness including a psychological report, criminal background check, and credit check, (8) committing to the highest Christian ideals of holy living, and (9) passing an examination of the board of ordained ministry including a written sermon.[64]

Associate members of an annual conference participate in the church's itinerant ministry. They are permitted to vote on all matters except: (a) constitutional amendments and (b) all matters of ordination, character, and conference relations of clergy.[65] There is a fellowship of local pastors and associate members organized in each annual conference.[66]

Provisional membership is held by those preparing for full membership and ordination as deacon or elder. Candidates may be elected to provisional membership by vote of the clergy members in full connection, upon recommendation of the board of ordained ministry when they meet requirements in the following areas: (1) Candidacy: The *Discipline* requires a candidate to have been certified as a candidate for provisional membership for at least one year and no more than twelve years.[67] (2) Service: Candidates will demonstrate their gifts for ministry and leadership according to the expectations of the district committee on ordained ministry.[68] There are a number of ways to fulfill the educational requirements. Many candidates fulfill the requirements for education through (3) an undergraduate bachelor's degree from an institution approved by the University Senate and (4) completion of a portion of the credits required for the particular order at the graduate level.[69]

Provisional elders are required to complete one-half of the credits toward a master of divinity degree including courses in Old Testament, New Testament, theology, church history, mission of the church in the world, evangelism, worship/liturgy, and United Methodist studies (these courses represent the basic graduate theological studies).[70] Provisional deacons may complete one-half of a master's degree from a United Methodist seminary or one approved by the University Senate, receive a master's degree in the area of specialized ministry in which they will serve, or complete one-half of the basic graduate theological studies.[71] There are other means to accomplish the educational requirements. For example, a local pastor may complete the following alternative educational requirements for provisional membership if they are forty years of age at the time of certification as a candidate: have a bachelor's degree and complete the five-year Course of Study for ordained ministry as well as an advanced course of study consisting of thirty semester hours of graduate theological study offered by a University Senate approved seminary.[72]

Receipt of provisional membership also requires an examination by the board of ordained ministry. This examination consists of written and oral (in the context of an interview) responses to a number of questions.

The examination questions for provisional membership focus for the most part on doctrinal standards of The United Methodist Church.[73] Candidates for provisional membership are also required to receive a recommendation from the district committee on ordained ministry with a minimum vote of three-fourths support to the board of ordained ministry and a recommendation from the board of ordained ministry with a minimum vote of two-thirds support to the clergy session.[74] Each candidate is required to undergo a psychological evaluation and provide a notarized statement of any criminal charges or complaints of sexual misconduct or child abuse.[75] Additionally, each candidate provides an autobiographical statement and report of good health.[76]

Provisional members are commissioned to their ministry roles during a worship service of the annual conference at which the bishop commissions each candidate by name to the ministry of deacon or elder: "Commissioning is the act of the church that publicly acknowledges God's call and the response, talents, gifts and training of the candidate. The church invokes the Holy Spirit as the candidate is commissioned to be a faithful servant leader among the people, to lead the church in service, to proclaim the Word of God and to equip others for ministry."[77] Following a service of commissioning the bishop appoints each provisional member to serve for a minimum of two years in preparation for full membership in the annual conference and ordination as deacon or elder.[78] Provisional members preparing for ordination as deacon or elder may be licensed for pastoral ministry.[79] Provisional members in extension ministries, graduate programs, or appointments beyond the local church are also accountable to the district superintendent and board of ordained ministry.[80] Provisional members have the right to vote on all matters except: (a) constitutional amendments, (b) election of delegates to jurisdictional and general conferences, and (c) all matters of ordination, character, and conference relations of clergy.[81] Provisional members are not eligible for election as delegates to general and jurisdictional conferences, but may serve on any board, commission, or committee of the annual conference with the exception of the board of ordained ministry.[82]

During one's provisional membership, in preparation for examination and election to full membership, as well as during candidacy in preparation for provisional membership, candidates participate in a program of mentoring: "Mentors shall be recommended by the cabinet, selected, trained and held accountable by the Board of Ordained Ministry."[83] There are two categories of mentors—the candidacy mentor and the clergy mentor[84]—and each is trained to provide counsel and guidance related to the candidacy process. Individuals are assigned to mentoring groups or to an individual mentor by the district committee on ordained ministry. According to the *Discipline*, "mentoring occurs within a relationship where the mentor takes responsibility for creating a safe place for reflection and growth. An effective mentor has a mature faith, models effective ministry, and possesses the necessary skill to help individuals discern their call to ministry."[85] Mentors are most often assigned to local pastors, provisional members, and those pastors transferring from other denominations, though mentors may be assigned as need is discerned.[86]

Evaluation and support of all members and pastors is an important aspect of nurturing and discerning ongoing effectiveness of ministry. The district superintendent facilitates the evaluation of those under appointment in consultation with the staff parish relations committee or other supportive body within the ministry appointment.[87] Boards of ordained ministry (at the annual conference level) develop criteria and processes used.[88] Evaluations of those under appointment in local churches and in extension ministry are evaluated annually by the pertinent bodies.[89] Complementary to one's ongoing posture of evaluation and discernment is support to enable continuing education and spiritual growth.[90] In addition to vacation and Sabbath is the need for ongoing spiritual and intellectual growth.[91]

Full membership or full connection is held by those ordained to the roles of deacon and elder. Provisional members may be elected to full membership following at least two years as provisional members of the annual conference and successful fulfillment of the disciplinary requirements for full membership. These requirements include the recommendation of the board of ordained ministry with at least two-thirds vote of support to the clergy session of the annual conference and two-thirds vote of the clergy members of the annual conference.[92] The additional requirements are similar to those for provisional membership:

(1) Candidates for full membership will have served effectively in full-time ministry for at least two years under the appointment of the bishop.[93] (2) Having previously received election to provisional membership, (3) candidates for full membership will complete the graduate educational requirements, most often the completion of seminary prior to receiving a full-time ministry appointment from the bishop.

Receipt of full membership, similar to provisional membership, also requires written and oral (in the form of an interview) examination by the board of ordained ministry. While the questions still refer to the United Methodist doctrinal standards, the focus shifts to the role and presence of the standards in the candidate's practice of ministry.[94] The examination also requires the preaching of at least one sermon, a project demonstrating fruitfulness in participating in the church's mission, and an ability to communicate clearly in both written and oral form.[95] Recommendation to full membership also requires the demonstration of good health.[96]

During the clergy session at which full members are considered for election, the bishop may choose to examine candidates, drawing from the historic questions. These questions, as well as the duties of the preachers, date back to John Wesley and Francis Asbury in the early generations of American Methodism. In 1787, the directions to the traveling preachers (the equivalent to elders in full connection today) included: "1. Be diligent. Never be unemployed. Never be triflingly employed. Never trifle away Time; neither spend any more Time at any Place than is strictly necessary." Another direction states: "Be punctual. Do every Thing exactly at the Time. And do not mend our Rules, but keep them; not for Wrath but Conscience sake."[97] Candidates elected to full membership at the clergy session of annual conference receive ordination from the laying on of hands by one's bishop during a service of ordination following the clergy session.

The United Methodist Church is committed to ecumenical partnerships and collaboration. United Methodist clergy members in full connection may be appointed annually to churches of other Christian denominations or to ecumenical shared ministries.[98] The *Discipline* also describes a commitment to opportunities for ministry in cooperative and other appointment or parish settings.[99] The following sections discuss in more detail the roles of elders and deacons in full connection. The participation of elders in full connection in the itinerant system is discussed in the next section. The appointment-making process is described in further detail in the next chapter on "Superintendency."

The Elder in Full Connection

Full-time ordained ministry in The United Methodist Church is most often carried out by elders in full connection or full membership: "Elders are ordained to a lifetime ministry of Word, Sacrament, Order, and Service."[100] Elders in full connection may supervise deacons in full connection as well as other local pastors and lay ministers. They most often serve as lead pastors in local churches. "By authority given in their ordination, they are authorized to preach and teach the Word of God, to provide pastoral care and counsel, to administer the sacraments of baptism and Holy Communion, and to order the life of the Church for service in mission and ministry."[101] Elders may also serve in appointments beyond the local church or extension ministries. In all settings the elder fulfills his or her calling "by leading the people of God in worship and prayer, by leading persons to faith in Jesus Christ, by exercising pastoral supervision, and by ordering the Church in mission to the world."[102]

The elder in full connection is given the authority to vote on all matters pertaining to those in or seeking membership as full members. The elder shares with the deacon in full connection responsibility for discerning matters of ordination and conference relations of clergy.[103] Elders, with deacons, may "vote on all matters in the annual conference except in election of lay delegates to the general and jurisdictional or central conferences (¶601a)."[104] Like deacons, as well as associate members, the elders also share in covenant relationship through the order of elders formed in each annual conference.[105]

Duties of an Elder

Responsibilities accompany the authority of ordination and full membership granted to elders in full connection. There are several paragraphs that offer descriptions and summaries of these responsibilities, but ¶¶340 and 341 are the clearest in their descriptions of the responsibilities and duties of this very important role—both in terms of what to do and what not to do. The following is drawn directly from ¶340, "Responsibilities and Duties of Elders and Licensed Pastors," and provides a detailed job description organized according to the fourfold ministry of the elder in all settings: word, sacrament, order, and service:

> Licensed pastors share with the elders the responsibilities and duties of a pastor for this fourfold ministry, within the context of their appointment.
>
> a) *Word and ecclesial acts:*
>   (1) To preach the Word of God, lead in worship, read and teach the Scriptures, and engage the people in study and witness.
>   (a) To ensure faithful transmission of the Christian faith.
>   (b) To lead people in discipleship and evangelistic outreach that others might come to know Christ and to follow him.
>   (2) To counsel persons with personal, ethical, or spiritual struggles.
>   (3) To perform ecclesial acts of marriage and burial.
>   (a) To perform the marriage ceremony after due counsel with the parties involved and in accordance with the laws of the state and the rules of The United Methodist Church. The decision to perform the ceremony shall be the right and responsibility of the pastor.
>   (b) To conduct funeral and memorial services and provide care and grief counseling.
>   (4) To visit in the homes of the church and the community, especially among the sick, aged, imprisoned, and others in need.
>   (5) To maintain all confidences inviolate, including confessional confidences, except in the case of suspected child abuse or neglect, or in cases where mandatory reporting is required by civil law.
> b) *Sacrament:*
>   (1) To administer the sacraments of baptism and the Supper of the Lord according to Christ's ordinance.
>   (a) To prepare the parents and sponsors before baptizing infants or children, and instruct them concerning the

significance of baptism and their responsibilities for the Christian training of a baptized child.

(b) To encourage reaffirmation of the baptismal covenant and renewal of baptismal vows at different stages of life.

(c) To encourage people baptized in infancy or early childhood to make their profession of faith, after instruction, so that they might become professing members of the church.

(d) To explain the meaning of the Lord's Supper and to encourage regular participation as a means of grace to grow in faith and holiness.

(e) To select and train deacons and lay members to serve the consecrated communion elements.

(2) To encourage the private and congregational use of the other means of grace.

c) *Order:*

(1) To be the administrative officer of the local church and to assure that the organizational concerns of the congregation are adequately provided for.

(a) To give pastoral support, guidance, and training to the lay leadership, equipping them to fulfill the ministry to which they are called.

(b) To give oversight to the educational program of the church and encourage the use of United Methodist literature and media.

(c) To be responsible for organizational faithfulness, goal setting, planning and evaluation.

(d) To search out and counsel men and women for the ministry of deacons, elders, local pastors and other church related ministries.

(2) To administer the temporal affairs of the church in their appointment, the annual conference, and the general church.

(a) To administer the provisions of the *Discipline*.

(b) To give an account of their pastoral ministries to the charge and annual conference according to the prescribed forms.

(c) To provide leadership for the funding ministry of the congregation.

(d) To model and promote faithful financial stewardship and to encourage giving as a spiritual discipline by teaching the biblical principles of giving.

(e) To lead the congregation in the fulfillment of its mission through full and faithful payment of all apportioned ministerial support, administrative, and benevolent funds.

(f) To care for all church records and local church financial obligations, and to certify the accuracy of all financial, membership, and any other reports submitted by the local church to the annual conference for use in apportioning costs back to the church.

(3) To participate in denominational and conference programs and training opportunities.

(a) To seek out opportunities for cooperative ministries with other United Methodist pastors and churches.

(b) To be willing to assume supervisory responsibilities within the connection.

(4) To lead the congregation in racial and ethnic inclusiveness.

d) *Service:*

(1) To embody the teachings of Jesus in servant ministries and servant leadership.

(2) To give diligent pastoral leadership in ordering the life of the congregation for discipleship in the world.

(3) To build the body of Christ as a caring and giving community, extending the ministry of Christ to the world.

(4) To participate in community, ecumenical and interreligious concerns and to encourage the people to become so involved and to pray and labor for the unity of the Christian community.[106]

Also important for the effective and faithful ministry of pastors is refraining from unauthorized conduct, which is clearly outlined in ¶341:

1. Pastors shall first obtain the written consent of the district superintendent before engaging for an evangelist any person who is not a general evangelist (¶¶630.3f, 1112.7), a clergy member of an annual conference, a local pastor, or a certified lay servant in good standing in The United Methodist Church.

2. No pastor shall discontinue services in a local church between sessions of the annual conference without the consent of the charge conference and the district superintendent.

3. No pastor shall arbitrarily organize a pastoral charge. (See ¶259 for the method of organizing a local church.)

4. No pastors shall hold a religious service within the bounds of a pastoral charge other than the one to which appointed without the consent of the pastor of the charge or the district superintendent. No pastor shall hold a religious service within the bounds of a pastoral charge or establish a ministry to a college or university campus served by The United Methodist Church without the consent of the pastor of the charge, or campus minister or chaplain serving the charge, or the district superintendent. If that pastor does not refrain from such conduct, he or she shall then be liable to the provisions of ¶363.1 and ¶2702.

5. All clergy of The United Methodist Church are charged to maintain all confidences inviolate, including confessional confidences, except in the cases of suspected child abuse or neglect or in cases where mandatory reporting is required by civil law.

6. Ceremonies that celebrate homosexual unions shall not be conducted by our ministers and shall not be conducted in our churches.

7. No pastor shall re-baptize. The practice of re-baptism does not conform with God's action in baptism and is not consistent with Wesleyan tradition and the historic teaching of the church. Therefore, the pastor should counsel any person seeking re-baptism to participate in a rite of re-affirmation of baptismal vows.[107]

Upon election to full membership and ordination, elders submit themselves to the bishop and participation in the *itinerant* system. The itinerant system continues to be the accepted method for appointment of ordained elders, provisional elders, and associate members in The United Methodist Church:[108] "Bishops and cabinets shall commit to and support open itineracy and the protection of the prophetic pulpit and diversity."[109] Since the leadership of John Wesley in the early Methodist movement, the appointment of clergy and traveling preachers, historically the most authoritative roles within the Methodist and Wesleyan traditions, has occurred through an itinerant system. Itineracy and appointment-making are discussed in more detail in the next chapter.

Extension Ministries

Elders in full connection and associate members may receive appointments to extension ministries even though they are full participants in the itinerant system and remain willing to receive an appointment from the bishop.[110] When possible, the hiring ministry will consult with the ordained minister's bishop to request approval prior to resolving an employment agreement.[111] Similarly, an elder desiring appointment extending the ministry of The United Methodist Church will consult with his or her bishop or district superintendent prior to interviewing for such a role.[112]

The *Discipline* specifies four categories of appointments in order to distinguish between the ministry to which all Christians are called and the ministry for which clergy are formed and authorized to practice within the itinerant system.[113] There are appointments (1) within the connectional structure of United Methodism. Within this category are subcategories including appointments to (a) positions for which the annual conference provides the pension (such as district superintendents and conference staff members), (b) general agencies, (c) a United Methodist institution or other ministry, and (d) an ecumenical agency.[114] Additional categories of appointments are (2) those to extension ministries endorsed by the General Board of Higher Education and Ministry, (3) those endorsed by the General Board of Global Ministries, and (4) those within other Christian denominations.[115]

Clergy appointed to extension ministries have the opportunity to meet annually with the bishop, district superintendent, and board of ordained ministry.[116] Clergy in extension ministries are expected to establish an affiliation with a local church in their home annual conference.[117] If serving outside the bounds of their annual conference of membership, they are expected to affiliate with a local church in the annual conference in which they serve.[118] Clergy are required to submit reports to their home bishop and district superintendent as well as the bishop and charge conference within the annual conference in which they serve.[119]

General Evangelist

The General Board of Discipleship sets standards for and facilitates the ministry of general evangelists. This role is filled by elders in full connection. According to the *Discipline*, "an elder who feels called by God to be a general evangelist should prepare definitely for such service under the guidance of the annual conference to which that person belongs."[120] The annual conference board of discipleship annually, in consultation with the board of ordained ministry, recommends to the bishop the appointment of individuals as general evangelists.[121] There may be one or more general evangelist(s) within an annual conference. General evangelists serve the annual conference by preaching and teaching widely to support the evangelistic witness of the annual conference.

The Deacon in Full Connection

The United Methodist Church established the current (permanent) role of deacon at the General Conference in 1996. The person filling this role is ordained and holds full membership in the annual conference; she or he also shares, with elders, responsibility for all matters of ordination, character, and conference relations of clergy.[122] The role of deacon, a role deeply rooted in Christian tradition, receives additional authority in comparison with preceding roles within the Methodist tradition.[123] Deacons within United Methodism "are ordained by a bishop to a lifetime ministry of Word, Service, Compassion, and Justice, to both the community and the congregation in a ministry that connects the two."[124]

Other diaconate roles preceded the current order of deacon within Methodist traditions. For example, the early Methodist renewal movement within Great Britain and the earliest embodiment of Methodism in America practiced a two-step ordination of deacon to elder[125]—a pattern that was in place until 1996.[126] Preceding the current role of deacon was that of diaconal minister, established among United Methodists in 1976.[127] This role developed from influential forces emerging from the ecumenical movement among the World Council of Churches.[128] According to the 1976 *Discipline*, "a diaconal minister is a person whose decision to make a professional career in the employed status in The United Methodist Church or its related agencies is accompanied by the meeting of standards for the office of diaconal minister, who has been certified or commissioned in the chosen field of service, and who has been consecrated by a bishop."[129] According to Kenneth Rowe, "diaconal ministers were laypersons called of God; employed by the church or an outside agency, either part-time or full-time; and set apart through consecration for specialized ministries of love, justice, and service."[130] While the service of the diaconal minister occurred primarily within the church, the current deacon serves primarily in the world.

Deacons serve both local churches and communities, acting as a bridge between the two: "In the congregation, the ministry of the deacon is to teach and to form disciples, and to lead worship together with other ordained and laypersons."[131] Deacons also work for justice, "serving with compassion as they seek to serve those on the margins of society."[132] Bishops appoint deacons, like elders, to their places of ministry, and while they do not itinerate, they may work in a range of contexts including local churches, agencies, schools, colleges, and theological schools within the United Methodist connection.[133] They may also be appointed to serve in educational, corporate, or other service industries beyond United Methodism.[134] According to the *Discipline*, "the General Board of Higher Education and Ministry, Division of Ordained Ministry, in order to assist the Boards of Ordained Ministry and cabinets, will provide guidelines for validating the appropriateness of appointment settings beyond the local church and will be available for consultation with bishops, cabinets, and Boards of Ordained Ministry."[135] Similar to elders in extension ministry, deacons are accountable to the bishop, district superintendent, and board of ordained ministry and affiliate with a local church in their home annual conference as well as with the connectional structure in the annual conference in which they serve, if other than their home.[136] Deacons and provisional deacons appointed to a local church hold membership in that charge conference (technically, though in addition to their membership in the annual conference). Those appointed beyond the local church, after consultation with the pastor and district superintendent related to that charge, also hold membership within a charge conference in the annual conference in which they are appointed.[137]

Conclusion

Whether a lay minister, local pastor, elder or deacon, or regular participant and committee member in a local church, all Christians are commissioned to ministry by our baptisms. While the variety of ministry roles for lay and ordained members within United Methodism may seem complex, these reflect ministry roles and their purpose from early Methodism until now. In the next chapter we will explore two additional roles of the superintendency and their work to facilitate the mission and ministry of the denomination.

– Chapter Five –

Superintendency

John Wesley is recognized as the first general superintendent of the Methodist renewal movement, particularly as it spread across Britain and then America.[1] Wesley named Francis Asbury and Thomas Coke as superintendents in 1784 to oversee the Methodist movement in America. Asbury and Coke in the context of the Christmas Conference then adopted the term *bishop* for their roles.[2] After the example of John Wesley, the United Methodists and those preceding them in the Wesleyan and Methodist traditions continue the role of superintending as an office of oversight facilitating the ministry of the connection. Superintendency is not unique to Methodism. Indeed, Wesley used the term *superintendency* as an alternative to *bishop*, reflecting Pietistic as well as Lutheran and Reformed themes. Within these traditions, but specifically across Pietism, superintendency appears as the translated term from scripture of *episkopos* to include facilitation of the work of societies or small groups (ecclesiolae in ecclesia) within the general or established church(es).[3]

As Thomas Frank points out, "the *Discipline* refers to the whole function as superintendency, but clearly names the discrete offices within it as 'bishop' and 'district superintendent' (the latter an extension of the former)."[4] The combined term *district superintendent* appears initially in 1908 in The Methodist Episcopal Church.[5] The Evangelical Association follows with its use in 1930, The Methodist Church (consisting of the amalgamation of Methodist Protestants and The Methodist Episcopal

Church, South, with The Methodist Episcopal Church) in 1939, and The Evangelical United Brethren Church in 1946.[6] As the work of facilitating the ministry of the connection has grown, the role of district superintendent, a key connector between laity and local churches, other clergy and bishops, has increased in complexity and significance.

According to the *Discipline*, "the task of superintending in The United Methodist Church resides in the office of bishop and extends to the district superintendent, with each possessing distinct and collegial responsibilities."[7] In this way district superintendents serve to extend the role of superintendency and the office of bishop, "to equip the Church in its disciple-making ministry" facilitating the mission of the Church.[8] Though the language of "general superintendency" is seldom used, the *Discipline* explains that "those who superintend [bishops and district superintendents] carry primary responsibility for ordering the life of the Church. It is their task to enable the gathered Church to worship and to evangelize faithfully."[9] Bishops and district superintendents are not ordained to their roles as a separate order, but rather are elected and appointed respectively from elders ordained as ministers of service, word, sacrament, and order.[10] This chapter will reflect on the history of the role, election or assignment, and responsibilities of the superintendency of both bishops and district superintendents.

Bishops

Despite the shift in terms from *superintendency* to *bishop* in the late eighteenth century, the episcopacy in American Methodism is firmly rooted in and continues the legacy of John Wesley. According to Bishops Coke and Asbury in their epigraph included in the 1798 *Discipline*, "nothing has been introduced into Methodism by the present episcopal form of government, which was not before fully exercised by Mr. Wesley."[11] That said, bishops in American Methodism clearly differentiated John Wesley's role as more authoritative and exceeding theirs.[12] While Francis Asbury's position of authority over his colleagues differed from that of Wesley, he nevertheless was able to have a significant impact because of his episcopal role, and so he indelibly shaped the role of the episcopacy in American Methodism.[13] Therefore, from its inception, the character of American Methodism was episcopal—a characteristic represented in its very name, Methodist Episcopal, until 1939.

Influenced by John Wesley and Francis Asbury's distinctive styles of leadership, birthed within the contexts of their formation and ministry, the episcopacy in America took on a peculiar character of its own. For example, the role of episcopacy within American Methodism may be seen as a parallel to the executive authority of the presidential office described in the Constitution of the United States. Episcopacy in American Methodism is embodied in the role of "the bishop as a missionary in a popular movement."[14] While American episcopacy includes the traditional roles of teacher and defender of Christian doctrine, its distinctive missional orientation is peculiar to the renewal movements of Methodism.[15] Consistent with much of contemporary Methodism, the practice of its episcopacy and ecclesiology allows for a responsiveness to God's vocation for the movement and its participation in God's unfolding reign.[16]

The episcopacy in American Methodism is protected by its Constitution, specifically Restrictive Rule 3: "The General Conference shall not change or alter any part or rule of our government so as to do away with episcopacy or destroy the plan of our itinerant general superintendency."[17] According to Richey and Frank, the episcopacy is one of a number of constitutional principles of The United Methodist Church along with the conference and Judicial Council.[18] The Constitution of The United Methodist Church is relatively new—revised in 1968 at the time of union with the Evangelical United Brethren—but the Restrictive Rules, a component of the current Constitution, date to 1808 and early American Methodism. The inclusion of the episcopacy and its itineracy among the Restrictive Rules demonstrates the deep rootedness of the episcopacy in American Methodism.

According to James E. Kirby, the story of episcopacy within American Methodism consists of two foci: (1) the significant impact of Francis Asbury on the role, and (2) the division of the church in 1844 into north and south.[19] Before assuming the role of bishop, Asbury declined Wesley's nomination to be appointed general superintendent and instead requested the consent of the preachers gathered, thereby shifting the authority to make such appointments to the conference.[20] Asbury promoted and modeled itinerant ministry and with his successors worked tirelessly for unity as the renewal movement grew swiftly.[21] The second focus emerged within a complex landscape of approaching civil war, economic shifts, and social struggles, among them slavery. In the midst of the dynamics contributing to the 1844 geographical split was a difference of vision for governance of the denomination. The Methodist Episcopal Church, South, was formed in large part to defend an "Asburian" ideal of episcopacy "as a co-equal branch of church government."[22] Alternatively, the north "affirmed the concept of a strong General Conference directing an episcopacy."[23] Elements of these divergent versions of governance—the competing authority of the episcopacy and General Conference—continue within contemporary United Methodism.

In 1939 The Methodist Episcopal Church; Methodist Episcopal Church, South; and the Methodist Protestants united to form The Methodist Church. At the time of union, the General Conference delegated to jurisdictional conferences (five regional and one racial— the Central Jurisdiction, which is discussed further in chapter 7) the historic power to elect bishops.[24] Richey and Frank point out another change that occurred following 1939: The *Discipline* required "that a bishop preside and make appointments in the annual conference(s) of his residency for all four years of a quadrennium."[25] Prior to 1939, the longstanding practice was for bishops to preside three out of four years, "with a fellow bishop designated to preside and make the appointments in one year out of the four."[26] The union of 1939 solidified the regionalization of the episcopacy and instituted the assignment of episcopal areas, a trend away from a general itinerating superintendency across the connection.[27]

Election and Assignment

Bishops within The United Methodist Church, according to the Constitution, "shall be elected by the respective jurisdictional and central conferences and consecrated in the historic manner."[28] The election process formally begins in the annual conference session immediately prior to the next regular session of the jurisdictional or central conference.[29] At this time an annual conference may name one or more nominees for episcopal election at the jurisdictional (or central) conference to follow.[30] However, in American Methodism the informal process often begins at the preceding annual conference more than one year prior to the jurisdictional conferences during the elections for general and jurisdictional conference delegates. Nominees most often emerge from the leading delegates as well as nominees from caucuses representing particular interest groups. Though not in every case, often an episcopal nominee will lead an annual conference delegation. In preparation for the formal nomination of episcopal candidates, jurisdictions and annual conferences may structure a process of interviews or conversations to inform the discernment process resulting in nominees.

The election of episcopal candidates occurs at jurisdictional and central conferences following an assessment of the leadership needs and the establishment of the number, if any, of bishops to be elected.[31] In the United States context, the jurisdictional conferences meet simultaneously during the month of July once every four years in their different locations. Each jurisdictional or central conference establishes the percentage of votes necessary to elect a bishop.[32] Delegates are directed to "give due consideration to the inclusiveness of The United Methodist Church with respect to sex, race, and national origin."[33] According to the *Discipline*, "consecration of bishops may take place at the session of the conference at which election occurs or at a place and time designated by the conference."[34] Notably, in United Methodism bishops are not ordained to another order, but *consecrated* to their role. In the American context the consecration of bishops most often occurs prior to the conclusion of the jurisdictional conference and includes bishops as well as episcopal representatives from other Christian communions.[35]

Upon election and consecration to the office of bishop, bishops hold membership in the Council of Bishops, composed of all active and retired United Methodist bishops. Bishops also hold membership in a College of Bishops, composed of those bishops assigned to a jurisdictional or central conference.[36] Drawing from a monarchical ecclesiology, bishops are set apart for life in the United States, though they remain in the same order with the other elders.[37]

In each jurisdiction a jurisdictional committee on episcopacy is organized and constituted of a clergy and lay delegate from each annual conference.[38] This committee is responsible for the assignment of bishops, which it achieves by consulting with the College of Bishops and making recommendations to the jurisdictional conference.[39] Most often bishops are assigned to a single, but sometimes to two or even three, annual conference(s). Assignments to episcopal areas, basically geographic regions, are considered following the election of episcopal delegates each quadrennium at jurisdictional conference.[40]

Responsibilities and Leadership

The responsibilities of bishops, not unlike district superintendents, have continued to increase in number and complexity. In the contemporary context, bishops are perhaps most known for their authority to appoint pastors to local churches (as well as extension ministries) and to preside at annual (and central) conferences. Bishops communicate with the connection in a variety of ways. One consistent medium is through the episcopal address given to General Conference and printed in the *Discipline*.[41] Often bishops also address the annual conferences in which they preside. The specific responsibilities of bishops are described by the *Discipline* in three categories: (1) leadership—spiritual and temporal; (2) presidential duties; and (3) working with ordained, licensed, consecrated, and commissioned personnel.[42] As these categories demonstrate, while bishops are authorized with appointment-making and presidential duties, these tasks are framed by the bishops' primary duty to spiritual and temporal leadership.

Bishops in The United Methodist Church, consistent with the role throughout Christian tradition, carry the responsibility of *spiritual and temporal leadership*. Tradition describes this most often as teaching and upholding the doctrines of the church, which is also included in the disciplinary description.[43] The 1848 *Discipline* describes bishops as in charge of appointing "a course of reading and study, proper to be pursued by candidates for the ministry for the term of four years."[44] Through their spiritual leadership, bishops "guard, transmit, teach, and proclaim, corporately and individually, the apostolic faith as it is expressed in Scripture and tradition, and, as they are led and endowed by the Spirit, to interpret that faith evangelically and prophetically."[45] Bishops fulfill this responsibility by traveling widely throughout the connection, encouraging and strengthening the local church, laity, and clergy.[46] Another important and distinctive responsibility of bishops, individually and corporately, is their ecumenical role through "leadership in the quest for Christian unity."[47] Bishops convene the orders of deacons and elders in their episcopal areas, working with the elected chairperson of each.[48] Bishops also organize missions authorized by General Conference, model and promote generous giving, and support the evangelical witness of the whole church.[49]

According to the *Discipline*, bishops "preside in the general, jurisdictional, central, and annual conferences."[50] An aspect of their *presidential duties* is presiding liturgically. For example, bishops are given the responsibility and privilege of consecrating other bishops, ordaining elders and deacons, consecrating diaconal ministers, and commissioning deaconesses, home missioners, and missionaries.[51] In addition to their public leadership convening conferences, bishops provide "general oversight for the fiscal and program operations" of the annual conferences to which they are assigned.[52] They serve on institutional boards and agencies, often presiding, but usually serving in a less direct capacity with regard to program and fiscal oversight.[53] Bishops often oversee processes for clergy and laity in involuntary administrative and some judicial proceedings, though with respect for separation of powers (¶2701). Bishops presiding in annual, central, or jurisdictional conferences hold the authority to decide all questions of law arising in the sessions of the respective conference. These questions, presented in writing, are recorded in the journal. The decisions of law administered by the bishop are authoritative upon review of the Judicial Council, which may affirm, modify, or reverse.[54]

According to the Constitution, "the bishops shall appoint, after consultation with the district superintendents, ministers to the charges."[55] Bishops work with set-apart ministers. They authorize the appointments of all clergy, including district superintendents, licensed local pastors, deaconesses, home missioners, and missionaries.[56] Additionally, bishops "make and fix appointments in the annual conferences, provisional annual conferences and missions as the *Discipline* may direct."[57] This includes approving appointments beyond the local church and fixing the charge conference membership of those ordained ministers and appointing deaconesses, home missioners, and missionaries to the General Board of Global Ministries.[58] Bishops oversee requests for transfer of annual conference memberships and appointments of associate, provisional, and full members "to attend any school, college, or theological seminary listed by the University Senate" or to participate in clinical pastoral education.[59] Bishops provide significant leadership to the denomination through their historic yet shifting role, which is complemented by the ministry of district superintendents.

District Superintendents

The office of district superintendent dates in many ways to the beginning of the Methodist renewal movement. The current office is most closely related to its predecessor of presiding elder. The office of presiding elder was officially recognized and its duties defined in 1792.[60] Similar to district superintendents, presiding elders were "chosen by, accountable to, and serv[ed] at the pleasure of the bishop, they were, and are, the load-bearing points of the Methodist system."[61] Presiding elders functioned as *de facto* bishops in the absence of episcopal leadership,[62] and in this way they assumed all the duties of the bishop, including presiding at annual conferences and making appointments, with the exception of carrying out ordination.[63]

District superintendents, as extensions of the general superintendency, are appointed by the bishop within an annual conference after consultation with the currently serving cabinet and committee on district superintendency.[64] Similar to the election of bishops, "in the selection of superintendents, bishops shall give due consideration to the inclusiveness of The United Methodist Church with respect to sex, race, national origin, physical challenge, and age, except for the provisions of mandatory retirement."[65] Following appointment, the district superintendent, though remaining in the order of elders, participates in the cabinet of district superintendents within an annual conference convened by the bishop.[66] The normal length of appointment for a district superintendent is up to six years, though this may be extended to eight years at the discretion of the bishop in consultation with the cabinet and committee on district superintendency.[67]

Responsibilities: Chief Missional Strategist

The district superintendent is the *chief missional strategist* of the district,[68] a key role in the midst of the connection. The language of chief missional strategist was introduced in the 2012 *Discipline* in large measure as a response to pressures for economic efficiencies and missional needs pushing annual conferences to better articulate and demonstrate their mission and purpose. This includes the district superintendent's commitment to and embodiment of inclusiveness through, for example, multicultural, multiracial, and cooperative ministries; promotion of generous Christian giving; and efforts to develop Christian unity for the purpose of extending the church's witness in the world.[69]

District superintendents, in their extension of the office of bishop, oversee the ministry of the clergy, those in local churches as well as in extension ministries. The district superintendent continues the spiritual and temporal leadership of the bishop's office as well as participating in the deployment of clergy and set-apart ministers by presiding at charge and district gatherings or delegating these responsibilities to other elders cultivating leadership across the district. In these capacities and in the overseeing of programs and administration of the district in the midst of the connection, district superintendents facilitate witness and service in the world.

The district superintendent, like the bishop, works with clergy during the appointment-making process, liaising with the board of ordained ministry and district committee on ministry to recruit candidates and help them in their discernment of and preparation for set-apart and ordained ministry.[70] District superintendents must also work with the bishop and cabinet as well as staff/pastor-parish relations committees to execute the deployment of clergy and set-apart ministers,[71] who they then supervise and to whom they provide "support, care, and counsel . . . concerning matters affecting their effective ministry."[72] This often includes the formation of covenant groups and other supportive structures for clergy, clergy families, and laity within the district.[73] At the same time, also to facilitate and promote the ministry and witness of the church in a district, the district superintendent provides leadership and support through charge conferences and other gatherings.[74]

In addition to their work providing spiritual leadership to clergy, laity, and local churches, district superintendents also practice administrative oversight. This takes the form of maintaining appropriate records of all clergy (including those in extension ministry) appointed to charges within the district.[75] Records are also maintained related to property, endowments, and other tangible assets of The United Methodist Church within the district.[76] The district superintendent, as an extension of the office of bishop, "shall interpret and decide all questions of Church law and discipline raised by the churches in the district, subject to review by the resident bishop of the annual conference."[77]

Appointment-Making

Itineracy is a foundational principle of Methodism overseen initially by Wesley in the British context and Asbury in the American context. Itineracy is a distinctive form of traveling ministry, directed by bishops and implemented by district superintendents, that allows for exchange of pastoral leadership and resources across the connection. Asbury, Coke, and their nineteenth-century episcopal descendants exercised substantial authority in the appointment of itinerant preachers. In the twentieth century, episcopal leadership, though still authoritative, shared the more complex responsibility of appointment-making with district superintendents. This practice of consultation in appointment-making emerged as the most significant revision to itinerant ministry during this period.

Beginning with John Wesley himself, itineracy emerged from a desire to meet the greatest needs and a willingness to travel to address those needs and eventually came to carry the momentum of the movement's mission to spread scriptural holiness over the land.[78] In Wesley's British Methodism, itineracy can be seen as a pragmatic embodiment of the movement's missional and connectional character that helped maintain doctrinal integrity. Flexible and mainly resilient in diverse geographies over the centuries, itineracy effectively established Methodism in the United States. Today the willingness to move still remains at the heart of Methodism's pivotal questions of polity and even doctrine.

Itinerating preachers manifested "the connexion" Wesley worked so diligently to establish and sustain. In early Methodism under Wesley's leadership, the connection was sustained by his authority to appoint itinerating preachers (after his death the conference inherited his authority). Through a clause included in the deed of every preaching house within the Methodist connection, Wesley maintained this authority. The clause stipulated the obligation of the trustees of the preaching house to accept preachers approved and appointed by Wesley. This clause helped ensure the trustees could not refuse these preachers. Alternatively, the trustees were entrusted with holding their preachers accountable to acceptable doctrine, namely "no other doctrine than that contained in Mr. Wesley's *Notes upon the New Testament* and four volumes of *Sermons*."[79] This shared practice and preservation of doctrinal faithfulness continues in the use of the trust clause in the deeds of United Methodist facilities. Preachers itinerated frequently in early Methodism. Initially preachers itinerated to a new circuit at least every three months; at most one might stay as long as two years.[80] The basic issue concerning the itineracy of full-time preachers was not that the preachers needed to move at particular intervals, but rather their sincerity of commitment to Methodism's mission. For Wesley this was demonstrated by their willingness to move.[81]

Francis Asbury continued Wesley's emphasis upon frequent itineracy of full-time preachers, though he experienced some dissent from other early American Methodist leaders, such as Joseph Pilmore and Richard Boardman. Thomas Coke and Asbury explained itineracy with the statement that "everything is kept moving as far as possible."[82] They cited biblical foundations and described itineracy as "the primitive and apostolic plan" after Wesley's example.[83] This peculiar Methodist polity, which complemented the cadre of local preachers, provided an incredibly effective method of expansion and fulfillment of Wesley's missional vision, planting Methodism not only across the ocean but also across the frontier.[84]

Itineracy continued in the spirit of Wesley, Coke, and Asbury in America until the middle of the nineteenth century, and, while deemed divinely prescribed, it was more immediately seen as immensely effective and therefore worth preserving. Like Wesley, American Methodists understood itineracy as a practice intimately related to the mission of the church in the world.[85] In the earliest itinerant practice, experienced by Pilmore and Boardman, preachers itinerated each quarter. In 1804, a two-year limit was established but with the normal appointment lasting one year. In 1864 The Methodist Episcopal Church set the limit at three years, increasing it later to an experimental duration of five years (albeit dropping this in 1900), while The Methodist Episcopal Church, South, set the limit at four years in 1866. With the settling of ministry and growth of the denomination, exceptions to these latter limits were not unusual, and in 1939 at the creation of The Methodist Church, no specific limits existed.[86]

Thus, itineracy has often served as a lens to focus and direct our most important conversations about the church's ministry and mission. However, one issue intimately related to itineracy seems still blurred: clergy compensation. This issue has remained noticeably absent in most historical and critical analyses of itineracy. Itineracy served Wesley's early Methodist movement as the central mechanism for fulfilling its mission. Could it be that itineracy is no longer merely a faithful practice emerging from the pursuit of God's mission for the church in the world? Instead, is it possible that itineracy has become captive to questions of clergy compensation such that its effectiveness in fulfilling God's mission is obscured?[87]

A number of principles guide current appointment-making within Methodism's itinerant system: First, clergy are appointed by the *bishop*. The bishop "is empowered to make and fix all appointments within the Episcopal area of which the annual conference is a part."[88] The bishops are empowered to appoint all clergy in full connection, including elders and deacons, as well as those in provisional and associate membership. Bishops making appointments consider the gifts and evidence of God's grace of those receiving appointments and the needs, characteristics, and opportunities of congregations, institutions, and communities.[89] Bishops appoint deacons in full connection in the annual conference in which they hold membership:[90] "The appointment shall reflect the nature of the ministry of the deacon as a faithful response of the mission of the church meeting the emerging needs in the world."[91] Though the bishop holds the authority to appoint all clergy, an appointment of a deacon in full connection may be initiated by the individual deacon, the agency seeking the deacon's service, the bishop, or the district superintendent.[92] Similarly, a change in appointment for an elder may be initiated by the pastor, a staff/pastor-parish relations committee, a district superintendent, or the bishop.[93]

A second guiding principle relates to the *receiving* of appointments. The call to serve a specific appointment within the United Methodist connection is a privilege. While appointments are guaranteed, signified by the language of "continuing availability for appointment,"[94] for elders in full connection, serving in a local church or extension ministry is an opportunity received in response to one's sacred vows taken at ordination. The 2012 General Conference considered the possibility of eliminating "guaranteed appointment" and worked toward this goal. However, the Judicial Council clarified the General Conference's action resulting in revisions to the process related to "evidence of continuing effectiveness" and limiting the authority of the bishop in such processes.[95]

A third guiding principle is the *openness* of itineracy within United Methodism. This "means appointments are made without regard to race, ethnic origin, gender, color, disability, marital status, or age, except for provisions of mandatory retirement."[96] Open itineracy is practiced in partnership by bishops and district superintendents as well as congregations. According to the *Discipline*, annual conferences provide training for staff/pastor-parish relations committees to "prepare congregations to receive the gifts and graces of appointed clergy without regard to race, ethnic origin, gender, color, disability, marital status, or age."[97] Open itineracy is a historic value held by United Methodism and its predecessor traditions. According to the *Discipline*, "the United Methodist Church promotes and holds in high esteem the opportunity of an inclusive church . . . with the formation of open itineracy."[98] John Wesley encouraged the preaching of laity and women with extraordinary calls and gifts, though he did not directly challenge the policies of the Church of England. Throughout Methodism's history, prophetic moments demonstrate our commitment to God's unfolding reign and the Spirit's witness in the midst of social resistance. For example, for many the ordination and appointment of women as well as people of color, including leading up to and following the dissolution of the Central Jurisdiction in 1968, represent such moments.

A final guiding principle of appointment-making within the itinerant system of United Methodism is *consultation*: "Consultation is the process whereby the bishop and/or district superintendent confer with the pastor and committee on pastor-parish relations, taking into consideration the criteria of ¶427, a performance evaluation, needs of the appointment under consideration, and mission of the Church."[99] As mentioned earlier in this section, the bishop, and by extension the district superintendent, are empowered to make appointments. However, the process of appointment-making includes consultation of all major parties involved in light of gifts, need, and mission, though this process may look different across annual conferences. According to the *Discipline*, "the process of consultation shall be mandatory in every annual conference."[100]

The criteria for appointment-making take into account several components, including "the unique needs of a charge, the community context, and also the gifts and evidence of God's grace of a particular pastor."[101] Profiles are developed in consultation with pastors and local churches to assist bishops, district superintendents, and cabinets with the discernment process. The *Discipline* describes the content of each profile, which is then reviewed annually by local churches and pastors. These profiles include descriptions of the congregational context, the pastor's gifts and graces, as well as the community context. The local church profile includes a description of the (1) general situation such as setting, size, financial condition, and lay leadership; (2) convictional stance (theology, spiritual life, prejudices—if any); (3) ministry of the congregation among the community; and (4) any special pastoral needs.[102] The pastor profile includes (1) spiritual and personal sensibility, (2) academic and career background, (3) skills and abilities, and (4) the pastor's ability to relate to a particular community setting.[103] The profile of the community context is often developed by the district superintendent in consultation with the pastor and staff/pastor-parish relations committee. These usually include (1) general demographic data such as age, gender, and racial-ethnic composition; (2) economic trends; (3) projected community changes; and (4) other aspects of the community surrounding the church.[104]

The process of consultation for the purpose of appointment-making, including those beyond the local church,[105] seeks to include all those affected by a possible change of appointment in the discernment process. As mentioned earlier, a change of appointment may be initiated by the pastor, staff/pastor-parish relations committee, district superintendent, or bishop. Requests for change of appointments are considered "in light of the profile developed for each charge and the gifts and evidence of God's grace, professional experience, and family needs of the pastor."[106] The district superintendent meets together or separately with the pastor and staff/pastor-parish relations committee to share the rationale for the change and describe the process.[107] "All appointments shall receive consideration by the bishop, the district superintendent(s), and the cabinet as a whole until a tentative decision is made."[108] The process of consultation continues with the district superintendent conferring with the pastor about a specific possible appointment with a number of steps depending on the nature of the appointment.[109] The district superintendent also confers with the receiving staff/pastor-parish relations committee about the nature of pastoral leadership.[110] If during the consultation process it is determined by the bishop and cabinet that an appointment will not be made, the process is repeated until the bishop determines an appointment will be made.[111] When the process is complete and an appointment is made, all those directly involved in the consultation process (cabinet, pastor, staff/pastor-parish relations committee) are informed before a public announcement is shared.[112]

Conclusion

The superintendency is a significant ministry (now set of ministries) within the Methodist tradition. Beginning with John Wesley, and followed by Francis Asbury, the role continues to develop to facilitate the mission of the church. This missional purpose is demonstrated through the responsibilities of bishops and, by extension, district superintendents. In the following chapters we will explore the role of local churches, conferences, councils, and agencies and their participation in the church's mission.

– Chapter Six –

The Local Church

The local church is often our primary context for experiencing church in United Methodism. The local church is the venue in which we worship together each week, study the scriptures, and share in the Lord's Supper. From our local churches we embark on journeys of outreach and ministry with neighbors near and far. It is the place in which children and loved ones are initiated into the body of Christ through baptism. Also in the local church we celebrate the covenants of marriage and commend those we cherish back to God in funeral services of remembrance. The local church in its many embodiments—of various sizes, architectural styles, and range of facilities—is most often the location where we encounter or prepare for the reign of God.

The local church as experienced by most United Methodists in the contemporary context is a relatively recent development. During the eighteenth-century Wesleyan renewal movement within the Church of England, Methodists participated in religious societies in the form of class and band meetings. Modeled on religious societies within the Church of England organized through the Society for Promoting Christian Knowledge,[1] these small groups populated a network of circuits eventually stretching across the British Isles. Wesley developed a comprehensive slate of leadership to nurture and oversee the growth of the movement, including class and band leaders, exhorters, stewards, and preachers. As the movement matured later in the eighteenth century and then following John Wesley's death, Methodists gathered in more ecclesial spaces referred to as *chapels*, distinguishing their non-conformist gatherings from churches within the Church of England.

Small groups also emerged as an early embodiment of American Methodism. These developed from a similar process beginning with societies consisting of class and band meetings linked within networks of circuits followed by the establishment and building of churches. Leadership within societies in the American Methodist movement followed a similar plan to their British counterparts. Under the influence and guidance of Bishop Francis Asbury, itinerant and local preachers were assigned to care for the expanding movement among the American colonies and then across the American frontier. Local preachers lived in particular communities and provided consistent pastoral care and nurture, while the itinerant preachers traveled the circuits presiding at the Lord's Supper. Interestingly, in early nineteenth-century *Disciplines*, the focus is upon practices related to society gatherings, for example "Of Public Worship," and "Of the Spirit and Truth of Singing," as well as orders of worship for baptism and the Lord's Supper.[2] In this way, the local church as a space for worship, sacraments, discipleship, and outreach cared for by an ordained elder is a somewhat recent development in the Methodist tradition.

Definition and Function of the Local Church

The language of "local church" came into use within American Methodism by the 1920s. However, prior to this emergence of what seems familiar conceptual terminology, the language of "local societies" was employed in the constitutional documents of The Methodist Episcopal Church General Conference as recently as 1904,[3] and the language of society was common in all branches of Methodism until 1939. In 1944, the section previously described as "Church Membership" was revised and renamed "Local Church." This revised and expanded section describes the local church "as a society of persons who have professed their faith and have joined together in the fellowship of a Christian congregation in order to pray together, to receive the word of exhortation, and watch over one another in love, that they may help each other to work out their salvation."[4] While the 1944 (and 1948) description(s) features the language of society, echoing themes of the Wesleyan renewal movement, in 1952 the description of "Local Church" becomes more ecclesial still, including a mention of sacraments:

> The local church is a connectional society of persons who have professed their faith in Christ, have been baptized, have assumed the vows of membership in The Methodist Church, and are associated in fellowship as a local Methodist church in order that they may hear the Word of God, receive the Sacraments, and carry forward the work which Christ has committed to his Church.[5]

While the description continues with reference to "a society of believers," the remainder of the paragraph proceeds to highlight further ecclesial concerns most likely influenced by the mid-twentieth century development of the ecumenical movement and establishment of the World Council of Churches.[6]

Although the annual conference has been officially stipulated as the basic organizational unit within Methodism since 1940 (and arguably functioned in this way since the Wesleys' eighteenth-century renewal movement), following the 1939 union the local church operationally continues to play a significant role within our polity and experience. For example, the location of the description of the "Local Church" in the *Discipline* occurs at the opening of part V, which addresses the topics of organization and administration. This prominent location represents the significance of the local church in contemporary United Methodist polity. However, location, similar to its language, has varied.

The description or definition of the "local church" included in the *Discipline* may seem familiar in that it echoes themes from the mission statement:

> *The local church provides the most significant arena through which disciple-making occurs.* It is a community of true believers under the Lordship of Christ. It is the redemptive fellowship in which the Word of God is preached by persons divinely called and the sacraments are duly administered according to Christ's own appointment. Under the discipline of the Holy Spirit, the church exists for

the maintenance of worship, the edification of believers, and the redemption of the world.[7]

This definition resonates with the denomination's mission statement and is informed by scripture—specifically Matthew 28—and tradition, particularly the Articles of Religion and Confession of Faith—as well as theology informed by a trinitarian perspective.

The description of the function of the local church begins with an orienting statement: "The church of Jesus Christ exists in and for the world." The local church is a "strategic base" from which Christians minister to and with others in society extending its relationship with the triune God: "The function of the local church, under the guidance of the Holy Spirit, is to help people to accept and confess Jesus Christ as Lord and Savior and to live their daily lives in light of their relationship with God."[8] The paragraph then adds the following to the list of the local church's functions: ministering to the surrounding community, providing nurture and training when appropriate, cooperating in ministry with other local churches in ministry, living in ecological responsibility, and participating in the worldwide mission of the church. These practices are described as "minimal expectations of an authentic church."[9]

While United Methodists often refer to their pastoral leaders as appointed to local churches, the technical and disciplinary language claims the *pastoral charge* as the formal assigned setting to which an ordained or licensed minister is or may be appointed, whether as pastor in charge, as a co-pastor, or associate pastor.[10] As indicated by the language of charge, the bishop charges, or authorizes and assigns, a pastor to pastoral oversight and ministry in a location. This language also indicates the role of the local church within the connectional nature of the denomination. A pastoral charge may consist of one or more churches organized and subject to the *Discipline* within a charge conference. A pastoral charge of two or more churches may be designated a circuit or a cooperative parish. In 2004, the General Conference stipulated that when it is not possible for an ordained or licensed minister to be appointed to a pastoral charge, it may be served by a qualified and trained layperson, lay minister, or lay missioner assigned by the bishop, upon recommendation of the cabinet.[11] Part V continues with descriptions of other forms for local ecclesial structures such as cooperative ecumenical parish, ecumenical shared ministries, and churches in transitional communities.

Church Membership in Historical Context

Church membership within the Wesleyan tradition began with participation in religious societies, most often referred to as classes and bands that complemented membership in the Church of England. The General Rules of the United Societies dating to the mid-eighteenth century, discussed in part 1, guided the participation and spiritual nurture of individuals. In The Methodist Episcopal Church, the 1848 *Discipline* was the first to include a section with language regarding the receiving of members. The section appears in this form through 1876.[12] While membership today in The United Methodist Church is inclusive in nature, these relatively early texts evidence the desire to "prevent improper persons from insinuating themselves into the Church." The stipulations for receiving members into the church included the following: recommendation "by a leader with whom they have met at least six months on trial" (and been baptized), "examination by the minister in charge before the Church," and "upon the correctness of their faith . . . their willingness to observe and keep the rules of the Church."[13] Also from 1848: "The official minister or preacher shall, at every quarterly meeting, read the names of those that are received into the Church, and also those that are excluded therefrom."[14] Such stipulations feature in a consistent way through 1912. Arguably, during the nineteenth and into the twentieth century as much attention was given to the receiving of members as to the excluding of them, in the spirit of a discreet accountable community of faith following an Anabaptist model.

The tone shifts in 1916 with chapter 1, "Membership," beginning with the section entitled "Admission into the Church" and the following introductory statement: "In order that the doors of the Church maybe open to any person seeking to be saved from his sins."[15] The statement continues with references to qualifications: "and yet the Church properly safeguarded against the hasty admission of any unworthy person; and in order that all those who have not had previous instruction in the doctrines of the Church may have the advantages of its means of grace."[16] In 1916, this chapter and section demonstrate a significant revision by providing for two main forms of membership: preparatory and full.

Preparatory membership was made available to those "expressing a desire to lead a godly life," but requiring "instruction by the Pastor, or properly appointed leaders, in the principles of the Christian life, as well as in the rules and regulations of the Methodist Episcopal Church." According to the *Discipline*, "such members shall be entitled to all the privileges of the Church, but may not become members of the Quarterly Conference, nor take part in judicial proceedings except as witnesses."[17]

Full membership was extended to "all baptized members . . . giving satisfactory evidence of the correctness of their faith and of their knowledge of the rules and regulations of the Methodist Episcopal Church." Full membership was extended to an individual following the recommendation of the official board or the board of stewards and the approval of the pastor.[18]

The 1916 *Discipline* also provides for a subsequent category of membership—*affiliated membership*—intended for "our young people, who are Church members, [and] are absent from home attending school." This allowed for individuals to receive "proper privileges . . . and pastoral oversight" in the local church proximate to one's school, ". . . but they shall be counted and reported only in the membership of their home Churches."[19]

The Christian formation of children, youth, and young adults was a priority for the Wesleys from early in the renewal movement. In 1864, a paragraph is included in the *Methodist Episcopal Discipline* describing the pastor's responsibility to "organize the baptized children of the Church when they shall have reached the age of ten years, or at an earlier age when it is deemed advisable."[20] The paragraph continues with guidance on frequency of and character of meetings as well as objectives such as "instruct them in the nature, design, and obligations of Baptism" and "to urge them to give regular attendance upon the means of grace."[21] This paragraph continues with only minor changes through 1936. In 1890, language describing "The Relation of Baptized Children to the Church" is included in the chapter on "The Membership of the Church."[22]

Other components of the current disciplinary material related to membership also resonate with earlier issues. In 1892, a third section entitled "Transfer of Membership" was added to the chapter on membership.[23] During the early twentieth century there were several additions regarding "Withdrawal" as well as "Non-Resident Membership" (1912)—revised to "Non-Resident Inactive Membership" (1924)—and the expansion of these paragraphs into a section entitled "Inactive Membership" including the above.[24] Additionally, in 1928, local churches were required to maintain both a record and register of membership. The latter included home address, date, and manner of membership to be signed upon admission.[25]

The Meaning of Church Membership Today

According to the 2012 *Discipline*, "the membership of a local United Methodist church shall include all people who have been baptized and all people who have professed their faith."[26] The descriptions of church membership echo earlier statements and are articulated in two main overlapping categories: baptized and professing membership. Both baptized and professing members of any local United Methodist church are members of both the worldwide United Methodist connection and members of the church universal. The *baptized membership* "of a local United Methodist church shall include all baptized people who have received Christian baptism in the local congregation or elsewhere, or whose membership has been transferred to the local United Methodist Church subsequent to baptism in some other congregation." *Professing members* of a local United Methodist church "shall include all baptized people who have come into membership by profession of faith through appropriate services of the baptismal covenant in the ritual or by transfer from other churches." The *Discipline* goes on to state, "For statistical purposes, church membership is equated to the number of people listed on the roll of professing members."[27]

Membership in The United Methodist Church includes hospitality to those connected to other denominations through affiliate and associate memberships:

> A professing member of The United Methodist Church, of an affiliated autonomous Methodist or united church, or of a Methodist church that has a concordat agreement with The United Methodist Church, who resides for an extended period in a city or community at a distance from the member's home church, may on request be enrolled as an *affiliate member* of a United Methodist church located in the vicinity.[28]

Affiliate members may participate in fellowship, receive pastoral care, and hold an office, though not one that allows a vote in a United Methodist body beyond the local church. Affiliate members are counted as members of their home church only. According to the *Discipline*, "a member of another denomination may become an *associate member* under the same conditions, but may not become a voting member of the church council."[29]

Membership in The United Methodist Church through baptism and profession of faith initiates one not only into a congregation but also into the body of Christ. As the *Discipline* explains, through the baptismal covenant persons are called into ministry and participate in Christian formation. Those baptized as infants are invited, when appropriate, to participate in rituals of confirmation, both a human act of commitment and the gracious action of the Holy Spirit strengthening and empowering discipleship.[30] Echoing the baptismal covenant included in *The Book of Worship*, the *Discipline* describes the covenant and promises made:

> When persons unite as professing members with a local United Methodist church, they profess their faith in God, the Father Almighty, maker of heaven and earth; in Jesus Christ his only Son, and in the Holy Spirit. Thus, they make known their desire to live their daily lives as disciples of Jesus Christ. They covenant together with God and with the members of the local church to keep the vows which are a part of the order of confirmation and reception into the Church:

1. To renounce the spiritual forces of wickedness, reject the evil powers of the world, and repent of their sin;

2. To accept the freedom and power God gives them to resist evil, injustice, and oppression;

3. To confess Jesus Christ as Savior, put their whole trust in his grace, and promise to serve him as their Lord;

4. To remain faithful members of Christ's holy church and serve as Christ's representatives in the world;

5. To be loyal to Christ through The United Methodist Church and do all in their power to strengthen its ministries;

6. To faithfully participate in its ministries by their prayers, their presence, their gifts, their service, and their witness;

7. To receive and profess the Christian faith as contained in the Scriptures of the Old and New Testaments.[31]

As baptized and professed members of the body of Christ and The United Methodist Church, each member is encouraged in their faith and held accountable to practice their faith in all aspects of life.[32]

Pastors are often given the privilege, as well as authority, to preside at the baptism and confirmation of individuals. A related primary responsibility of pastors is for the spiritual well-being of those members and preparation for membership. While the pastor is primarily responsible, the congregation shares in this nurture. According to the *Discipline*, "because the redeeming love of God revealed in Jesus Christ extends to all persons, and because Jesus explicitly included the children in his kingdom, the pastor of each charge shall earnestly exhort all Christian parents or guardians to present their children to the Lord in baptism at an early age."[33]

Before administering baptism (or confirmation) to an infant or child, "the pastor shall diligently instruct the parents or guardians" on the meaning of the sacrament or ritual and the promises to be made and the same in the case of an adult seeking baptism or confirmation. In the event of the baptism of an infant, at least one parent, guardian, or sponsor must be a member of a Christian church.[34] Baptism (of adults and children) is ideally a communal event located in a local church and administered during regular worship.[35] However, if an individual is not able to be present at such a time and place, laity representing the congregation may be present for the baptismal/confirmation rite.[36] Similar to adults, while responsibility for the nurture of members is primarily that of the pastor, particularly when a child is baptized, the entire congregation shares in the responsibility to nurture the child in the Christian faith.

Additional guidelines for appropriate practices of baptism and confirmation are provided in the *Discipline*. Especially noteworthy is the *Discipline's* instruction against re-baptism, mentioned previously in chapter 4.[37] Although re-baptism is not permitted, the rituals of confirmation and reaffirmation of the baptismal covenant are permitted and even encouraged.[38] According to the *Discipline*, "there are many occasions as people mature in the faith when the Holy Spirit's confirming action may be celebrated, such as in the reaffirmation of the Baptismal Covenant or other services related to life passages."[39]

As has been mentioned previously, all baptized persons are called to ministry in Christ's church. Therefore, all members of The United Methodist Church are called to ministry and "to be a servant of Christ on mission in the local and worldwide community."[40] The *Discipline*, Christian tradition, and scripture—each to various extents—inform our discipleship in the body of Christ, which is a gift. We are invited to participate in God's reign through the body of Christ, and therefore membership in Christ's church, including The United Methodist Church. Such participation is a response to the triune God's invitation to relationship with God and one another, forgiveness for sins, and reconciliation of all things. Participation is not a duty to earn God's love. That love is unconditional.

It is hoped that individuals received into membership in The United Methodist Church will continue for the whole of their lives to participate in congregations, whether as United Methodists or in another Christian tradition. However, in rare circumstances a member may not fulfill the expectations of his or her membership. For example, it is possible for a baptized or professing member to be confronted about breaking his or her promises made in the baptismal covenant if he or she is regularly absent from the worship of the church without reason.[41] In these cases, the pastor is advised to visit with the individual and discuss his or her spiritual well-being and any difficulties he or she may have fulfilling his or her obligations. While serious offenses are rare, the *Discipline* provides for procedures to address such situations.[42]

As an aspect of The United Methodist Church's mission, the local church led by the pastor and supported by the members of the church council facilitates the spiritual growth and participation of its members and "continually . . . aid[s] the members to keep their vows to uphold the Church by attendance, prayers, gifts, service [and witness]."[43] As described in the section on "Care of Members," spiritual nurture and oversight of members may be organized in a number of ways, including the implementation of small groups.[44] According to the *Discipline*, "the Church has a moral and spiritual obligation to nurture its nonparticipating and indifferent members and to lead them into an active church relationship."[45]

Occasionally, a professing member may cease to be active in the life of the congregation. As mentioned above, the pastor and church council "shall do all in its power to reenlist the member in active fellowship of the church." If the member resumes active membership, a reaffirmation of the baptismal covenant may occur to mark the return to living in community. If the member, for whatever reason, does not resume active membership, he or she may request transfer to another United Methodist church, arrange a transfer to a particular church of another denomination, or request withdrawal. The process for removing a member's name (a member who has not recently died, moved, or chosen to be removed) is outlined in detail in the *Discipline* ¶228. The basic requirements of the process include the pastor and membership secretary reporting the member's name to the church council while also pursuing possibilities for the member's reengagement or transfer. According to the *Discipline*, "if the member does not comply with any of the available alternatives over a period of two years, the member's name may be removed." [46] The "Care of Members" is an important aspect of the life of the local church for the purpose of facilitating members' spiritual well-being and participation in the church's mission. The balance of membership, as a response to God's gift of relationship and reconciliation with accountability to one's baptismal covenant, is delicate.

A more pragmatic component of the "Care of Members" is the proper and responsible maintenance of membership records, described in considerable detail in ¶¶230–33 of the *Discipline*. However, the manner in which membership records are kept has evolved significantly over time, as demonstrated by previous *Disciplines* and a number of guidebooks published over the years, often entitled "Membership Manuals." One 1958 text describes its purpose:

> We are particularly interested in the changes in the terms of church membership. Put briefly, at first the problem faced by the individual member was keeping his [or her] name on the rolls; now the problem faced by the congregation is getting the name off the rolls. In the early days the Methodist was required quarterly to prove his [or her] faith and loyalty, else he [or she] was dropped. Today the Methodist is likely to find his [or her] name still enrolled, despite nonattendance, indifference, nonresidence, iniquitous living, or even death.[47]

It is important to note that membership records—and the subsequent rolls for constituency (not members), affiliate, and associate members—are kept in order to support the church's mission and the spiritual nurture of individuals, to occupy space or energy to undermine that mission and nurture.

The Organization of the Local Church

Organization of local churches has increased in flexibility over the last several quadrennia, allowing local churches to create a structure appropriate to the gifts and needs within a community. Beginning in 1972, following the amalgamation of The Evangelical United Brethren and Methodist Churches to form The United Methodist Church, local church organization and structure mirrored that of denominational organizations such as the council on ministry and administrative board. In 1980, as well as in subsequent years, significant revisions to local church organization have occurred with the purpose of flexibly supporting our shared mission, "reaching out and receiving with joy all who will respond; encouraging people in their relationship with God and inviting them to commitment to God's love in Jesus Christ;

providing opportunities for them to seek strengthening and growth in spiritual formation; and supporting them to live lovingly and justly in the power of the Holy Spirit as faithful disciples."[48] In the midst of such flexibility some structure has nevertheless been maintained for the purpose of continuity within the connectional and itinerant system. The following administrative units are mandated for every local church: (1) charge (church) conference, (2) church council, (3) committee on staff/pastor-parish relations, (4) board of trustees, (5) committee on finance, and (6) committee on lay leadership or nominations.[49]

United Methodist local churches are meant to be fundamentally *connectional* in nature. Therefore, their primary governing body is a unit that facilitates the connectional system: the *charge conference*. According to the *Discipline*, "Within the pastoral charge the basic unit in the connectional system of The United Methodist Church is the charge conference."[50] The *Discipline* explains that the charge conference shall be organized from the local church (or churches—a charge may consist of more than one church/congregation) as set forth in the Constitution.[51] The charge conference meets annually, though special sessions may be called by the district superintendent after consultation with the pastor, or by the pastor with written consent of the district superintendent.[52] Normally the district superintendent is present for charge conference meetings; however, he or she may designate an elder to preside, though the district superintendent sets the date and time for the meeting.[53] The charge conference determines the place of the meeting.[54] The charge conference membership includes "all members of the church council or other appropriate body, together with retired ordained ministers and retired diaconal ministers who elect to hold their membership in said charge conference."[55] The members present and voting constitute a quorum.[56] According to the *Discipline*, "Notice of time and place of a regular or special session of the charge conference shall be given at least ten days in advance by two or more of the following (except as local laws may otherwise provide): from the pulpit of the church, in its weekly bulletin, in a local church publication, or by mail."[57]

According to Thomas Frank, "local churches cannot make major decisions about such items as facilities, elected officers, pastoral salary, removal of members from the rolls, or candidates for ordained ministry, without the sanction of the representative of the connection, the district superintendent."[58] Therefore, usually the connectional representative, or district superintendent, presides over the crucial decisions in the life of the church with the participation of the pastoral and lay leadership. The primary positions and bodies connected to the charge conference, beyond the district superintendent and pastor(s), include a recording secretary, church historian, a committee on records and history, and sundry elected officers serving on church organizational committees with encouragement for full representation of the congregation.[59]

The *Discipline* describes the charge conference's power and duties, noting that "the charge conference shall be the connecting link between the local church and the general Church and shall have general oversight of the church council(s)."[60] The primary responsibilities of the charge conference, particularly in the annual meeting, are "to review and evaluate the total mission and ministry of the church (¶¶120–24), receive reports, and adopt objectives and goals recommended by the church council that are in keeping with the objectives of The United Methodist Church."[61] The main tasks carried out by the charge conference include: to recommend (and to renew) candidates for ordained ministry, candidates for Church-related vocations including inquiring annually of lay speakers, and certified lay ministers; to receive reports of volunteer in mission teams; set the compensation of the pastor(s) and other staff appointed by the bishop; and, when authorized, to provide for the sponsorship of satellite congregations.[62]

The *church conference* is very similar to the charge conference, its job being "to encourage broader participation by members of the church." In order to do this, "the charge conference may be convened as the church conference, extending the vote to all professing members of the local church present at such meetings."[63] The church conference is also authorized by the district superintendent and may be called under similar circumstances, through including a written request from the church council or 10 percent of the professing membership of the local church.[64] The additional policies governing the charge conference apply to the church conference.[65] The charge conference or church conference shall elect upon recommendation by the committee on nominations and leadership development or by nomination from the floor at least the following leaders: chairperson of the church council, committee on nominations and leadership development (chaired by the pastor), chairperson and members of the pastor-parish relations committee, chairperson and members of the finance committee including the financial secretary and church treasurers (if not paid employees of the local church), trustees, lay leader and lay members of annual conference, and a recording secretary—with special attention given to inclusivity.[66] While a church conference may fulfill similar purposes to the charge conference, to do so requires the presence or authorization of the district superintendent. Additionally, a church conference, though overlapping in purpose and participation, is distinct from a charge conference when all professing members are invited to participate.[67]

The *church council*, an administrative agent of the charge conference,[68] cares for the church's organization and temporal life for the purpose of implementing a program for nurture, outreach, and witness. It meets at least quarterly, but the chairperson or pastor may call special meetings. The charge conference determines the size of the church council, which may consist of as few as eleven persons and include representatives of program ministries (described further in the *Discipline*), and must constitute a quorum for voting to occur.[69] The membership shall include, but not be limited to, chairperson, lay leader, chairperson or representative of the staff/pastor-parish relations committee, chairperson or representative of the finance committee, chairperson or representative of the trustees, church treasurer, lay member to annual conference, presidents or representatives from United Methodist Men and Women, a young adult representative, a representative from the United Methodist Youth, and the pastor.[70]

The church council offers local churches a flexible structure from which to govern its ministry and programs. Local churches have a number of options in this regard. They may continue with the administrative board model created in 1968—a model that incorporates elements of both Methodist and Evangelical United Brethren local church polity and includes a separate council on ministries that carries out programming and receives reports from various program divisions (such as age-level and family ministries, education, evangelism, missions, stewardship, and worship). On the other hand, churches may opt to utilize the simpler administrative council model introduced in 1980. In this model, administration and program are under one governing body with four programmatic divisions: nurture, outreach, witness, and age-level and family ministries. The administrative council model is generally recommended, although it is often implemented flexibly.[71] According to the *Discipline*, the church council provides planning and implementation for nurture, outreach, witness, and resources in the local church.[72] The *Discipline* goes on to state that the church council shall provide for the administration of the local church as well as envisioning, planning, implementing, and annual evaluation of the mission and ministry of the local church.[73]

The purpose of the *committee on nominations and leadership development* is "to identify, develop, deploy, evaluate, and monitor Christian spiritual leadership for the local congregations."[74] To inform its prayerful work of identifying spiritual gifts and abilities of members, the committee engages in biblical and theological reflection upon the mission of the church,[75] and meets throughout the year to guide the church council, or alternative administrative structure, on leadership matters (other than employed staff) to facilitate the church's mission. The committee also recommends to the charge conference at its annual session names of those willing and able to serve in leadership. Membership is to be composed of not more than nine persons, in addition to the pastor and lay leader, with at least one young adult, all elected by the charge conference with attention given to inclusivity. The pastor serves as chair. The vice chair is a layperson elected by the committee. The committee is divided into three rotating classes to provide stability and experience.[76]

The *staff/pastor-parish relations committee* is elected annually at the charge/church conference from the professing membership including associate members.[77] Like all committees, this group also pursues biblical and theological reflection to inform its prayerful work of supporting the pastor and staff in their ministry and leadership roles. The committee shall be composed of no fewer than five nor more than nine persons representative of the total charge. Members must include a young adult, a lay leader, *and* a lay member of annual conference. No staff member or immediate family member of a pastor or staff member may serve on the committee. In order to provide stability and experience, the committee membership is divided into three rotating classes.[78]

The committee must meet at least quarterly, though it may meet more often, and may only meet with the knowledge of the pastor or district superintendent. The *Discipline* provides some qualifications:

> The pastor shall be present at each meeting of the committee on pastor-parish or staff-relations except where he or she voluntarily excuses himself or herself.
>
> The committee may meet with the district superintendent without the pastor or appointed staff under consideration being present. However, the pastor or appointed staff under consideration shall be notified prior to such meeting with the district superintendent and be brought into consultation immediately thereafter.
>
> The committee shall meet in closed session, and information shared in the committee shall be confidential.[79]

In addition to offering the pastor and staff support and consultation, evaluation, and accountability as well as facilitating spiritual renewal and continuing education, the committee also annually recommends lay preachers and candidates for ordination to the charge conference.[80]

The purpose of the *finance committee* is to compile a complete annual budget for the local church and submit it to the church council for review and adoption. It also develops and implements plans to raise sufficient funds to meet the budget adopted by the church council,[81] although it is not authorized to decide how the local church will spend that money. The finance committee membership is composed of the chairperson, pastor(s), lay member of the annual conference, the chairperson of the church council, the chair or representative from the staff/pastor-parish relations committee, a representative of the trustees selected by the trustees, the chairperson of the ministry group on stewardship, the lay leader, the financial secretary, the treasurer, the church business administrator, and other members that may be added by the charge conference. Notice that there is a chair of this committee in addition to a financial secretary and treasurer. Following appropriate practices with regard to finances, including counting the offering, is essential for the protection of both the local church and pastor. With regard to counting the offering at least two persons not of the same immediate family or residing in the same household must be designated to report a record of all funds received.[82]

The *board of trustees* must consist of no fewer than three and no more than nine members. It is recommended that at least one third be laywomen. The trustees must be of legal age as determined by law, and at least two-thirds shall be professing members of The United Methodist Church. No pastor is a voting member of the board of trustees unless elected as a member.[83] This committee is also divided into three rotating classes. The board of trustees elects its own chair unlike other administrative units whose chairs are elected by charge conference.[84] Trustees shall have (subject to the charge conference) supervision, oversight, and care of all real property owned by the local church[85] and shall meet at the call of the pastor or of its chairperson at least annually at such times and places with appropriate notice to each trustee.[86] While the local church may own property—in that it is financially obligated to pay mortgage(s) and other loans, as well as to maintain and renovate church property in order to comply with legal and safety policies—such property is held in trust for The United Methodist Church. The United Methodist Church is unable to hold title property, therefore local churches and other structures within the denomination hold property in trust, and all deeds must contain the trust clause specified in ¶2503.[87] The United Methodist Church as a whole is *not* a legal entity.[88]

There are a number of key roles held by laypersons within the local congregation; these include the chairs of the church council, staff/pastor-parish relations committee, finance committee, and board of trustees and vice chair of the committee on nominations and leadership development, in addition to the lay leader and lay members of the annual conference. The lay leader is an *ex officio* member of the charge conference, church council, finance committee, and committee on nominations and leadership development, as well as the staff/pastor-parish relations committee. The lay members of the annual conference are also *ex officio* members of the charge conference, church council, staff/pastor-parish relations committee, and finance committee. Each of these lay representatives must have held membership in The United Methodist Church for at least two years. The pastor is an *ex officio* member of the charge conference, church council, and finance committee and chairs the committee on nominations and leadership development; she or he is also a member of both the United Methodist Women and United Methodist Men.

The pastor and persons fulfilling these key lay leadership roles share in the responsibility for discerning the local church's specific practices to fulfill the church's mission. The pastor's ability to exercise wisdom in recognizing, and, with the leadership of the church, then continuing to cultivate such persons in their spiritual well-being and leadership is essential. As has already been mentioned, ongoing biblical study, theological reflection, and prayerful consideration shape the most faithful and effective communities of faith.

Conclusion

The local church is arguably the most significant organizational body within the denomination. It is the context in which members and visitors participate most directly in the mission of the church. The number of membership categories within the local church attempts to maintain continuity with our early Methodist tradition as well as provide opportunities for individuals to express their Christian faith and discipleship in its many embodiments. The function and purpose of the local church is structured to facilitate participation in the broader church's mission, both locally as well as through the connectional structure. The following section will discuss conference gatherings as well as councils and agencies. In their various forms, these continue to facilitate the broader church's mission to make disciples for the transformation of the world.

PART III

United Methodist Practice:
Conferencing and Governance

– Chapter Seven –

Conferences

In the Wesleyan tradition, conferencing remains a means of grace, and it is also, alongside the local church, a significant gathering for our experience in Christian community as United Methodists. Beginning with John Wesley's leadership, gathering for worship, fellowship, and planning the work of ministry was a means to receive and to share God's grace.[1] As the early Methodist movement spread across the British Isles and increased in numbers, Wesley gathered the preachers in conference. These gatherings demonstrated and embodied the interrelated spiritual and operational dynamics of the connection that facilitated the ministry of the early Methodist movement. In our strongest and most faithful moments, United Methodism continues this tradition as an aspect of our connectionalism in conference gatherings.

Most, if not all, of the Methodist and Wesleyan traditions across the world continue to practice a form of conferencing. In The United Methodist Church conferencing is embodied in both temporal and geographic terms—in bodies that meet at regular intervals from regions with clear boundaries[2]—and in a structure of conferences with interrelated accountability and support that visibly represents connection and guides the ministry of the church. In recent years pressure upon conference structures has increased. For United Methodism in the United States, declining membership presents a need to consolidate bureaucratic structures, particularly within and between annual conferences, restructuring to create efficiencies. In other parts of the world, increasing membership presents a different set of issues requiring expanded support structures, including additional annual conferences within central conferences, to facilitate the ministry of the church.

The highest legislative body in The United Methodist Church is the General Conference. Next in the connectional organization are jurisdictional conferences—of which there are five in the continental United States—and seven central conferences—in regions around the world—which carry out delegated duties from the General Conference. Jurisdictional and central conferences mediate between the General Conference and annual conferences. In the United States, district conferences support the annual conference and missionary annual conferences, connecting it with local congregations. These conferences are described in the following pages.

General Conference

The General Conference is the highest legislative body in the denomination. Its origins date to 1792 in the conference gatherings of early Methodism in Britain as well as in the United States.[3] According to the *Discipline*, "the General Conference has full legislative power over all matters distinctively connectional."[4] This power is granted by the Constitution,[5] which also offers further description of connectional matters. For example, the legislative power of General Conference relates to matters of church membership, orders and types of ministry, conferences (including duties and boundaries), episcopacy, judicial system, official resources such as the hymnal and ritual, fiscal resources, establishment of commissions, as well as matters relating to membership in all agencies, programs, and institutions in The United Methodist Church.[6] As a balance to the significant power granted to the General Conference, the Constitution also provides for Restrictive Rules to guide the General Conference's practice of power.[7]

Only the General Conference holds the authority to speak on behalf of the denomination: "No person, no paper, no organization, has the authority to speak officially for The United Methodist Church, this right having been reserved exclusively to the General Conference under the Constitution."[8] According to the Constitution, the General

Conference meets for approximately two weeks in late April and early May each quadrennium (every four years), although it may meet at additional times for special sessions.[9] The usual pattern of meeting every four years can pose challenges as the denomination seeks to contribute to various questions and advocate on particular issues in a timely manner. However, the General Conference's sole authority to speak for the denomination is a distinctive characteristic that allows for representation of a vast and complex connection.

Framed by worship and fellowship, representatives from the Council of Bishops preside over each session of General Conference. In advance of the gathered sessions, the General Conference receives legislative petitions from official bodies such as conferences, agencies, and councils as well as individuals.[10] Each petition receives attention in pertinent committees with foci such as finance, ministry, theological education, and mission.[11] Committees compose motions from the numerous petitions for deliberation on the floor of General Conference and possible adoption by a positive vote among a quorum of the General Conference's delegates.[12] This process results in new legislation as well as resolutions to guide the ministry of the denomination. New legislation and resolutions are incorporated respectively into the *Book of Discipline* and the *Book of Resolutions*, which are published following General Conference each quadrennium.

In light of the General Conference's significant responsibilities for The United Methodist Church as a whole, the composition of its membership is very important. According to the *Discipline*, membership consists of an equal number of clergy and lay delegates elected by annual conferences at a session one to three years prior to the General Conference,[13] and "the number of delegates to which an annual conference is entitled shall be computed on a two-factor basis: the number of clergy members [active and retired] of the annual conference, and the number of members of local churches in the annual conference."[14] The *Discipline* goes on to explain in detail the formula used by the secretary (an elected office that may be held by a lay or clergy member of the church)[15] that defines the minimum and maximum number of delegates to a General Conference.[16] According to the Constitution, "the General Conference shall be composed of not less than 600 nor more than 1,000 delegates, one half of whom shall be clergy and one half lay members, to be elected by the annual conferences."[17]

As United Methodist membership grows in the "global south," and declines in the "global north," particularly United Methodism in the United States, the delegations to General Conference represent an increasingly international constituency. For example, in 1968 at the time of the merger between The Evangelical United Brethren and Methodist Churches, Africans consisted of 1.5 percent of United Methodist membership globally.[18] Interesting, by 2006, that number of Africans grew to 32.5 percent of the global membership.[19] During the same time period the membership of United Methodism in the United States declined from 92.5 to 64.6 percent of the total global membership.[20] At this rate, it is plausible for the majority of United Methodist members and therefore General Conference delegates to represent constituencies beyond the United States in the next few decades.

Jurisdictional Conferences

Jurisdictional conferences were established by the Constitution of the newly formed Methodist Church in 1939 to assume particular duties or powers delegated by the General Conference.[21] Jurisdictional conferences are unique to United Methodism in the United States, though central conferences serve similar purposes in other contexts across global Methodism. While the *Discipline* does not offer a distinctive definition of powers for the jurisdictional conferences as it does for the General Conference,[22] outlines of the jurisdictional conferences' powers and duties conferred by the General Conference are provided by the Constitution. These powers and duties include promoting ministry, electing bishops, establishing jurisdictional boards, determining boundaries of annual conferences, and appointing a committee on appeals.[23]

When jurisdictional conferences were organized in 1939, six were established: five organized by geographic region to cover the continental United States and one racially segregated jurisdiction made up of nineteen African American missionary conferences that covered the entire nation. The sixth racially segregated jurisdiction was called the Central Jurisdiction. While the large majority of delegates across the amalgamating denominations at the time voted in favor of this configuration, the sentiment among African American delegates was much different: "Of the forty-seven African American delegates to the General Conference, thirty-six voted against the Plan of Union and eleven abstained."[24] The membership of the Central Jurisdiction during the time of its existence remained relatively stagnant, around 300,000–350,000, neither losing nor gaining many members.[25]

The Central Jurisdiction allowed for African American Methodists to develop their own leadership in national agencies and as bishops, electing twelve bishops in the first twenty years compared with two in the previous 150 years. However, the Central Jurisdiction undoubtedly embodied the sin of segregation within ecclesial structures imposed by the white majority upon African Americans. The 1952 General Conference laid the groundwork for Amendment IX to the Constitution and the eventual abolition of the Central Jurisdiction at the time of union with the Evangelical United Brethren, which was not a segregated church, beginning in 1968 and culminating by 1972.[26]

The jurisdictional conferences equally share "the same status and privileges of action within the limits fixed by the Constitution."[27] According to the Constitution, each jurisdictional conference meets quadrennially (with allowance for special sessions), and simultaneously, that is, at the same time as other jurisdictional conferences, usually in July of the same year as the General Conference, which meets in April or May.[28] Representatives of the College of Bishops, consisting of each bishop serving an episcopal area within the jurisdiction, preside over the sessions of jurisdictional conferences.[29] The Constitution also stipulates "the General Conferences shall fix the basis of representation in the jurisdictional conferences, provided that the jurisdictional conferences shall be composed of an equal number of clergy and lay delegates to be elected by the annual conferences, the missionary conferences and the provisional annual conferences."[30] Jurisdictional conference delegates are elected by annual conferences following those elected as delegates to General Conference.[31] Delegates to jurisdictional conference serve as alternate delegates to General Conference. Additional alternate or reserve delegates for jurisdictional conference are also elected.[32] Alternate delegates attend the general and jurisdictional conferences in order to ensure the maximum number of voting members on the floor at all times.

The jurisdictional conferences of The United Methodist Church established by the Constitution include the following geographic areas:

Northeastern—Bermuda, Connecticut, Delaware, District of Columbia, Maine, Maryland, Massachusetts, New Hampshire, New Jersey, New York, Pennsylvania, Rhode Island, Vermont, the Virgin Islands, West Virginia.

Southeastern—Alabama, Florida, Georgia, Kentucky, Mississippi, North Carolina, South Carolina, Tennessee, Virginia.

North Central—Illinois, Indiana, Iowa, Michigan, Minnesota, North Dakota, Ohio, South Dakota, Wisconsin.

South Central—Arkansas, Kansas, Louisiana, Missouri, Nebraska, New Mexico, Oklahoma, Texas.

Western—Alaska, Arizona, California, Colorado, Hawaii, Idaho, Montana, Nevada, Oregon, Utah, Washington, and Wyoming and the territory of the United States in the Pacific region.[33]

According to the Constitution, "changes in the number, names, and boundaries of the jurisdictional conferences may be effected by the General Conference upon the consent of a majority of the annual conferences of each of the jurisdictional conferences involved."[34]

The two most prominent duties of the jurisdictional conferences are to establish annual conference boundaries and to elect bishops. One of the main committees within the jurisdictional conference is the committee on episcopacy, which relates to the interjurisdictional committee on episcopacy.[35] The members of the committee on episcopacy consist of one lay and one clergy delegate to jurisdictional conference from each annual conference.[36] The members of the interjurisdictional committee on episcopacy are elected by the General Conference from those nominated to serve on the jurisdictional committees on episcopacy from annual conference delegations.[37] The jurisdictional committee on episcopacy recommends boundaries of episcopal areas (consisting of at least one annual conference) and the assignment of bishops, determines the number of effective bishops eligible for assignment, and deals with related matters to appropriately execute these duties.[38]

Jurisdictional conferences hold the authority to appoint or elect agencies directed by the General Conference or as it deems necessary.[39] The *Discipline* authorizes the provision of a jurisdictional body to coordinate ministry programs of the general agencies within the jurisdiction alongside jurisdictional program agencies related to general program agencies.[40] Additional bodies authorized by the *Discipline* to fulfill the duties of the jurisdictional conferences include: archives and history, jurisdictional youth ministry organization convocation, committee on ordained ministry, United Methodist Women, and United Methodist Men.[41]

Central Conferences

Central conferences emerged as early as 1884 when The Methodist Episcopal Church recognized an established body in India. Predecessors of The United Methodist Church participated in mission work outside of the United States during the nineteenth century resulting in the organization of a variety of ecclesial institutions such as congregations, schools, and hospitals.[42] Central conferences emerged as a way to obtain training for lay and clergy leaders, as well as accountability and control of ecclesial matters.[43] The Constitution provides for the organization of central conferences,[44] whose duties include promotion of ministry, election of bishops, determination of boundaries of annual conferences, and appointment of a judicial court and committee on appeals within central conferences.[45] As will be discussed later in this section, central conferences may adapt portions of the *Discipline* to accommodate local needs.

The following describe the central conferences of The United Methodist Church, as recognized by the 2016 General Conference, and the countries within which they minister:

a) Africa Central Conference: Angola, Botswana, Burundi, Ethiopia, Kenya, Malawi, Mozambique, Namibia, Rwanda, Swaziland, South Africa, South Sudan, Uganda, Zambia, Zimbabwe;

b) Central and Southern Europe Central Conference: Albania, Algeria, Austria, Belgium, Bulgaria, Croatia, Czech Republic, France, Hungary, Republic of Macedonia, Poland, Romania, Serbia, Slovak Republic, Switzerland, Tunisia;

c) Congo Central Conference: Central African Republic, Democratic Republic of Congo, Republic of Congo, Tanzania, Zambia;

d) Germany Central Conference: Germany;

e) Northern Europe and Eurasia Central Conference: Belarus, Denmark, Estonia, Finland, Kazakhstan, Kyrgyzstan, Latvia, Lithuania, Moldova, Norway, Russia, Sweden, Tajikistan, Ukraine, Uzbekistan;

f) Philippines Central Conference: Philippines;

g) Southeast Asia and Mongolia Central Conferences: Laos, Mongolia, Thailand, Vietnam;

h) West Africa Central Conference: Burkina Faso, Cameroon, Cote d'Ivoire, Guinea, Guinea-Bissau, Liberia, Mali, Niger, Nigeria, Senegal, Sierra Leone.[46]

The *Discipline* explains, "A provisional central conference may become a central conference upon the fulfillment of the necessary requirements and upon the authorization of the General Conference."[47] Also, "in territory outside the United States, annual conferences, provisional annual conferences, missionary conferences, mission conferences, and missions, in such numbers as the General Conference by a two-thirds vote shall determine, may be organized by the General Conference into central conferences or provisional central conferences."[48] Central conferences meet within the year following General Conference with the date and place of the initial gathering usually set by the bishops of the respective central conferences.[49] They require a minimum of thirty clergy and thirty lay delegate representatives as described in the *Discipline*.[50]

While the central conference is the foremost category for describing these organizational units, they emerge from, retain, and continue to develop into a range of forms. The *Discipline* includes a number of categories beyond central conferences such as provisional central conferences, autonomous Methodist churches, affiliated autonomous Methodist churches, affiliated united churches, covenanting churches, concordat churches, provisional annual conferences, missions, and missionary conferences.[51] Central conferences, similar to jurisdictional conferences, "shall fix the boundaries of the annual conferences, provisional annual conferences, missionary conferences, and missions within its bounds."[52]

With many duties similar to jurisdictional conferences, such as setting boundaries of annual and other conferences and electing and assigning bishops, central conferences are conferred additional powers and duties by the General Conference. These powers allow the interpretation, adaptation, and even changes to the *Discipline* "as the special conditions and the mission of the church in the area require."[53] The denomination has worked over the last several years, mostly through the committee to study the worldwide nature of the church, to make progress toward creating a more equitable church structure.[54] One result is a "global" or General *Book of Discipline* allowing for adaptation prompted by local needs. While committees continue to work on clarifications for consideration at the 2020 General Conference, the 2012 General Conference confirmed the following paragraphs as belonging to the global *Discipline* and subject to change only by General Conference action: the Constitution, doctrinal standards, theological task, "The Ministry of All Christians," and the Social Principles.[55]

Duties of the central conferences include advising annual conferences to set standards for church membership,[56] establishing a judicial court as well as a court of appeals,[57] translating and adapting the "Ritual" (including marriage) to conform to cultural norms,[58] providing theological education, and publishing a *Discipline.*[59] Central conferences possess the authority, "through a duly incorporated property-holding body or bodies . . . to purchase, own, hold, or transfer property for and on behalf of . . . The United Methodist Church within the territory of that central conference."[60] This broader spectrum of powers and duties allows central conferences to practice agility in its participation in the mission of the Church in its many and diverse contexts.

Annual Conferences

According to the Constitution, "the annual conference is the basic body in the Church."[61] While the local church functions as a primary unit in the imagination of most United Methodists, according to the Constitution and demonstrated by the attention given to the annual conference in the *Discipline* (approximately one hundred pages), the annual conference is the basic organizational unit. The centrality of the annual conference to the life of the church points to the connectional nature of United Methodism. From its earliest embodiment during the leadership of John Wesley in Britain and Francis Asbury in the United States, the annual conference initially provided a time and space for clergy and laity to gather for worship, fellowship, and to plan the work of ministry. The church's adoption of the mission statement by General Conference in 1996 informed the shared purpose of the annual conferences, local churches, and other ecclesial bodies. According to the *Discipline*, "the purpose of the annual conference is to make disciples of Jesus Christ for the transformation of the world by equipping its local churches for ministry and by providing a connection for ministry beyond the local church; all to the glory of God."[62]

John Wesley presided over the first annual conference in 1744, consisting of a relatively small number of clergymen.[63] Since that time laity and women were added to the membership of predecessor Methodist churches and women included among the clergy of The Methodist Church in 1956.[64] In American Methodism, The Methodist Church at its formation in 1939 adopted from the Methodist Protestants the practice of including laity.[65] In 1976, this practice was clarified to include an equal number of laity and clergy, including retired clergy, among its membership, resulting in the need for districts to elect additional at-large lay members.[66] The Constitution describes an extensive list of those composing the membership of the annual conference, from clergy members such as deacons and elders in full connection, provisional and associate members, as well as local pastors under appointment, to lay members such as diaconal ministers, active deaconesses, conference presidents of the United Methodist Women and Men, conference lay leader, president of the conference youth and young adult organizations, as well as those elected by pastoral charges and districts.[67]

Upon Methodism's shift to America, bishops presided over annual conferences, and today, bishops preside over the annual conference(s) located in the episcopal area to which they are assigned.[68] The bishop also decides the time for holding annual conference each year.[69] Special sessions of annual conference are possible, but these sessions are authorized only to exercise such powers as stated in the call.[70] Each annual conference elects a lay leader as an officer of the annual conference "to participate in annual conference sessions as a partner in ministry with the bishop."[71]

To fulfill its mission, the annual conference is provided with rights by the Constitution. These rights include voting upon all constitutional amendments, electing clergy and lay delegates to the general and jurisdictional or central conferences, and making decisions relating to clergy members, including ordination.[72] When voting upon delegates to general and jurisdictional or central conferences, the Constitution requires that only ordained members in full connection elect ordained delegates, and only lay members of the annual conference elect lay delegates.[73] Lay members are not permitted to vote on matters of ordination, character, and conference relations of clergy, except if they serve on the board (or district committee) of ordained ministry.[74] The disciplinary paragraphs regarding the annual conference's "Composition and Character" provide additional detail regarding the voting privileges of each constituent member of the annual conference.[75]

The duties of the annual conference vary as it seeks to support the work of ministry to fulfill the church's mission, but they focus on three main areas: (1) the admission, support, and accountability of clergy; (2) the recognition, support, and accountability of local churches; and (3) the financial implications of both.[76] While laypersons hold membership in local churches, when an individual is elected to provisional or licensed membership in an annual conference his or her membership shifts to the annual conference. In this way, the annual conference is responsible for its clergy members in a manner distinctive from the laity. With regard to local churches, the annual conference holds authority to inquire into the membership status of local churches as well as financial status.[77] However, "an annual conference cannot financially obligate any organizational unit of The United Methodist Church except the annual conference itself."[78]

The annual conference is authorized, as are other organizational units, to organize itself in the best manner necessary, with flexibility in the midst of some minimal constraints, to fulfill its mission programmatically.[79] As a mediating agency between the general and local church, the annual conference often embodies a creative tension. With most, if not all, annual conferences holding property as incorporated entities, annual conferences are both connectional and distinct within the connection. At the time of the annual conference session, the fullness of both these characteristics may be witnessed. At annual conference sessions the business of the conference is framed by worship and fellowship as reports are heard from various committees and decisions made within the practice of governance. Annual conference sessions also often include separate sessions of laity and clergy for the purpose of making inquiry into the moral and spiritual well-being of its members. Throughout the year, the various committees and other bodies authorized to facilitate the annual conference's mission continue in their connectional ministries between the general and local church. A significant aspect of the annual conference's ability to fulfill its mission is the commitment of local churches, charges, and districts to participate in the payment of apportionments to the annual conference.[80] The conference council on finance and administration sets the formula in each annual conference for the payment of apportionments.[81] Apportionments support annual conference as well as general church entities, with the majority of funds going to outreach.

The *Discipline* describes numerous roles related to the organization and ministry of the annual conference such as secretary, treasurer, archivist, chancellor, lay leader, director of communications, and the chairs and officers of the many committees and other bodies. Among the committees facilitating ministries of the annual conference are board of ordained ministry, orders of deacons and elders, board of laity, administrative review committee, commission on equitable compensation, committee on ethnic local church concerns, commission on the small membership church, committee on Native American ministry, committee on disability concerns, United Methodist Women and Men, as well as conference councils on youth, young adult, and older adult ministry. These are in addition to conference agencies that are parallel organizations to general agencies such as council on finance and administration, committee on episcopacy, boards of discipleship, higher education and ministry, church and society, global ministries, Christian unity and interreligious concerns, religion and race, pensions, and the commission on the status and role of women. Through these agencies, the annual conference provides for the equipping of local churches to make disciples through multifaceted support.

Missionary Annual Conferences

Missionary annual conferences are organized in the same manner and with the same privileges as an annual conference with a small number of exceptions.[82] There are currently three missionary annual conferences within the United States: Alaska, Oklahoma Indian, and Red Bird. The Rio Grande Annual Conference was recently a missionary annual conference. Following approval from the South Central Jurisdiction in 2012, in February 2014 the Rio Grande and Southwest Texas Annual Conferences voted to join, forming the Rio Texas Annual Conference. According to the *Discipline*, only the General Conference can create a missionary conference or change a conference's status (for example, from provisional annual conference to annual conference).[83] Missionary annual conferences are designated as a result of particular mission opportunities, strategic regional or language considerations, and unique leadership requirements, as well as its limited membership and resources.[84] The General Board of Global Ministries provides support in the form of administrative guidance and financial assistance, including property matters.[85] Missionary annual conferences are most similar in rights and privileges to central conferences.[86]

Episcopal supervision for the missionary annual conference is exercised from the College of Bishops.[87] Missionary annual conferences may elect clergy and lay delegates to general and jurisdictional conferences on the same terms as annual conferences.[88] Missionary annual conferences may also vote to establish the right of full ministerial membership.[89] According to the *Discipline*, "with approval and consent of the bishops or other judicatory authorities involved, appointments are to be made by the resident bishop of the conference in which the clergy person is to serve."[90]

District Conferences

District conferences serve important functions within the connection despite the relatively few pages dedicated in the *Discipline* to describing them. According to the Constitution, "there may be organized in an annual conference, district conferences composed of such persons and invested with such powers as the General Conference may determine."[91] District conferences and district functions may be held if directed by the annual conference upon the call of the district superintendent.[92] Districts provide connection between annual conferences and local churches to facilitate their ministries.

Composed of members as determined by the annual conference, giving attention to inclusiveness, there are a number of key roles, such as the district superintendent (appointed by the bishop to preside) and district lay leader (elected by the district).[93] One of the most significant bodies within the district is the district committee on ordained ministry, which works with the board of ordained ministry to oversee the process of candidacy and approve candidates for ministry.[94] Districts may organize a district board of laity "to foster an awareness of the role of laity both within the local congregation and through their ministries in the home, workplace, community, and world in achieving the mission of the Church."[95] Districts also include a number of other committees—committee on district superintendency, United Methodist Men, and United Methodist Women.[96] They may also include a district council on youth ministry and district committee on lay speaking ministries.[97] Similar to annual conferences, districts may appoint directors to liaise with conference and more broadly connectional organizations such as directors of church and society, ethnic local church concerns, and religion and race.[98]

Conclusion

Conferences remain the most significant connectional structures and gatherings within United Methodism. The annual conference, both currently and historically, is the basic organizational unit of the denomination as it connects local churches with the broader governing structure to facilitate a comprehensive participation in the mission of the church. The general, jurisdictional, and central conferences provide a thoughtful and agile structure for a growing international connection. As United Methodism continues to shift, this structure may experience even more pressure to reflect the growing vitality of its witness and mission in international contexts.

– Chapter Eight –

Councils and Agencies

A number of councils and agencies function within the governance and polity of The United Methodist Church. In this chapter, we will look at the Judicial Council, Council of Bishops, Connectional Table, and University Senate as well as introduce the general boards and agencies. Each of these bodies functions in distinctive and significant ways to connect and integrate ministries and resources across the denomination. As an introduction to the "Agencies and General Agencies," the *Discipline* states, "Connectionalism is an important part of our identity as United Methodists."[1] These entities, at their best, provide leadership and contributions to the life of the denomination for the purpose of fulfilling our mission to participate in God's reign in the world.

Judicial Council

According to the *Discipline*, "the Judicial Council is the highest judicial body in The United Methodist Church. The Judicial Council shall have authority as specified in the Constitution, ¶¶55-57, and in ¶¶2609-2612."[2] Sometimes referred to as the "Supreme Court" of United Methodism, the Judicial Council decides on specific matters and

is required to review each decision on a point of law made by a bishop during an annual conference session. Other cases come from lower church courts, or from an official body of the church requesting a declaratory decision as to the legality of a particular action. There usually are several requests during General Conference for declaratory decisions.[3]

The *Discipline* continues with some admonishment regarding fundamental principles for trials, stating, "Church trials are to be regarded as an expedient of last resort."[4] The Judicial Council relies upon an accountable covenant shared by all members in every role within The United Methodist Church—including bishops, clergy members of annual conferences, elders and deacons, local pastors, diaconal ministers, clergy on various locations, as well as professing members of the local churches. According to Belton Joyner, longtime member and secretary of the Judicial Council, "the Judicial Council works if it provides a system for authoritative judgments that clears confusion so connectional ministry for making disciples of Jesus Christ for the transformation of the world can occur."[5] While sin and the brokenness of individuals and systems mean that problems will arise, the council provides helpful and constructive oversight of judicial process to discern and minister in the midst of the "not yet-ness" of God's inbreaking reign. According to the *Discipline*, "only after every reasonable effort has been made to correct any wrong and adjust any existing difficulty should steps be taken to institute a trial."[6]

The Constitution offers provision for the Judicial Council, placing the responsibility for determining the number and qualifications of its members, terms of office, and method of elections, including filling vacancies, with the General Conference.[7] The Judicial Council is given authority to provide for its own methods of organization and procedure (as will be described below) and has authority to determine the constitutionality of acts of General Conference and bishops' decisions and their appeals, in addition to any other duties and powers as may be conferred by the General Conference.[8] According to the Constitution, "all decisions of the Judicial Council shall be final."[9]

History

Methodist clergy historically have been guaranteed the right of trial and appeal. The Constitution states, "The General Conference shall establish for the Church a judicial system that shall guarantee to our clergy a right to trial by a committee and an appeal, and to our members a right to trial before the Church, or by a committee, and an appeal."[10] However, this has taken a variety of forms prior to the current structure characterized by the Judicial Council. The earliest Judicial Council was established in 1934 by the General Conference of The Methodist Episcopal Church, South (MECS). It emerged from its inclusion in a proposed plan for union with The Methodist Protestant and Methodist Episcopal Churches presented by a Joint Commission on Unification that met regularly from 1916–1918. This plan led to the proposal of a revised Constitution to be adopted by The Methodist Episcopal Church, South, General Conference in 1930, and although the revised Constitution was rejected, a separate amendment pertaining to the Judicial Council was adopted by a nearly five to one margin.[11] As a result, the council was established as a part of The Methodist Episcopal Church, South, Constitution in 1934 and then informed the Judicial Council implemented in 1939 when The Methodist Episcopal Church; Methodist Episcopal Church, South; and The Methodist Protestant Church merged to create The Methodist Church.

Sally Curtis AsKew provides a brief instructive history of the Judicial Council in her article in *Methodist History*,[12] describing the preceding structures for addressing a right to appeal among those traditions that constitute The United Methodist Church and the discussions that raised the need for an effective way to deal with appellate cases.[13] For example, in The Methodist Episcopal Church there was a committee on the judiciary and in The Methodist Episcopal Church, South, and Methodist Protestant Church a committee on appeals, but trials of clergy appealed by those involved could wait as many as four years for resolution.[14] In The Methodist Episcopal Church, the General Conference provided the final interpretation of any question of law, while in The Methodist Episcopal Church, South, the College of Bishops held this authority.[15] In The Methodist Protestant Church, the conference presidents ruled on questions of law, but these decisions still needed to be reported to the General Conference and receive approval prior to implementation.[16] In The Evangelical United Brethren Church, which united with the other churches in 1968, "interpretations made by the Board of Bishops were only effective until the next General Conference" and in order to be established required action by General Conference.[17]

Membership

The Judicial Council continues to be composed of nine members. Initially, membership consisted of five clergy and four laity, but from 1980, the composition of this ratio was made to alternate every four years so that for every other two quadrennial laity constituted the majority. All members were required to be forty years of age or older until the minimum age requirement was dropped in 1972.[18] Lay members sometimes have a legal or political background. Members have included judges, a major corporation's legal affairs vice president, a prominent figure in Illinois politics, and the first African American mayor of Cincinnati.[19]

The term of office continues to be eight years, though a member may be reelected. According to the *Discipline*, "a member may serve a maximum of two consecutive eight-year terms, with a minimum of four years before reelection to the council."[20] Members are elected by General Conference, resulting in eight-year terms coinciding with the quadrennium of the church's governance. It is essential that all members of the Judicial Council practice confidentiality with the exception of securing pertinent facts and statements for the facilitation of process.[21] According to the *Discipline*, "the members of the Judicial Council will not permit discussion on matters pending before them or that may be referred to them for determination, save and except before the Judicial Council is in session."[22]

At each quadrennial session of the General Conference, the Council of Bishops nominates by majority vote three times the number of persons to be elected, preserving the balance of clergy and lay, as well as "reflect[ing] the diversity of The United Methodist Church, including racial, age, ethnic, gender, jurisdiction and central conferences, and congregational size."[23] At the same time such nominations are made, additional nominations may be made from the floor of the General Conference, and then the names, biographies, and conference to which the nominee belongs are published in "the *Daily Christian Advocate* at least forty-eight hours prior to the time of election."[24] Elections are made without discussion, by ballot and majority vote.[25] Alternate members will be included among those elected, specifically six alternates for clergy and six alternates for laity.[26] The term of the alternate members of Judicial Council is four years.[27] Full and alternate members of the Judicial Council are "ineligible to serve as delegates to the general, jurisdictional, or central conference or to serve in any general, jurisdictional, or central conference board or agency."[28]

Organization and Process

From its establishment, the Judicial Council has held the authority to provide for its own method of organization and procedure within disciplinary provisions.[29] The *Discipline* requires the Judicial Council to "meet at the time and place of the meeting of the General Conference continuing in session until the adjournment of that body, and at least one other time in each calendar year and at such other times as it may deem appropriate."[30] Otherwise, the Judicial Council establishes the date, place, frequency, and length of meetings.[31] It maintains its own "Rules of Practice and Procedure," which may be amended at any time.[32] The Rules, consisting of sixteen pages inclusive of procedures and appendices, appear on the Judicial Council portion of The United Methodist Church's website.[33]

The Judicial Council elects its own officers for terms of four years. While officers were initially elected for one term without the possibility of reelection, this rule was dropped prior to 1980 and officers are routinely reelected to the same office.[34]

Most often questions come to the Judicial Council for attention from the General Conference and the Council of Bishops. These groups possess the authority to ask for a decision on any act or legislation. Most appeals come from annual conferences, which—during session—may ask for a "declaratory decision" or for a decision of law by a bishop.[35] However, declaratory decisions may also be petitioned by the General Conference, Council of Bishops, a majority of the bishops assigned to a specific area, or any body created or given authority by the

General Conference or other conference structure relating to or affecting the work of that body:[36]

> Decisions are based on the Constitution of The United Methodist Church and on the specific paragraphs of the *Book of Discipline* cited in a case, but may refer to other relevant paragraphs. Conflicting paragraphs must be resolved before a decision is reached. The *Discipline* instructs the court not to go "further than is necessary to decide the question of church law involved."[37]

The Judicial Council issues two types of opinions: (1) decisions and (2) memoranda.[38] The basic distinction is the length of the opinion, with decisions being longer and more detailed. Recent memoranda usually consist of statements of no jurisdiction.[39] Generally, individuals do not possess authority to appeal to the Judicial Council, though there are some exceptions related to decisions of a jurisdiction or central conference court of appeals.[40] Such appeals may only be made on matters of church law in which only two questions are to be decided: "(a) Does the weight of the evidence sustain the charge or charges? [and] (b) Were there such errors of church law as to vitiate the verdict and/or the penalty?"[41] There is no statute of limitations on questions of child and sexual abuse.[42]

The *Discipline* explains in detail the current jurisdiction and powers of the Judicial Council in ¶2609. These remain largely consistent with the authority and several duties given to the Judicial Council at its establishment: (1) The Judicial Council determines the constitutionality of any act of the General Conference when requested by one-fifth of the members of the General Conference or a majority of the Council of Bishops; (2) The council determines the constitutionality of any act of central or jurisdictional conference on the appeal of the majority of the College of Bishops or one-fifth of the members of the jurisdictional or central conference; (3) The Judicial Council determines the legality of any action taken by any General Conference board or jurisdictional or central conference board or body; (4) The Judicial Council hears and passes on all decisions of law made by bishops in annual conferences; (5) A fifth power was considered between 1940 and 1944 and added to give the Judicial Council authority to rule on declaratory decisions allowing the council to consider questions of lack of clarity, conflict in or among disciplinary paragraphs, and the proper authority of conferences to take certain actions.[43]

The Rules require all materials related to docket items be in the possession of the Judicial Council secretary no later than sixty days in advance of the twice-yearly meetings.[44] The precise nature of the materials is described in the Rules, but perhaps most distinctly these include provision for thirteen copies in addition to those required for persons identified as "interested parties."[45] The *Discipline* requires that no request for a declaratory decision be heard until at least thirty days following publication of docket items.[46] While no such advance notice is required for bishops' decisions of law, the same deadline is used.[47] All decisions of the Judicial Council are published on The United Methodist Church's website.[48]

The longtime procedure practiced by the Judicial Council to accomplish its work is for the president, in consultation with the vice president and secretary, to assign specific docket items to judicial members for research and composition of draft opinions prior to meetings.[49] According to the Judicial Council's rules and procedures, "at least two persons are assigned each docket item, but any member may write on any docket item whether assigned or not."[50] Each member authoring a draft opinion reads the opinion aloud to the council following the distribution of copies to the members. The question is then discussed by the entire council. One draft opinion is adopted as a working paper with an invitation for suggestions of additions and deletions before two members collaborate on a second draft. Most decisions go through several drafts before becoming final and given a decision or memorandum number. The final decisions are not signed by an individual member since these are representative of and contributed to by the entire membership of the Judicial Council, though if a member writes a concurring or dissenting opinion, it is signed and placed at the end of the majority opinion.[51] The Judicial Council has considered approximately 1,250 questions of law. With the exception of a higher-than-average trajectory during the decade of union (1960s), the number of decisions has steadily increased each year and quadrennium.

Complaints

When confronted with accusations in the form of a formal complaint, all are given the right of fair process as described in the *Discipline*. Complaints are a means of seeking just resolution in the midst of brokenness, particularly the breaking of promises made in one's ordination, which along with membership in an annual conference of The United Methodist Church is a sacred trust demonstrated by the fulfillment of qualifications and duties that flow from the gospel of Jesus Christ.[52]

If the effectiveness of a clergyperson, either an associate or full member, is questioned, the bishop will pursue a supervisory process.[53] If such a process does not result in sufficient improvement the bishop and district superintendents may request the clergyperson to be placed on administrative location. This process includes deliberations, such as fair process hearings,[54] and recommendation from the conference relations committee, board of ordained ministry and clergy session of the annual conference.[55]

If a clergyperson—local pastor, associate, provisional, or full member—is accused of violating the sacred trust, the membership of his or her ministerial office shall be subject to review.[56] According to the *Discipline*, "a complaint is a written and signed statement claiming misconduct as defined in ¶2702.1." A supervisory response by the bishop is pastoral and administrative and, like all review responses, seeks just resolution, reconciliation, and healing. Possible outcomes may include suspension, referral, or dismissal.[57] Responses may include continuing education, leave of absence (voluntary or involuntary), early retirement or involuntary retirement, sabbatical leave, honorable location, surrender of ordained ministerial office, personal counseling or therapy, program of career evaluation, peer support and supervision, or private reprimand.[58]

If the bishop determines a complaint is based on allegations of one or more offenses listed in ¶2702.1, the complaint may be referred to counsel for the church and categorized as a judicial complaint.[59] The *Discipline* describes the following chargeable offenses as constitutive of a judicial complaint that may be brought against a clergy person within The United Methodist Church: (a) immorality, (b) practices declared by The United Methodist Church to be incompatible with Christian teaching, (c) crime, (d) disobedience to the order and discipline of The United Methodist Church, (e) doctrines contrary to established standards of doctrine, (f) undermining the ministry of another pastor, (g) child abuse, (h) sexual abuse, (i) sexual misconduct including the use or possession of pornography, (j) harassment including sexual harassment, (k) racial or gender discrimination, or (l) fiscal malfeasance.[60] In the case of charges brought against a clergy person, including a bishop, elder, deacon, or diaconal minister, a trial may be held when the appropriate body recommends involuntary termination.[61]

A professing lay member of a local church may be charged with the following offenses, and if so, may choose a trial: (a) immorality, (b) crime, (c) disobedience to the order and discipline of The United Methodist Church, (d) dissemination of doctrines contrary to the established standards of doctrine of The UMC, (e) sexual abuse, (f) sexual misconduct, (g) child abuse, (h) harassment, including, but not limited to racial or sexual harassment, (i) racial or gender discrimination, (j) relationships and behaviors that undermine the ministry of persons serving within an appointment, or (k) fiscal malfeasance.[62] Similar to an administrative process, a supervisory response seeks just resolution through possible suspension, referral, or dismissal. Once referred to church counsel, the complaint may be sent to the committee on investigation and then dismissed or brought to trial.[63]

As mentioned previously, while clergy and, more recently, laity continue to be guaranteed the right of trial and appeal within United Methodism, this right is provided as a last resort to facilitate just and fair resolution within our covenantal community. Relationships and community require faithful discipline and rely upon the Holy Spirit for flourishing. Reconciliation in the midst of baptismal and ordination covenants within the body of Christ is a spiritual gift and means of grace. Turning to judicial and other processes are a means to resolve difficult questions and hopefully maintain community, but they also benefit from a deep respect that does not take lightly the cost of such processes on all involved.

Council of Bishops

Bishops, while elected by jurisdictions and central conferences, are general superintendents and representatives of the whole connection. Similar to ordained ministers, who are elected from local churches into membership of an annual conference, bishops are elected from their appointments within annual conferences to membership in the Council of Bishops. Here they are bound in covenant with one another to fulfill their servant leadership and practice mutual accountability. According to the *Discipline*, "the Council of Bishops is a faith community of mutual trust and concern responsible for the faith development and continuing well-being of its members."[64] The Council of Bishops is required to meet at least annually by the Constitution,[65] but meets at least semiannually, and it is "charged with the oversight of the spiritual and temporal affairs of the whole Church, to be executed in regularized consultation and cooperation with other councils and service agencies of the Church."[66] All active and retired bishops make up its body.[67]

If the General Conference is considered the highest *legislative* body, the Judicial Council the highest *judicial* body, the Council of Bishops is considered the highest *executive* body. The Council of Bishops offers leadership to the denomination through its roles of presiding as well as through written statements.[68] Each quadrennium, the Council of Bishops, led by a colleague selected from its membership, drafts an "Episcopal Address," which is revised within the Council of Bishops and is then delivered by the selected bishop to General Conference. The writing of the address occurs in addition to the composition of "Episcopal Greetings" that opens each *Book of Discipline*. At the 2012 General Conference, a proposal to set aside a full-time president of the Council of Bishops was considered, but did not receive approval. The Council of Bishops also makes statements on particular issues (accessible through the denomination's website), thereby providing an episcopal perspective on serious and sometimes controversial concerns facing the church in the world, concerns such as care for creation, war, global health, sexual abuse, and church membership. The Council of Bishops serves as a key body for ecumenical conversation and efforts.

Connectional Table

The Connectional Table, formed by the 2004 General Conference, is an advisory body that provides vision and leadership for the denomination in connection with the various resources, including financial resources, available from across the denomination. According to the *Discipline*, "there shall be a Connectional Table in The United Methodist Church where ministry and money are brought to the same table to coordinate the mission, ministries, and resources of The United Methodist Church."[69] The establishment of the Connectional Table followed the dissolution of the General Council on Ministries. Similarly to the General Council on Ministries, the Connectional Table is accountable to the General Conference in consultation with the Council of Bishops.[70]

Membership

The Connectional Table structure, organization, and membership reflect the desire to include representation from across the denomination to inform the implementation of the mission of the church for the transformation of the world.[71] Currently there are forty-nine voting members,[72] and the *Discipline* provides significant care and detail in describing the representative character of this membership:

a) Twenty-eight persons elected through jurisdictional and central conferences, one from each of the central conferences by their own nomination processes and 21 from the jurisdictional conferences elected by the jurisdictional nomination process. Jurisdictional membership shall include one person from each jurisdiction and the balance of the jurisdictional members shall be allocated by the Secretary of the General Conference so as to insure to the extent possible that the members represent the proportionate membership of the jurisdictions based upon the combined clergy and lay membership.

b) An effective bishop, selected by the Council of Bishops, serves as the chair of the Connectional Table.

c) The ecumenical officer of the Council of Bishops and the presidents of the following agencies: General Board of Church and Society, General Board of Discipleship, General Board of Global

Ministries, General Board of Higher Education and Ministry, General Commission on Religion and Race, General Commission on Status and Role of Women, General Commission on United Methodist Men, General Commission on Communications, and General Commission on Archives and History, program-related agencies that are accountable to the Connectional Table (as expressed in ¶702.3), and the president of the General Council on Finance and Administration shall also sit with voice and vote on the Connectional Table.

d) One youth and one young adult elected by the Connectional Table upon nomination by the membership of the Division on Ministries with Young People from among its members shall serve on the Connectional Table.

e) One member from each of the racial ethnic caucuses as elected by the Connectional Table upon nomination from: Black Methodists for Church Renewal, Methodists Associated to Represent Hispanic Americans, Native American International Caucus, National Federation of Asian American United Methodists and Pacific Islanders National Caucus United Methodist.

f) The general secretaries of the above named agencies and the General Board of Pension and Health Benefits and the president and publisher of The United Methodist Publishing House shall sit at the Table and have the right of voice but no vote.

g) Jurisdictional, central conferences, and other groups involved in the nominating and election of persons to the Connectional Table shall ensure the diversity objectives of, insofar as possible, fifty percent clergy, fifty percent laity, fifty percent female, fifty percent male, not less than thirty percent members of racial/ethnic groups (excluding central conference members), and not less than ten percent youth and young adults, ensuring diversity as otherwise provided in ¶705.4b.

h) Vacancies of members elected from central and jurisdictional conferences occurring between sessions of the general conference shall be filled by the College of Bishops where the vacancy occurred, in so far as possible from the same annual conference.[73]

Among those represented include general agencies through voice (general secretaries) and vote (agency presidents), each ethnic caucus, as well as youth.[74] The organization and structure of the Connectional

Table includes an advisory team that coordinates leadership through a rotating membership to facilitate the work of a number of task groups. These task groups focus upon select objectives of the Connectional Table's work and are responsible for sharing information with the entire body distributing the work to implement the denomination's mission.[75] Officers other than the chair are elected from the Connectional Table and may serve for a quadrennium or until a successor is elected.[76] The Connectional Table meets at least semiannually and as necessary to be determined by the president or on written request of one-fifth of its members.[77]

Objectives

The objectives of the Connectional Table are to (1) provide a forum for vision and implementation; (2) enable flow of information and communication; (3) coordinate program life of the global church; (4) evaluate the missional effectiveness of agencies; (5) recommend changes for agency effectiveness; (6) provide leadership in planning and research; and (7) collaborate with the General Council on Finance and Administration (GCFA) to develop the budget.[78] While the Connectional Table is accountable to the General Conference, it works closely with the Council of Bishops, which offers leadership and collaboration.[79]

The United Methodist website describes the work of the Connectional Table as collaboratively "identifying four areas of focus for churchwide ministry; [s]ponsoring research on the state of the Church; and [l]aying the groundwork for equitable change as the Church grows worldwide."[80] The Table has also responded to the Council of Bishops's fall 2009 "call to action" that sought a "focused, in-depth study of The UMC to understand what concrete changes are needed for a more fruitful future" resulting in the "Call to Action" report.[81] This report named challenges to the church's flourishing and led to a multiagency initiative focused on vital congregations in addition to the four areas of focus. The four areas of focus for church-wide ministry include developing principled Christian leaders for the church and the world, creating new places for people by starting new congregations and renewing existing ones, engaging in ministry with the poor, and combating the diseases of poverty by improving health globally.[82] While there continues to be progress in articulating and implementing the ministry and purpose of the denomination, proposals to restructure denominational organizations submitted to the 2012 General Conference generally did not succeed.

General Agencies

As mentioned previously, general agencies of the church contribute to the overall mission and demonstrate an aspect of our connectionalism. According to the *Discipline*, "connectionalism is an important part of our identity as United Methodists."[83] General agencies represent connectionalism as an expression of General Conference powers in their work to implement and fulfill the mission of the church.[84] The *Discipline* continues,

> [Connectionalism] is a vital web of interactive relationships (¶132) that includes the agencies of the Church, as defined in ¶¶701.2 and 701.3, with the purpose of equipping local churches for ministry and by providing a connection for ministry throughout the world, all to the glory of God. It provides us with wonderful opportunities to carry out our mission in unity and strength.[85]

The creation of the current structure of general agencies dates to the amalgamation of The Evangelical United Brethren and Methodist Churches, when a structure study commission was established in 1968 to bring a report to the 1972 General Conference. The report described a proposed structure to combine the strengths of both denominational traditions. From this many of our general boards and agencies were formed.

The *Discipline* goes on to explain the term *agency*, noting that "wherever it is used in the *Book of Discipline*, [it] is a term used to describe the various councils, boards, commissions, committees, divisions or other units constituted within the various levels of Church organization (general, jurisdictional, central, annual, district, and charge conferences) under the authority granted by the *Book of Discipline*."[86] Paragraph 703 outlines in more detail the "Definitions, Structures, and Titles" of the six distinct terms that are included in the term *general agencies*. These include the following:

1. *General Council*—An organization created by the General Conference to perform defined responsibilities of review and oversight on behalf of the General Conference in relation to the other general agencies and to perform other assigned functions shall be designated as a general council. General councils are amenable and accountable to the General Conference and report to it. The General Council on Finance and Administration is a council.

(Note: The Council of Bishops and Judicial Council are authorized by the Constitution and are not created by the General Conference.)

2. *General Board*—A continuing body of the Church created by the General Conference to carry out assigned functions of program, administration, and/or service shall be designated as a general board.

3. *General Commission*—An organization created by the General Conference for the fulfillment of a specific function for an indefinite period of time.

4. *Study Committee*—An organization created by the General Conference for a limited period of time for the purpose of making a study ordered by the General Conference. The Connectional Table shall provide for coordination with and among the study committees except where General Conference otherwise designates.

5. *Program-Related General Agencies*—The general boards and commissions that have program and/or advocacy functions shall be designated as program-related general agencies. These agencies are amenable to the General Conference, and between sessions of the General Conference are accountable to the Connectional Table for those functions outlined in the 900 ¶s: the General Board of Church and Society, the General Board of Discipleship, the General Board of Global Ministries, the General Board of Higher Education and Ministry, the General Commission on Religion and Race, the General Commission on United Methodist Men, and the General Commission on the Status and Role of Women. In all matters of accountability, episcopal oversight as provided in ¶422 is assumed.

6. *Administrative General Agencies*—The general boards and

commissions that have primarily administrative and service functions shall be designated as administrative general agencies. These agencies are the General Board of Pension and Health Benefits, The United Methodist Publishing House, and the General Commission on Archives and History and General Commission on Communication, the last two of which also carry program-related responsibilities for which they are accountable to the Connectional Table.[87]

The general agencies may be organized into categories. For example, the Connectional Table and the General Council on Finance and Administration are supervisory councils.[88] Following General Conference in 1972, the four basic program components were identified as General Board of Church and Society—Advocacy; General Board of Discipleship—Nurture; General Board of Global Ministries (including the United Methodist Commission on Relief)—Outreach; and General Board of Higher Education and Ministry—Vocation. With these four program boards, three other general commissions are listed among them in the *Discipline*: the General Commission on Religion and Race, the General Commission on United Methodist Men, and the General Commission on the Status and Role of Women.[89] Administrative units include the remaining agencies of the General Board of Pension and Health Benefits, the publishing house, the General Commission on Archives and History, the General Commission on Communication, the Standing Committee on Central Conference Matters, and JUSTPEACE Center for Mediation and Conflict Transformation.[90] United Methodist Women, the most recent agency approved by the General Conference in 2012, is membership-based, elects its own leadership, and reports to General Conference.

University Senate

The University Senate of The United Methodist Church is one of the oldest accrediting bodies in the nation, dating to the General Conference of 1892.[91] The University Senate continues the aspirations of John and Charles Wesley, Francis Asbury, and Thomas Coke to provide quality higher education as an aspect of the ministry of United Methodism and its predecessors in the spirit of the well-known hymn line:

Unite the pair so long disjoin'd
Knowledge and vital Piety[92]

The University Senate is facilitated by an associate general secretary of the General Board of Higher Education and Ministry. While the Senate was originally made up of sixteen members and gathered four times in eight years, the current membership totals twenty-five and meets at least twice annually. Two subordinate bodies, the Commission on Theological Education and the Commission on Institutional Review, carry out the work of the Senate. The former supports the mission of seminaries and graduate schools of theology whose degrees provide credentials for pastors and practitioners in the church. The latter supports the mission and work of undergraduate institutions. The University Senate seeks not to duplicate the work of current regional and other accrediting bodies, such as the Association of Theological Schools, but rather implements accountability to guidelines, sometimes similar, for church-related institutions.

Conclusion

In this chapter several select councils and agencies have been explored demonstrating the connectional nature of the denomination and its efforts to participate in God's mission. Each of these distinctive bodies, from the Judicial Council to the Council of Bishops and the Connectional Table as well as the University Senate and general boards and agencies, support and enable the ministries of the church—individuals, local churches, and conferences.

PART IV

UNITED METHODIST ORGANIZATION:
STRUCTURE AND LANGUAGE

Conference Organization Chart

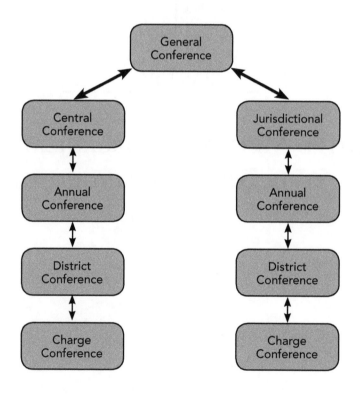

The United Methodist Church Organization Chart

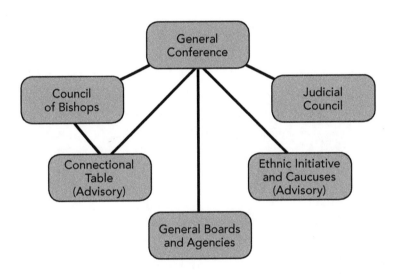

Conclusion: Sent to the World

This book opens with a chapter on the nature and mission of The United Methodist Church to introduce United Methodist polity and organization. As described in chapter 1: "The mission of the Church is to make disciples of Jesus Christ for the transformation of the world. Local churches provide the most significant arena through which disciple-making occurs."[1] While definitions of mission vary, one way to understand mission, drawing from biblical themes, is as *sending*. For example, the Latin phrase *missio dei*, or "mission of God," refers to God's sending Jesus Christ in ministry to the world. Similarly, Jesus Christ sends the disciples—and the church—in ministry to and with the world. In John 20:19-22 we read,

> It was still the first day of the week. That evening, while the disciples were behind closed doors because they were afraid of the Jewish authorities, Jesus came and stood among them. He said, "Peace be with you." After he said this, he showed them his hands and his side. When the disciples saw the Lord, they were filled with joy. Jesus said to them again, "Peace be with you. As the Father sent me, so I am sending you." Then he breathed on them and said, "Receive the Holy Spirit."

Drawing on these biblical themes, we may understand our identity and purpose related to God's call upon us as a gathered community sent by God in Jesus Christ through the Holy Spirit to minister to and with the world. This is not to constrain the ministry of individuals and groups to a perceived "going out" or "to bring something to or to fix the other."

Rather, to understand United Methodism as missional, in light of its mission statement, is to draw on biblical themes to inform an imagination and impetus to seek the Holy Spirit through the other—near or far—by ministering to, with, and receiving ministry from and through the other. In this way, we hope to participate with the Holy Spirit in God's unfolding reign, to bring the gospel and love of God in Jesus Christ, but also to receive that gospel and love expanding our imaginations for what ministry to and with the world can be.

When understood within biblical and theological frames, mission, polity and organization take on dimensions beyond the mere mechanics of governance and the execution of policies and legislation. Our polity and organization undergird and facilitate our mission providing a means within which to fulfill that mission. From doctrinal standards and ministry roles to conferences and councils, the aspects of our polity and organization benefit from biblical and theological frames grounded in the Wesleyan tradition in order to make sense of them and live into their full purpose. How we understand these components informs our identity and purpose as a church—one that is already and not yet—as we seek to participate in the unfolding reign of God. Such an understanding of United Methodism is consistent with John and Charles Wesley's vision for the early Methodist renewal movement within the Church of England. As mentioned previously, in the "Large" *Minutes,* John Wesley summarized his understanding of Methodism's purpose: "What may we reasonably believe to be God's design in raising up the Preachers called Methodists? A. To reform the nation and, in particular, the Church; to spread scriptural holiness over the land."[2]

While the Wesleys' birthing of a renewal movement has resulted in a number of challenges when considering an ecclesiology for United Methodism, there is a profound simplicity in the early movement's purpose. The Wesleys were less concerned with doctrinal disagreements than with an imperative to share and demonstrate the gospel of Jesus Christ. This is to say, difficulties of polity and organization, availability of resources and leadership, will persist. However, our Wesleyan heritage offers helpful guidance for continued response to God's calling and sending United Methodism to participate in God's reign.

I hope this book encourages current and future denominational leaders to understand practices of polity and administration as a theological endeavor and key component of our ministries. Consistent with our Wesleyan heritage, understanding our practices of leadership as theological helps us navigate default mind-sets and metrics created by worldly temptations, while still being accountable to our purpose and mission.

Framing our practices of polity, much less our identity and purpose, theologically and missionally is difficult in the midst of what many describe as a crisis of identity and purpose for United Methodism in the United States. Some ask, *Is the church declining, even failing, in some locations because of a loss of identity and purpose?* And, *Will reclaiming our identity and purpose renew the church?* While I believe such a reclaiming is significant, if not essential, to the viability of United Methodism, particularly in the United States, this may not necessarily occur in the way we expect. For example, it is important for General Conference as well as jurisdictional conferences, central conferences, and annual conferences to legislate for renewal, facilitating the embodiment of our beliefs for the fulfillment of our shared mission. However, renewal seems most often to come from communities of faith—or institutions of the faithful—sent by God in Jesus Christ through the Holy Spirit to participate in the reign of God. These communities and institutions exist in a variety of locations, many outside the United States, where United Methodism and Christianity are experiencing significant growth in grace and numbers. Polity and organization facilitate our shared mission as United Methodists in a worldwide connection.

In the midst of a complicated and shifting religious landscape, in the United States and internationally, United Methodism has much to celebrate. In light of our roots as a renewal movement, we enjoy an agility in response to the Holy Spirit's leading. This agility is characterized by a number of strengths discussed throughout the preceding chapters—the relationship of beliefs and practice, ordered for ministry, and a missional worldwide connection.

Beliefs and Practice

From spiritual formation of individuals in small groups to challenging systemic injustices and crossing boundaries, United Methodism, as well as its Wesleyan heritage, continues to hold together Christian beliefs and practice. This synergy is demonstrated by the multiple genres of doctrine, such as constitutional standards, as well as contemporary statements, that often function as operational doctrine. Constitutional standards within United Methodism articulate our beliefs, which reflect alignment with historic and scriptural Christianity traced initially through the Church of England, the ecclesial home of the Wesleys. United Methodist doctrinal standards describe these Christian beliefs through a series of articles informed by the Church of England of Wesley's day, John Wesley's General Rules for the United Societies, his *Sermons* and *Notes upon the New Testament*, and The Evangelical United Brethren Church's Confession of Faith. Methodism in the United States grew from a missional imperative, embodying those beliefs in practices of disciple-making and renewal. Contemporary statements include "Our Doctrinal Heritage," "Our Doctrinal History," and "Our Theological Task;" the Social Creed, Social Principles, and the *Book of Resolutions*, as well as liturgical resources—*The United Methodist Hymnal* and *The United Methodist Book of Worship*. While these contemporary statements receive occasional revisions by the General Conference or with its approval, these statements serve as guides for interpreting the relationship of our beliefs and practices as a denomination in the contemporary context sent in ministry to and with the world.

Ordered for Ministry

Inspired by the leadership of the early Methodist renewal movement in Great Britain, United Methodism encourages contemporary leadership to emerge through a variety of roles, including lay and ordained, while at the same time holding one another accountable to authentic vocations, substantial criteria and requirements, as well as training for those roles. Whether as a member of a local church, certified lay servant or speaker, deaconess or home missioner, licensed local pastor, deacon or elder, associate, provisional, or full member of an annual conference, all baptized Christians are called to "proclaim the good news and live according to the example of Christ."[3] Though the proliferation of roles may seem complex, and even confusing, the various roles provide a number of entry points and accessibility to those responding to the Holy Spirit's call upon lives to share gifts in ministry. That being said, through study commissions, the denomination pursues ongoing revision and efforts to clarify these roles.

The superintendency within Methodism follows the examples of John Wesley and Francis Asbury, and in the contemporary context includes the offices of bishop and district superintendent. Bishops traditionally hold responsibility for teaching and defending the faith. However, within Methodism they also carry a distinctive missional role. The role of bishop, protected by the Constitution and Restrictive Rules, has changed some in response to needs and opportunities within the denomination. Bishops itinerate in a more limited way than in previous generations. Bishops once exchanged responsibilities for appointments with a colleague bishop once in every four years. Today, bishops are assigned each quadrennium, or every four years (following general and jurisdictional as well as possibly central conferences), to episcopal areas within jurisdictional or central conferences. District superintendents extend the office of bishop through their assistance in overseeing smaller geographic regions within annual conferences. A well-known responsibility of the district superintendent is assisting the bishop in administering an itinerant system through the appointment-making of clergy and licensed or set-apart ministers. The 2012 *Discipline* describes district superintendents as "chief missional strategists."[4] District superintendents recruit, assess, and deploy pastoral leadership within the district, both lay and ordained, to facilitate the ministry of local churches and those in extension ministries.

A Missional Worldwide Connection

In the United States since the mid-twentieth century, the local church has functioned operationally as the most significant organizational component within the denomination. This makes sense in that individuals in more recent generations tend to experience church in the context of local church worship, a distinction from earlier generations of Methodists who identified most closely with small groups such as classes, bands, and subsequently, Sunday schools. According to the

Discipline, the annual conference continues to function as the basic organizational unit within United Methodism, a function rooted in the early Methodist renewal movement. Annual conferences may not embody a significant physical entity; however, they shape the imaginations and programs for ministry within the United Methodist connection. While the local church remains significant for its role in nurturing disciples and the regular administration of the sacraments, the annual conferences possess a distinctive missional character and flexibility as participants in God's unfolding reign sent in ministry to and with the world.

As membership declines in many annual conferences in the United States, United Methodism grows steadily worldwide. Though this brings challenges related to practices of polity, organization, and governance, it brings many more opportunities to receive and learn from these vibrant communities in a worldwide connection. Gifted with vital and authentic ministries, local churches, annual conferences, and other ecclesial institutions within the worldwide connection are responding to God's sending United Methodism in ministry to and with the world.

United Methodism enjoys a connectional structure that enables the interrelationship of organizational bodies, from local churches to annual, jurisdictional, and central conferences, general boards and agencies, the Council of Bishops and Connectional Table to the General Conference. This complicated structure sometimes lacks clear lines of accountability. However, connection, which dates to the early Methodist renewal movement, at its best continues to facilitate the missional character of the denomination in ministry to and with the world.

Whether new to United Methodism as a congregational member or candidate for ordained ministry, or a longstanding member and denominational leader, I pray the Holy Spirit continues to guide and challenge us in our shared vocations to extend God's love in Jesus Christ. May we find hope and purpose in our identity as United Methodists, a connection of missional and worldwide Christians.

– Notes –

Introduction

1. John Wesley, "The Character of a Methodist," in *The Bicentennial Edition of the Works of John Wesley*, vol. 9, *The Methodist Societies: History, Nature, and Design*, ed. Rupert E. Davies (Nashville: Abingdon Press, 1989), 30–46. Wesley poses such questions as well as providing answers in his 1742 essay, cited above and quoted in Russell E. Richey, *United Methodism and American Culture*, vol. 5, *Marks of Methodism: Theology in Ecclesial Practice*, with Dennis M. Campbell and William B. Lawrence (Nashville: Abingdon Press, 2005), 2.

2. Richey, *Marks of Methodism*, 2–6.

3. Ibid., 6.

4. Ibid., 7.

5. Ibid.

6. Ibid., 6.

7. Ibid.

8. Ibid., 8.

9. Ibid., 9.

10. *The Works of the Rev. John Wesley, A.M.*, ed. Thomas Jackson, 14 vols. (London: Wesleyan Conference Office, 1872), VIII, 275, quoted in Richey, *Marks of Methodism*, 11.

11. Richey, *Marks of Methodism*, 11.

12. Albert C. Outler, "Do Methodists Have a Doctrine of the Church?" in *The Wesleyan Theological Heritage*, ed. Thomas C. Oden and Leicester R. Longden (Grand Rapids: Zondervan, 1991), 211–26. The essay was originally published in an earlier (1964) volume as the lead article derived from a lecture given at the 1962 Oxford Institute on Methodist Theological Studies.

13. Geoffrey Wainwright, *The Ecumenical Moment: Crisis and Opportunity for the Church* (Grand Rapids: Eerdmans, 1983), 220–21.

14. Outler, "Do Methodists Have a Doctrine of the Church?," 226.

15. Linda Bloom, "Global Delegates Mean Multiple Languages," United Methodist News Service (UMNS), June 13, 2012, http://www .umc.org/news-and-media/global-delegates-mean-multiple-languages.

16. Ibid.

17. Ibid.; and Skyler Nimmons, "GC2012: Covenant for a Worldwide Church Debuts," UMNS, April 26, 2013, http://www.umc.org /news-and-media/gc2012-covenant-for-a-worldwide-church-debuts.

18. Nimmons, "GC2012."

19. 2012 *Discipline*, ¶101, p. 43: "The following parts and paragraphs are not subject to change or adaptation except by action of the General Conference . . . Parts I, III-V[:] I. Constitution ¶¶1–61. III. Doctrinal Standards and Our Theological Task ¶¶102–105. IV. The Ministry of All Christians ¶¶120–143. V. Social Principles Preface, Preamble, and ¶¶160–166" (2012 *Discipline*, ¶101.).

20. Ibid., ¶125, pp. 93–94.

21. Ibid., ¶701, p. 507.

22. Ibid.

23. Thomas Frank, *Polity, Practice and the Mission of the United Methodist Church* (Nashville: Abingdon Press, 2006), 275.

24. Brian Beck, "Connexion and Koinonia: Wesley's Legacy and the Ecumenical Ideal," in *Rethinking Wesley's Theology for Contemporary Methodism*, ed. Randy Maddox (Nashville: Abingdon Press, 1998), 131.

25. Ibid., 130.

26. Ibid., 131.

27. Russell E. Richey, "Connection and Connectionalism," in *Oxford Handbook of Methodist Studies*, ed. William J. Abraham and James E. Kirby (Oxford: Oxford University Press, 2009), 213.

28. Ibid., 217.

29. Ibid., 215.

1. The Nature and Mission of the Church

1. While this is largely true, a brief mention of John Wesley's rogue acts of ordination seems appropriate. Wesley ordained, a practice reserved for the episcopacy, three ministers prior to their departure for America for the sake of the movement, implying a polity dispute.

2. Scott J. Jones, *United Methodist Doctrine: The Extreme Center* (Nashville: Abingdon Press, 2002), 246.

3. Ibid.

4. Outler, "Do Methodists Have a Doctrine of the Church?" 212.

5. Jones, *United Methodist Doctrine*, 247.

6. Richard Heitzenrater, "Wesleyan Ecclesiology: Methodism as a Means of Grace," in *Orthodox and Wesleyan Ecclesiology*, ed. ST Kimbrough Jr. (Crestwood, NY: St. Vladimir's Seminary Press, 2007), 119–28.

7. For more attention to Wesley's means of grace see John Wesley, "Sermon 16: The Means of Grace," in *The Bicentennial Edition of the Works of John Wesley*, vol. 1, *Sermons I*, ed. Albert C. Outler (Nashville: Abingdon Press, 1984), 37897; see also Henry Knight, *The Presence of God in the Christian Life: John Wesley and the Means of Grace* (Lanham, MD: Scarecrow Press, 1992).

8. Scott J. Jones, *The Evangelistic Love of God and Neighbor: A Theology of Witness and Discipleship* (Nashville: Abingdon Press, 2003), 151.

9. Ibid.

10. Ibid. According to Jones, "These are not the only ways in which God gives grace to persons. After all, prevenient grace is given to persons whether or not the church is present in their lives at all. But where the church is present, God's grace is available in more explicit ways" (Jones, *United Methodist Doctrine*, 255.).

11. Jones, *United Methodist Doctrine*, 255. John Wesley described both instituted and prudential means of grace. Instituted means of grace were "instituted" by Jesus Christ and appear in the Gospels. Prudential means of grace are prudent forms and practices for Christians in community to pursue to deepen faith through discipleship.

12. Ibid.

13. Ibid., 247.

14. Ibid.

15. 2012 *Discipline*, ¶104, p. 66.

16. Jones, *United Methodist Doctrine*, 247.

17. 2012 *Discipline*, ¶103, pp. 60–61.

18. Ibid., ¶104, p. 71.

19. Jones, *United Methodist Doctrine*, 247.

20. Ibid., 248.

21. Ibid.

22. 2012 *Discipline*, ¶102, p. 47.

23. Ibid.

24. Ibid., ¶102, pp. 47–48.

25. Jones, *United Methodist Doctrine*, 256.

26. "The Baptismal Covenant I" and "The Baptismal Covenant II," in *The United Methodist Hymnal* (Nashville: The United Methodist Publishing House, 1989), 35 and 40.

27. Jones, *United Methodist Doctrine*, 255.

28. In 1745 the Methodist Conference under John's leadership decided to experiment with preaching wherever opportunities arose.

The results of the experiment were definitive. Methodist small groups organized by Wesley provided essential Christian spiritual formation for a vast majority of those awakened by the preaching. Because of un-equivocal results the experiment ceased in 1748, and the Conference returned its priority to the organization of small groups. See William Abraham, *The Logic of Evangelism* (Grand Rapids: Eerdmans, 1989), 54–55; Theodore Runyon, *The New Creation: John Wesley's Theology Today* (Nashville: Abingdon Press, 1998), 115; and Richard P. Heitzenrater, *Wesley and the People Called Methodists* (Nashville: Abingdon Press, 1995), 165.

29. 2012 *Discipline*, ¶121, p. 91.

30. Ibid.

31. Matthew 28:16-20; Mark 16:1-8; Luke 24:44-49; John 20:19-23; Acts 1:8.

32. Sarah Heaner Lancaster, "Our Mission Reconsidered: Do We Really 'Make' Disciples?" *Quarterly Review* 23, no. 2 (Summer 2003): 117–30.

33. Ibid.

34. 2012 *Discipline*, ¶121.

35. Amy-Jill Levine, "'To All the Gentiles': A Jewish Perspective on the Great Commission," *Review and Expositor* 103 (Winter 2006): 144.

36. 2012 *Discipline*, ¶121, p. 91

37. Bosch, "The Structure of Mission," 84.

38. Ibid.

39. Ibid., 84–85.

40. Levine, "'To All the Gentiles,'" 144.

41. David Bosch, "The Structure of Mission: An Exposition of Matthew 28:16-20," in *The Study of Evangelism*, ed. Paul W. Chilcote and Laceye C. Warner (Grand Rapids: Eerdmans, 2008), 85. While Levine uses different examples, she demonstrates a similar dynamic to Bosch. See Levine, "'To All the Gentiles,'" 144–45. For Levine, the

linguistic issue prompts the question: "Does the Great Commission include the witness to the Jews, or does it prompt the evangelization of the Gentile world only?" (145).

42. Levine, "'To All the Gentiles,'" 146.

43. Ibid.

44. Ibid.

45. Bosch, "The Structure of Mission," 85.

46. Levine, "'To All the Gentiles,'" 147. See also Ulrich Luz, *Matthew 21–28: A Commentary* (Minneapolis: Fortress Press, 2005), 629. Luz concurs that the language used in Matthew 28:16-20 indicated both "nations" and "Gentiles," not merely one. Luz's position is outlined in pp. 629–31.

47. Levine, "'To All the Gentiles,'" 147.

48. Musa W. Dube, "Go Therefore and Make Disciples of All Nations (Matt. 28:19a): A Postcolonial Perspective on Biblical Criticism and Pedagogy," in *Teaching the Bible*, ed. Fernando Segovia and Mary Ann Tolbert (Maryknoll, NY: Orbis Books, 1998), 224–25; here summarized by Daniel Patte et al., *The Gospel of Matthew: A Contextual Introduction for Group Study* (Nashville: Abingdon Press, 2003), 116, referenced in Levine, "'To All the Gentiles,'" 148.

49. Mortimer Arias and Alan Johnson, *The Great Commission: Biblical Models for Evangelism* (Nashville: Abingdon Press, 1992), 18.

50. Ibid., 20–21.

51. Ibid., 18, 22–24.

52. Ibid., 20.

53. Ibid.

54. Ibid.

55. Ibid.

56. 2012 *Discipline*, ¶122, p. 92.

57. Ibid.

58. Mortimer Arias, "Centripetal Mission or Evangelization by Hospitality," *Missiology* 10 (January 1982): 69–71.

59. Ibid., 74.

60. Ibid., 74–75, italics mine.

61. Ibid., 75.

62. Brad J. Kallenberg, *Live to Tell: Evangelism in a Postmodern World* (Grand Rapids: Brazos Press, 2002), 21.

63. Ibid., 54.

64. Ibid., 32.

65. Ibid., 41

66. Ibid.

67. 2012 *Discipline*, ¶122, p. 92.

68. Ibid., ¶123, p. 92.

69. Ibid., ¶124, p. 92.

70. Ibid., ¶125, p. 93.

71. Ibid., ¶125, p. 94.

2. Defining Documents: Doctrinal Standards

1. James Logan, "The Evangelical Imperative: A Wesleyan Perspective," in *Theology and Evangelism in the Wesleyan Heritage*, ed. James Logan (Nashville: Kingswood Books, 1994), 16.

2. John Wesley, "The 'Large' *Minutes*, A and B (1753, 1763)," in *The Bicentennial Edition of the Works of John Wesley*, vol. 10, *The Methodist Societies: The Minutes of Conference*, ed. Henry D. Rack (Nashville: Abingdon Press, 2011), 845.

3. John Wesley, "A Plain Account of the People Called Methodists," in *The Bicentennial Edition of the Works of John Wesley*, vol. 9, *The Methodist Societies: History, Nature, and Design*, ed. Rupert E. Davis (Nashville: Abingdon Press, 1989), 254.

4. Ibid., italics mine.

5. Ibid., 9:254–55.

6. For further discussion of the implications of Wesley's emphases see Kenneth L. Carder and Laceye C. Warner, *Grace to Lead: Practicing Leadership in the Wesleyan Tradition* (Nashville: The General Board of Higher Education and Ministry, 2011), 24–25; and Laceye C. Warner, "Spreading Scriptural Holiness: Theology and Practices of Early Methodism for the Contemporary Church," *The Asbury Journal* 63, no. 1 (Spring 2008): 121–22.

7. Randy Maddox, "Formation for Christian Leadership: Wesleyan Reflections," *American Theological Library Association Summary of Proceedings* 57 (2003): 115.

8. Ibid., 116. See also Warner "Spreading Scriptural Holiness," 122.

9. 2012 *Discipline*, ¶1, p. 23. The Plan of Union followed the adoption of the Constitution at the Uniting Conference in Dallas on April 23, 1968.

10. 2012 *Discipline*, preamble, p. 23.

11. Ibid.

12. 2012 *Discipline*, ¶¶1–7, pp. 23–25.

13. Jones, *United Methodist Doctrine*, 43.

14. Ibid., 44.

15. Ibid.

16. Ibid.

17. Ibid.

18. Heitzenrater, *Wesley and the People Called Methodists*, 5.

19. Ibid.

20. Ibid., 8.

21. Ibid. Each of these sources came primarily from Cranmer a decade earlier.

22. 2012 *Discipline*, ¶103, p. 57.

23. Jones, *United Methodist Doctrine*, 48. For a list of those articles omitted, see ibid., 65–66n42.

24. Ibid., 48. For a list of articles revised by Wesley, see ibid., 66n43.

25. Ibid., 48. For further detail, see ibid., 66nn44–45.

26. Ibid., 48.

27. 2012 *Discipline*, ¶102, p. 49.

28. Ibid.

29. Ibid.

30. Jones, *United Methodist Doctrine*, 60–61. For a comprehensive overview of John Wesley's theology, see also Randy L. Maddox, *Responsible Grace: John Wesley's Practical Theology* (Nashville: Abingdon Press, 1994).

31. J. Steven O'Malley, "The Distinctive Witness of the Evangelical United Brethren Confession of Faith in Comparison with the Methodist Articles of Religion," in *Doctrines and Disciplines: United Methodism and American Culture*, ed. Dennis M. Campbell, William B. Lawrence, and Russell E. Richey (Nashville: Abingdon Press, 1999), 55–56. The original documents were both composed in German and later translated into English. These groups represent the largest North American denominations emerging from German American revival activities (56).

32. 2012 *Discipline*, "Our Doctrinal History," ¶103, p. 60.

33. Ibid.

34. Ibid.

35. O'Malley, "The Distinctive Witness," 55. This essay provides a helpful overview to the topic (pp. 55–76). See 2012 *Discipline*, "Our Doctrinal History," ¶103, p. 62.

36. James E. Will, "The 1962 Evangelical United Brethren Confession of Faith," in *The Making of an American Church*, ed. Robert L. Frey (Lanham, MD: Scarecrow Press, 2007), 62.

37. Ibid., 56, 60.

38. Ibid., 63–64. According to Will, twenty amendments were submitted in writing to the bishops resulting in what he describes as friendly revisions. The United Methodist *Discipline* claims, "A new Confession, with sixteen articles, of a somewhat more modern character than any of its antecedents, was presented to the General Conference of 1962 and adopted *without amendment*" (2012 *Discipline*, "Our Doctrinal History," ¶103, p. 62, italics mine.).

39. O'Malley, "The Distinctive Witness," 60. O'Malley's descriptions are in reference to The Evangelical United Brethren Confession and Evangelical Association Articles of Faith. However, the descriptions continue to demonstrate pertinence.

40. 2012 *Discipline*, ¶103, p. 55.

41. O'Malley, "The Distinctive Witness," 55.

42. Jason Vickers, "The Confession of Faith and the Twenty-Five Articles of Religion Compared: Assessing the EUB Contribution to Methodist Standards of Doctrine," *Methodist History* 46, no. 4 (July 2008): 238.

43. Ibid., 239.

44. Ibid.

45. O'Malley, "The Distinctive Witness," 75.

46. Ibid., 76.

47. Warner, "Spreading Scriptural Holiness," 124.

48. John Wesley, "Sermon 24: Upon Our Lord's Sermon on the Mount: Discourse the Fourth," in *The Bicentennial Edition of the Works of John Wesley*, vol. 1, *Sermons I*, ed. Albert C. Outler (Nashville: Abingdon Press, 1984), 533–34.

49. Warner, "Spreading Scriptural Holiness," 124.

50. Heitzenrater, *Wesley and the People Called Methodists*, 21. The Society for Promoting Christian Knowledge has its roots in the religious societies founded by Anthony Horneck in the 1670s, the English counterparts to the *collegia pietatis* organized by Philipp Jakob Spener.

51. Wesley, "A Plain Account of the People Called Methodists," in Davies, *Works*, II.5, IX.2, X.2, XI.4, 9:254–80.

52. Thomas R. Albin, "An Empirical Study of Early Methodist Spirituality," in *Wesleyan Theology Today: A Bicentennial Theological Consultation*, ed. Theodore Runyon (Nashville: Kingswood Books, 1985), 277. In relation to awakening and conviction, lay people are mentioned three times more frequently than clergy, twice as often in relation to the new birth, and four times more often in relation to sanctification. Interestingly, in many accounts there is no human catalyst identified. See ibid., 278.

53. Ibid., 278.

54. Ibid. One individual in the study received such an experience after forty-eight years, creating a mean of two years and four months between conviction and conversion in this study for overall time people participated in society prior to receiving a spiritual experience.

55. 2012 *Discipline*, ¶104, p. 76. Wesley composed the rules after he expelled sixty-four persons from the Newcastle society in February 1743. See Jones, *United Methodist Doctrine*, 50.

56. 2012 *Discipline*, ¶104, p. 76.

57. Ibid., 75–78.

58. Maddox, "Formation for Christian Leadership," 122. See also Wesley, "Sermon 16: The Means of Grace," in Outler, *Works*, 1:376–97.

59. Joerg Rieger, "Between God and the Poor: Rethinking the Means of Grace in the Wesleyan Tradition," in *The Poor and the People Called Methodists*, ed. Richard P. Heitzenrater (Nashville: Kingswood Books, 2002), 86; based on John Wesley, "Sermon 92: On Zeal," in *The Bicentennial Edition of the Works of John Wesley*, vol. 3, *Sermons III*, ed. Albert C. Outler (Nashville: Abingdon Press, 1986), 313.

60. 2012 *Discipline*, ¶17, p. 29.

61. Jones, *United Methodist Doctrine*, 48.

62. Ibid., 52.

63. 2012 *Discipline*, ¶103, p. 58.

64. Ibid., pp. 62–63.

65. Ibid., p. 56; See also Jones, *United Methodist Doctrine*, 52.

66. Jones, *United Methodist Doctrine*, 55.

3. Contemporary Statements: Operational Doctrine

1. Jones, *United Methodist Doctrine*, 44. According to Jones, "there are also [beyond Parts II, III, and IV] explicitly doctrinal statements embedded in various places in Part V of the *Discipline* titled 'Organization and Administration.'"

2. 2012 *Discipline*, ¶102, pp. 45–54.

3. Ibid., ¶103, pp. 54–63.

4. Ibid., ¶104, pp. 63–78.

5. Ibid., ¶105, pp. 78–89.

6. Ibid., ¶102, p. 45.

7. Ibid., pp. 45–46.

8. Ibid., p. 46.

9. Ibid., p. 49, italics mine.

10. Ibid.

11. Ibid.

12. Ibid., pp. 49–52.

13. Ibid., p. 52.

14. Ibid., ¶103, p. 60.

15. Randy Maddox, "Reclaiming an Inheritance: Wesley as Theologian in the History of Methodist Theology," in *Rethinking Wesley's Theology for Contemporary Methodism*, ed. R. L. Maddox (Nashville: Kingswood Books, 1998), 214, 223.

16. Ibid., 220–22.

17. Ibid., 223–25.

18. Randy Maddox, "'Honoring Conference': Wesleyan Reflections on the Dynamics of Theological Reflection," in *The Renewal of United Methodism: Mission, Ministry, and Connectionalism*, ed. Rex D. Matthews (Nashville: The General Board of Higher Education and Ministry, 2012), 57. The term *quadrilateral* was introduced to capture the fourfold character of Wesley's practice in an interim report submitted to a special session of General Conference in 1970 in a section on "The Wesleyan Concept of Authority." This material drew from a previously published article of Outler's from 1968 (58).

19. Ibid., 58. Interestingly, the term was absent from the final report of the commission. According to Maddox, Outler soon regretted coining the term as a result of "literal-minded people who would construe it in geometrical terms and draw the unintended inference that this downgraded the primacy of Scripture."

20. Ibid., 59.

21. Ibid., 57.

22. Ibid.

23. Ibid.

24. 2012 *Discipline*, ¶105, pp. 79–80.

25. Ibid., pp. 80–86.

26. Scott Jones, "The Rule of Scripture," in *Wesley and the Quadrilateral: Renewing the Conversation*, ed. W. Stephen Gunter (Nashville, Abingdon Press, 1997), 40.

27. Ibid., 53.

28. Ted A. Campbell, "The Interpretive Role of Tradition," in *Wesley and the Quadrilateral: Renewing the Conversation*, ed. W. Stephen Gunter (Nashville, Abingdon Press, 1997), 65.

29. For a survey of the multiple facets of experience employed during Wesley's time and context, see Randy Maddox, "The Enriching Role of Experience," in *Wesley and the Quadrilateral: Renewing the Conversation*, ed. W. Stephen Gunter (Nashville, Abingdon Press, 1997), 108–12.

30. Ibid., 113.

31. Rebekah L. Miles, "The Instrumental Role of Reason," in *Wesley and the Quadrilateral: Renewing the Conversation*, ed. W. Stephen Gunter (Nashville, Abingdon Press, 1997), 77.

32. 2012 *Discipline*, ¶105, p. 86.

33. Ibid.

34. Donald K. Gorrell, "The Social Creed and Methodism Through Eighty Years," in *Perspectives on American Methodism Interpretive Essays*, ed. Russell E. Richey, Kenneth E. Rowe, and Jean Miller Schmidt (Nashville: Abingdon Press, 1993), 387. According to Gorrell, "nor do they [most persons] appreciate the unique relationship of this literary genre." (386).

35. Ibid., 388.

36. Ibid.

37. Ibid.

38. Ibid.

39. *Journal of the General Conference of the Methodist Episcopal Church* (1908), 547, quoted in Gorrell, "The Social Creed," 388.

40. Gorrell, "The Social Creed," 389.

41. Ibid.

42. Ibid.

43. Ibid.

44. Ibid., 390.

45. Ibid.

46. See Priscilla Pope-Levison, "A 'Thirty Year War' and More: Exposing Complexities in the Methodist Deaconess Movement," *Methodist History* 47, no. 2 (January 2009): 101–16.

47. Gorrell, "The Social Creed," 390.

48. Ibid., 391.

49. Ibid.

50. Ibid., 394.

51. Ibid., 394–95.

52. 2012 *Discipline*, ¶166, p. 142.

53. Gorrell, "The Social Creed," 396.

54. Ibid., 397. For a comprehensive analysis of the Social Principles, including their composition, see Darryl W. Stephens, "A Witness of Words: The United Methodist Social Principles as Moral Discourse and Institutional Practice" (PhD diss., Emory University, 2006), 147–152.

55. Gorrell, "The Social Creed," 397–98.

56. Stephens, "A Witness of Words," 49.

57. 1968 *Discipline*, ¶97, pp. 63, 127–28, described in Darryl W. Stephens, "Face of Unity or Mask over Difference? The Social Principles in the Central Conferences of The United Methodist Church," *Thinking About Religion* 5 (2005): 2.

58. 2012 *Discipline*, ¶161C, pp. 109–10.

59. Ibid., ¶¶161–63, pp. 109–34.

60. Ibid., preface to Social Principles, p. 103. See also Jones, *United Methodist Doctrine*, 231–32. There are a number of study guides to the Social Principles that have been published, including J. Richard Peck, ed., *When the Church Speaks: A Guide to the Social Principles* (Nashville: Cokesbury, 2001).

61. Stephens, "Face of Unity or Mask over Difference?," 2. See 2012 *Discipline*, ¶543.7, pp. 373–74.

62. Heather Hahn, "Effort to Make Social Principles More Global," UMNS, May 9, 2013, http://www.umc.org/news-and-media/effort-to-make-social-principles-more-global.

63. Ibid. The legislation was adopted with a vote of 589 to 319.

64. Ibid.

65. See Connectional Table, "Revising the Social Principles: A Draft of a Work Plan," accessed January 21, 2013, http://www.umc

.org/atf/cf/%7Bdb6a45e4-c446-4248-82c8-e131b6424741%7D
/REVISING%20THE%20SOCIAL%20PRINCIPLES%202.PDF.

66. Stephens, "A Witness of Words," 9.

67. 2012 *Discipline*, ¶510.2.a, p. 355: "Those [resolutions] that have expired shall not be printed in subsequent editions of the *Book of Resolutions*."

68. Jones, *United Methodist Doctrine*, 45.

69. 2012 *Discipline*, ¶16.6, p. 28.

70. *Via Saluis* is Latin for "the way of salvation."

71. Heitzenrater, *Wesley and the People Called Methodists*, 231.

72. Brian Beck, "Rattenbury Revisited: The Theology of Charles Wesley's Hymns," *Epworth Review* 26, no. 2 (April 1999): 71.

73. Ibid., 72. See John R. Tyson, *Charles Wesley: A Reader* (New York: Oxford University Press, 1989), 13, 212–20. See also Thomas R. Albin, "Charles Wesley's Other Prose Writings," in *Charles Wesley: Poet and Theologian*, ed. ST Kimbrough Jr. (Nashville: Kingswood Books, 1992), 91.

74. A. Raymond George, "Methodism," in *Singing the Faith: Essays by Members of the Joint Liturgical Group on the Use of Hymns in Liturgy*, ed. Charles Robertson (Norwich: The Canterbury Press, 1990), 135; Terry Heisey, "Singet Hallelujah! Music in the Evangelical Association, 1800–1894," *Methodist History* 28, no. 4 (July 1990): 237.

75. Beck, "Rattenbury Revisited," 71, 75, 77.

76. Thomas A. Langford, "Charles Wesley as Theologian," in *Charles Wesley: Poet and Theologian*, ed. ST Kimbrough Jr. (Nashville: Kingswood Books, 1992), 99. Namely Ernest Rattenbury.

77. Beck, "Rattenbury Revisited," 74.

78. Langford, "Charles Wesley as Theologian," 104.

79. For further discussion of this point see Warner, "Spreading Scriptural Holiness," 123–24.

80. Kenneth E. Rowe, "The United Methodist Hymnal: An Historical Overview," *Arts* 2, no. 1 (Fall 1989): 13.

81. Ibid., 8. Interestingly, Jacob Albright (1759–1808), the founder of The Evangelical Association, was drawn to Methodism not as a result of the distinctive singing of its members but by their preaching and their *Discipline* (Heisey, "Singet Hallelujah!," 237.). The first hymnbook published by The Evangelical Association numbered fifty-six pages and consisted of German Evangelical hymnody (237–38). Six years later the denomination compiled an official hymnal of 436 pages also consisting largely of traditional German Lutheran hymnody (237).

82. Rowe, "The United Methodist Hymnal," 8. See also Karen B. Westerfield Tucker, *American Methodist Worship* (Oxford: Oxford University Press, 2001), 9.

83. Rowe, "The United Methodist Hymnal," 8.

84. Ibid.

85. See Ibid., 9.

86. Lester Berenbroick, "An Introduction to the Hymns in the 1989 United Methodist Hymnal," *The Drew Gateway* 60 (Fall 1990): 79. See also Carol Doran and Thomas H. Troeger, "The United Methodist Hymnal," *Worship* 65, no. 2 (March 1991): 160.

87. Doran and Troeger, "The United Methodist Hymnal," 168.

88. Ibid., 160.

89. Ibid., 161.

90. Ibid., 160.

91. For example, see Carlton R. Young, *Companion to the United Methodist Hymnal* (Nashville: Abingdon Press, 1993). Young served as editor to both the 1964 and 1989 *Hymnals*. He also participated with two additional authors in the *Companion to the Hymnal: A Handbook to the 1964 Methodist Hymnal* (Nashville: Abingdon Press, 1970).

92. Westerfield Tucker, *American Methodist Worship*, 6. According to Westerfield Tucker, Wesley preferred Methodists to gather for public

worship on Sundays, an expectation that did not prove viable for all due to the distance between and among circuits. See Westerfield Tucker for further detail regarding the services and their content composed by and distributed by Wesley for the new church in America.

93. Ibid., 8.

94. Ibid.

95. Ibid., 9.

96. Ibid., 16.

97. Ibid.

98. Ibid., 20.

99. Ibid., 21.

100. Ibid., 36.

101. Ibid., 36, 53.

4. Pastoral Roles and Ordained Ministry

1. 2012 *Discipline*, ¶305, p. 221.

2. Ibid., ¶127, p. 95.

3. Ibid.

4. Ibid., ¶128, p. 95: "The church as the community of the new covenant has participated in Christ's ministry of grace across the years and around the world."

5. Ibid.

6. Ibid., ¶¶266.6, 267, 268, pp. 211–13.

7. Ibid., ¶270, p. 213.

8. Ibid., ¶271.2, p. 214.

9. Ibid., ¶1314, p. 623.

10. Ibid., ¶¶266.6, 270, 271, pp. 211–14: "While lay speakers are engaged in a variety of ministries, their purpose is to complement and support, not replace, pastors." (211) Similarly, the lay servants *assist*

with priestly roles, such as distributing the elements of Holy Communion (266.3.e, p. 211). "While lay missioners are engaged in a variety of ministries, their purpose is to complement, not replace, pastors." (213). And, finally, certified lay ministers serve "as a part of a ministry team with the supervision and support of a clergyperson" (214).

11. Ibid., ¶266.3, pp. 210–11.

12. Ibid.

13. Ibid., ¶267.1.b, p. 212.

14. Ibid., ¶267.3, p. 212.

15. Ibid., ¶268.2, p. 212–13.

16. Ibid., ¶266.6, p. 211.

17. Ibid. Though not ordained, lay speakers serve in accordance with ¶341.1.

18. Ibid., ¶266.6, p. 211.

19. Ibid., p. 212.

20. Ibid., ¶269, p. 213.

21. Ibid., ¶270, p. 213.

22. Ibid.

23. Ibid., ¶271, p. 214.

24. Ibid.

25. Ibid.

26. Ibid., ¶¶271.3, 271.4, pp. 214–15.

27. Ibid., ¶271.5, p. 215.

28. Ibid., ¶1314, p. 623. For additional historical context regarding deaconesses see chapter three and the discussion of the Social Creed.

29. Ibid.

30. Ibid., ¶¶1314.3 and 1314.4, pp. 623–24.

31. Ibid., ¶1314.4, p. 624.

32. Ibid., ¶1314.5, p. 624.

33. Ibid., ¶1316, p. 625.

34. Ibid., ¶303, p. 217.

35. 1787 *Discipline*, section V, p. 7. In addition to a board of ordained ministry, in each annual conference there is also a board of laity. 2012 *Discipline*, ¶635, p. 456 and ¶631, p. 438 respectively.

36. 2012 *Discipline*, ¶303.2, pp. 217–18.

37. 1892 *Discipline*, ¶189, p. 104.

38. 2012 *Discipline*, ¶339, p. 267.

39. Ibid., ¶303.3, pp. 217–18, italics mine.

40. Ibid., ¶303.3, p. 218.

41. Ibid., ¶303.4, p. 218.

42. Ibid., ¶304.2, p. 219.

43. Ibid., ¶304.1, p. 218.

44. Ibid., ¶304.1, p. 219.

45. *The Christian as Minister: An Exploration into the Meaning of God's Call* (Nashville: General Board of Higher Education and Ministry, 2009).

46. 2012 *Discipline*, ¶310, p. 223.

47. Ibid., ¶315, p. 229.

48. Ibid., ¶315, pp. 229–30. See Ibid., ¶312, p. 226 for "Orientation to Ministry."

49. 1787 *Discipline*, section VII, p. 11.

50. Ibid., section VII, p. 13.

51. Ibid.

52. 2012 *Discipline*, ¶316, p. 230. For all the duties of a pastor see ¶340.

53. Ibid., ¶316.1, p. 230.

54. Ibid., ¶318.1, p. 231.

55. Ibid., ¶318.1c, pp. 231–32. See ¶318.1c for other educational opportunities. Full-time local pastors receive compensation equal to or larger than the minimum salary established by the annual conference (¶318.1b, p. 231).

56. Ibid., ¶318.2b, p. 232.

57. Ibid., ¶318.2d, p. 232. Part-time local pastors receive less than the total minimum compensation set by the annual conference (¶318.2c, p. 232).

58. Ibid., ¶318.3b, p. 232.

59. Ibid.

60. Ibid., ¶318.3c, p. 232. Students of other denominations may also serve as local pastors upon the recommendation of the board of ordained ministry and affirmative vote of the clergy members in full connection (¶318.4, p. 233).

61. Ibid., ¶318.5, p. 233.

62. Ibid.

63. For a discussion of types of local church membership, see chapter 6.

64. 2012 *Discipline*, ¶322, p. 236. Student pastors are members of their charge conference.

65. Ibid., ¶321, p. 235.

66. Ibid., ¶323, p. 237.

67. Ibid., ¶324.1, p. 238.

68. Ibid., ¶324.2, p. 238.

69. Ibid., ¶¶324.3, 324.4, p. 238.

70. Ibid., ¶¶324.4a, 324.4b, pp. 238–39.

71. Ibid., ¶324.4c, p. 238.

72. Ibid., ¶324.6, pp. 239–40. For additional means of fulfilling the educational and other requirements for provisional membership, see ¶324.

73. Ibid., ¶324.9, p. 240. For the examination questions required for provisional membership, see ¶324.9. Annual conference boards of ordained ministry may present these in alternative form or include additional questions/requirements, such as a recorded sermon and manuscript as well as a Bible study curriculum.

74. Ibid., ¶324.10, p. 241.

75. Ibid., ¶324.12, p. 242.

76. Ibid., ¶¶324.8, 324.13, pp. 240, 242.

77. Ibid., ¶325, p. 242.

78. Ibid., ¶¶325, 326, pp. 242–43.

79. Ibid., ¶¶326.1, 326.2, p. 243.

80. Ibid., ¶¶326.3, 327.5, pp. 243–44.

81. Ibid., ¶327, p. 244.

82. Ibid., ¶327.3, p. 244.

83. Ibid., ¶349, p. 283.

84. Ibid.

85. Ibid., ¶349.2, p. 284.

86. Ibid., ¶¶349.2, 349.3, p. 284.

87. Ibid., ¶350.1, p. 284.

88. Ibid.

89. Ibid., ¶350.2, p. 285.

90. Ibid., ¶¶351, 352, pp. 285–86.

91. For discussion of voluntary leaves, see ibid., ¶354, pp. 287–90.

92. Ibid., ¶335, p. 259.

93. Ibid.

94. Ibid., p. 260. For specific questions see pp. 260–62.

95. Ibid., p. 260.

96. Ibid.

97. 1787 *Discipline*, section VII, p. 11. These directions echo question 19 of the historic questions in the 2012 *Discipline*, ¶336.19, p. 263.

98. 2012 *Discipline*, ¶345, p. 278.

99. Ibid., ¶¶428, 431, pp. 340–41, 342–44, respectively.

100. Ibid., ¶332, p. 256.

101. Ibid.

102. Ibid.

103. Ibid., ¶334, p. 257.

104. Ibid.

105. Ibid., ¶332, p. 256.

106. Ibid., ¶340, pp. 267–70.

107. Ibid., ¶341, pp. 270–71.

108. Ibid., ¶338, p. 264.

109. Ibid., ¶338, pp. 264–65.

110. Ibid., ¶344, p. 272.

111. Ibid., ¶343.2, p. 272.

112. Ibid., ¶343.3, p. 272.

113. Ibid., ¶344, pp. 272–73.

114. Ibid.

115. Ibid., pp. 273–74.

116. Ibid., ¶344.2b, p. 275.

117. Ibid., ¶344.3, p. 276.

118. Ibid., ¶344.3b, p. 277.

119. Ibid.

120. Ibid., ¶1112.7, p. 591.

121. Ibid., ¶630.3f, p. 436.

122. Ibid., ¶330, p. 247.

123. Charles Yrigoyen, Jr., "The Office of Deacon: A Historical Summary," *Quarterly Review* (Winter 1999): 327. Yrigoyen's article is a helpful outline of the wider historical context tracing the origin, evolution, and significance of the diaconate throughout Christian tradition. Yrigoyen concludes, "The offices of deacon and deaconess have evolved considerably since the first century. There remains diversity among the churches regarding the nature and authority of those who occupy these places in Christ's ministry. Whatever their status, lay or ordained, deacons occupy a critical ministry in the body of Christ" (340). An earlier embodiment of the role of deacon within Methodism was transitional as a preparatory office for elder. The revision to the current role occurred in 1996.

124. 2012 *Discipline*, ¶329.1, p. 247.

125. Kenneth E. Rowe, "The Ministry of Deacons in Methodism from Wesley to Today (1998)," *Quarterly Review* (Winter 1999), 344. See also 1812 *Discipline* for the earliest mention of the two-step process describing deacon as predecessor to elder with a time limit (section VII, p. 36).

126. Rowe, "The Ministry of Deacons in Methodism," 344. For a discussion of all preceding diaconate roles including Asbury and Otterbein, as well as Lucy Rider Meyer and Jane Bancroft Robinson, see ibid.

127. Ibid., 352.

128. Ibid., 350–52.

129. 1976 *Discipline*, ¶303, p. 162.

130. Rowe, "The Ministry of Deacons in Methodism," 353.

131. 2012 *Discipline*, ¶329.1, p. 247.

132. Ibid.

133. Ibid., ¶331, pp. 251–56.

134. Ibid.

135. Ibid., ¶331.4d, p. 253.

136. Ibid., ¶331.5, p. 253.

137. Ibid., ¶331.9b, p. 255.

5. Superintendency

1. For an interrogation and alternative proposals to this statement, which is asserted by most scholars, see a helpful analysis of the role including current implications in Russell E. Richey and Thomas Edward Frank, *Episcopacy in the Methodist Tradition: Perspectives and Proposals* (Nashville: Abingdon Press, 2004).

2. Frank, *Polity, Practice and the Mission* (Nashville: Abingdon Press, 2007), 232.

3. Ibid., 231.

4. Ibid., 232.

5. Ibid., 249.

6. Ibid.

7. 2012 *Discipline*, ¶401, p. 315.

8. Ibid.

9. Ibid.

10. Ibid., ¶402, p. 315. (See 1 Peter 2:9; John 21:15-17; Acts 20:28; 1 Peter 5:2-3; 1 Timothy 3:1-7.)

11. *The Doctrines and Disciplines of the Methodist Episcopal Church, in America* (Philadelphia: Henry Tuckniss, 1798), 40.

12. Richey and Frank, *Episcopacy in the Methodist Tradition*, 58.

13. Ibid., 13. "No individual was more significant in shaping Methodist episcopacy than Asbury. He both held and personified the office of bishop in American Methodism for the first three decades of its existence" (James E. Kirby, *The Episcopacy in American Methodism* [Nashville: Kingswood Books, 2000], 9.).

14. Richey and Frank, *Episcopacy in the Methodist Tradition*, 91.

15. Ibid. This missional component contributes to the insufficient development of theological foundations or ecclesiology.

16. Ibid.

17. 2012 *Discipline*, ¶19, p. 29.

18. Richey and Frank, *Episcopacy in the Methodist Tradition*, 91.

19. Kirby, *The Episcopacy in American Methodism*, 9–10.

20. Ibid., 9.

21. Ibid.

22. Ibid., 10.

23. Ibid.

24. Ibid., 98.

25. Richey and Frank, *Episcopacy in the Methodist Tradition*, 98.

26. Ibid., 99.

27. Ibid.

28. 2012 *Discipline*, ¶46, p. 37.

29. Ibid., ¶405, p. 318.

30. Ibid.

31. Ibid., ¶404, pp. 317–18.

32. Ibid., ¶405.2b, p. 319: "It is recommended that at least 60 percent of those present and voting be necessary to elect."

33. Ibid., ¶405.2, p. 319.

34. Ibid., ¶405.2c, p. 319.

35. Ibid.

36. Ibid., ¶¶47–48, pp. 37–38.

37. Frank, *Polity, Practice and the Mission*, 229.

38. 2012 *Discipline*, ¶524, p. 362.

39. Ibid., ¶406, p. 319.

40. Ibid: "A bishop may be recommended for assignment to the same residence for a third quadrennium. . . . A newly elected bishop shall be assigned to administer an area other than that within which his or her membership was most recently held, unless by a two-thirds vote the jurisdictional committee shall recommend that this restriction be ignored and by majority vote the jurisdictional conference shall concur."

41. Richey and Frank, *Episcopacy in the Methodist Tradition*, 19. The episcopal address is an innovation of William McKendree, though after 1808 it arguably contributed to the loss of individual voices.

42. 2012 *Discipline*, ¶¶414–16, pp. 330–32.

43. Ibid., ¶414.5, p. 330: "5. To teach and uphold the theological traditions of The United Methodist Church."

44. 1848 *Discipline*, section I, p. 35.

45. 2012 *Discipline*, ¶414.3, p. 330.

46. Ibid., ¶414.2, p. 330.

47. Ibid., ¶414.6, p. 330.

48. Ibid., ¶414.10, p. 331.

49. Ibid., ¶¶414.7, 414.8, 414.11, pp. 330–31.

50. Ibid., ¶415.1, p. 331.

51. Ibid., ¶415.6, p. 331.

52. Ibid., ¶415.2, p. 331: "This may include special inquiry into the work of agencies to ensure that the annual conference and general church policies and procedures are followed."

53. Frank, *Polity, Practice and the Mission*, 229. As Frank explains, United Methodist episcopacy combines aspects of a monarchical and administrative ecclesiology.

54. 2012 *Discipline*, ¶51, p. 39.

55. Ibid., ¶54, p. 40.

56. Ibid., ¶¶415.7, 416.1, p. 331.

57. Ibid., ¶416.1, p. 331. See also ¶¶425–29 on "Appointment-Making."

58. Ibid., ¶¶416.4, 416.3, p. 332.

59. Ibid., ¶416.6, p. 332. These latter appointments are not extension ministry appointments.

60. Kirby, *The Episcopacy in American Methodism*, 55.

61. Ibid.

62. Ibid.

63. Ibid.

64. 2012 *Discipline*, ¶417, p. 332.

65. Ibid, p. 333.

66. Ibid., ¶424, pp. 336–37.

67. Ibid., ¶418, p. 333: "No superintendent shall serve for more than eight years in any consecutive eleven years. No elder shall serve as district superintendent more than fourteen years."

68. Ibid., ¶419.1, p. 333.

69. Ibid.

70. Ibid., ¶¶419.3, 419.11, pp. 334, 335.

71. Ibid., ¶¶419.4, 419.9, pp. 334, 335.

72. Ibid., ¶419.6, p. 334.

73. Ibid., ¶¶419.4, 419.5, p. 334.

74. Ibid., ¶419.4, p. 334.

75. Ibid., ¶419.8, p. 334.

76. Ibid.

77. Ibid., ¶419.10, p. 335.

78. Richard Heitzenrater, "Connectionalism and Itineracy: Wesleyan Principles and Practice," in *Connectionalism: Ecclesiology, Mission, and Identity*, ed. Russell E. Richey, Dennis M. Campbell, and William B. Lawrence, vol. 1, *United Methodism and American Culture* (Nashville: Abingdon Press, 1997), 31.

79. Ibid.

80. Ibid., 33.

81. Ibid., 33, 34–35. Although local preachers (those who did not travel or itinerate but worked with a single circuit or society) assisted, they were not granted the same authority as full-time traveling

preachers or preachers in full connection (33). Historically, recognition as a traveling preacher and admission to membership in the annual conference was not linked to ordination, as early preachers were not ordained until 1784.

82. Frederick Norwood, *The Story of American Methodism* (Nashville: Abingdon, 1974), 137.

83. Ibid.

84. Ibid., 146.

85. E. Dale Dunlap, "The United Methodist System of Itinerant Ministry," in *Perspectives in American Methodism*, ed. Russell Richey, Kenneth Rowe, and Jean Miller Schmidt (Nashville: Kingswood Books, 1993), 419.

86. Norwood, *The Story of American Methodism*, 10, 364.

87. For a description of "Support for Elders" including equitable compensation, see 2012 *Discipline*, ¶342, p. 271. While there is a description and setting of minimum salaries, there is not a discussion of maximum salaries.

88. Ibid., ¶425.1, p. 337.

89. Ibid., ¶¶425, 430, pp. 337, 342.

90. Ibid., ¶430, p. 342.

91. Ibid. See also ¶331.

92. Ibid., ¶430, p. 342.

93. Ibid., ¶428.1, p. 340.

94. Ibid., ¶324.2a, p. 258. Though this language occurs elsewhere, this paragraph (324) is significant on this topic. Essentially, if a clergy refuses an appointment, they discontinue themselves volunteering for limited itineracy.

95. See ibid., ¶324.2c, p. 258, and Judicial Council decisions 1226 and 1216.

96. Ibid., ¶425.1, p. 337.

97. Ibid., p. 338.

98. Ibid., ¶425.3, p. 338.

99. Ibid., ¶426, p. 338. Consultation with the itinerating preacher most likely first occurred in 1940 in The Methodist Church. Eventually the pastor-parish relations committee was also consulted, which was approved by The United Methodist Church in 1972.

100. Ibid., ¶426.1, p. 338.

101. Ibid., ¶427, p. 339.

102. Ibid., ¶427.1, p. 339.

103. Ibid., ¶427.2, pp. 339–40.

104. Ibid., ¶427.3, p. 340.

105. Ibid., ¶428.9, p. 342.

106. Ibid., ¶428.2, p. 340.

107. Ibid., ¶428.3, p. 340.

108. Ibid., ¶428.4, p. 340.

109. Ibid., ¶428.5, p. 341.

110. Ibid., ¶428.6, p. 341.

111. Ibid., ¶428.8, p. 342.

112. Ibid., ¶428.10, p. 342.

6. The Local Church

1. Heitzenrater, *Wesley and the People Called Methodists*, 21. Samuel Wesley became connected with the society while serving as rector of the Epworth Parish. His son John joined the society as a corresponding member. The approach of the Society for Promoting Christian Knowledge was to renew society through transforming one individual at a time.

2. 1812 *Discipline*, sections XXIII and XXIV respectively, pp. 80–83. Despite the brevity of sections and the *Discipline* generally, there is mention of "Do not suffer the people to sing too slow." There is also counsel to maintain separation of women and men, particularly in seating, but also in singing (pp. 81–82).

3. Frank, *Polity, Practice, and the Mission*, 174.

4. 1944 *Discipline*, ¶102, p. 38.

5. 1952 *Discipline*, ¶102. For further discussion of sacramental practices (baptism and Lord's Supper respectively) in contemporary United Methodism, see "By Water and the Spirit" and "This Holy Mystery."

6. 1952 *Discipline*, ¶102: "Such a society of believers, being within The Methodist Church and subject to its *Discipline*, is also an inherent part of the Church Universal, which is composed of all who accept Jesus Christ as Lord and Saviour, and which in the Apostles' Creed we declare to be the holy catholic Church."

7. 2012 *Discipline*, ¶201, p. 143, italics mine.

8. Ibid., ¶202, p. 143.

9. Ibid., pp. 143-44—much of this statement was added in 1972. Specifically, "Therefore, the local church is to minister to persons in the community where the church is located, to provide appropriate training and nurture to all . . . as minimal expectations of an authentic church."

10. Ibid., ¶205.1, p. 144.

11. Ibid., ¶205.4, p 145.

12. Omitting 1860.

13. 1848 *Discipline*, section II, p. 24. The 1880 edition is very similar, and similar themes persist into the twentieth century.

14. Ibid., section II, p. 25.

15. 1916 *Discipline*, chapter I, ¶48, p. 51.

16. Ibid.

17. Ibid., part 1, chapter I, ¶48.2, p. 51.

18. Ibid., ¶48.3, p. 51–52.

19. Ibid., chapter 1, ¶57, p. 56.

20. 1864 *Discipline*, part I, chapter II, ¶54, section 2.2, p. 53.

21. Ibid.

22. 1890 *Discipline*, part I, chapter II, ¶49, p. 39.

23. 1892 *Discipline*, part I, chapter IV, ¶49, p. 37.

24. 1924 *Discipline*, chapter I, part V, a section entitled "Nonresident-Inactive Membership" is contained in ¶58, p. 57.

25. 1928 *Discipline*, ¶48.5, p. 52.

26. 2012 *Discipline*, ¶215, p 151.

27. Ibid.

28. Ibid., ¶227, p 159, italics mine.

29. Ibid., italics mine.

30. Ibid., ¶216.1a, p. 152.

31. Ibid., ¶217, p. 153.

32. Ibid., ¶221, p. 154: "Accountability." There is little, if any, emphasis upon requirements for specific doctrinal beliefs beyond these basic Christian principles described in the baptismal covenant. For early discussions of this dynamic see Charles Wesley Flint, "Doctrinal Requirements for Membership in the Methodist Episcopal Church," *The Methodist Review* 28, no. 1 (January 1912): 81–92; and Leila Bagley Rumble, *Membership Manual of the Methodist Church for Teen-Agers* (Nashville: The Methodist Publishing House, 1951), 51.

33. 2012 *Discipline*, ¶226.1, p. 156.

34. Ibid.

35. Ibid., ¶226.2, p. 157.

36. Ibid., ¶224, pp. 155–56.

37. Ibid., ¶341.7, p. 271: "No pastor shall re-baptize. The practice of re-baptism does not conform with God's action in baptism and is not consistent with Wesleyan tradition and the historic teaching of the church. Therefore, the pastor should counsel any person seeking re-baptism to participate in the rite of re-affirmation of baptismal vows."

38. Ibid., ¶216.2, pp. 152–53.

39. Ibid., ¶216.2, p. 152.

40. Ibid., ¶220, p. 154.

41. Ibid., ¶¶221; 228.2.b.1, pp. 154–55, 159.

42. Ibid., ¶2702.3, p. 777.

43. Ibid., ¶228.1, p. 159.

44. Ibid., ¶228.2, pp. 159–62.

45. Ibid., ¶228.1, p. 159.

46. Ibid., ¶228.2b.3, p. 161. The practice has evolved from the public reading of names over five consecutive years to three years in 1964, to two years in 1996. Until 1996 the practices included "listing the name in the church bulletin, circulating it throughout the parish, and reading it from the pulpit."

47. Frederick A. Norwood, *Church Membership in the Methodist Tradition* (Nashville: The Methodist Publishing House, 1958), 11. For further examples of perspectives on membership within the Methodist tradition, see also Rumble, *Membership Manual of the Methodist Church*; C. Lloyd Daugherty, *Manual for the Local Church Commission on Membership and Evangelism* (Nashville: Methodist Evangelistic Materials, 1960); and from British Methodism, Leonard Barnett, *Here Is Methodism* (London: Epworth Press, 1966).

48. 2012 *Discipline*, ¶243, p. 168.

49. Ibid., ¶244, pp. 168–69.

50. Ibid., ¶246.1, p. 169; and Frank, *Polity, Practice, and the Mission*, 185.

51. 2012 *Discipline*, ¶43, p. 37.

52. Ibid., ¶246.7, p. 170.

53. Ibid., ¶246.4-5, p. 170.

54. Ibid., ¶246.4, p. 170.

55. Ibid., ¶246.2, p. 170.

56. Ibid., ¶246.6. With the exception of the board of trustees, a quorum is not required at any of the required units (p. 170).

57. Ibid., ¶246.8, p. 170.

58. Frank, *Polity, Practice, and the Mission*, 185.

59. 2012 *Discipline*, ¶247.2, 4-5, p. 171.

60. Ibid., ¶247.1, p. 170.

61. Ibid., ¶247.3, p. 171.

62. Ibid., ¶247, p.170.

63. Ibid., ¶248, p. 174.

64. Ibid.

65. See ibid., ¶¶246–247, pp. 169–174.

66. Ibid., ¶249. "All local church offices and all chairs of organizations within the local church may be shared between two persons, with the following exceptions: trustee, officers of the board of trustees, treasurer, lay member of annual conference, member and chairperson of the committee on staff- or pastor-parish relations" (¶249.8, p. 175).

67. A church conference must be called to seek approval for a building program (Ibid., ¶2544.6, p. 754.).

68. Ibid., ¶252.1, p. 178.

69. Ibid., ¶252.6, p. 180.

70. Ibid., ¶252.5, pp. 179–80.

71. Frank, *Polity, Practice, and the Mission*, 187.

72. 2012 *Discipline*, ¶251, pp. 176–78.

73. Ibid., ¶251.3, pp. 177–78.

74. Ibid., ¶258.1, p. 191.

75. Ibid.

76. Ibid., ¶258.1.a-e, pp. 190–92.

77. Ibid., ¶258.2, pp. 192–97.

78. Ibid., ¶258.2.a-d, pp. 192–93.

79. Ibid., ¶258.2.e, p. 193.

80. Ibid., ¶258.2.g, pp. 194–97.

81. Ibid., ¶258.4, pp. 197–98.

82. Ibid.

83. Ibid., ¶2525, p. 737.

84. Ibid., ¶¶2526, 2530.2, pp. 737–38, 742.

85. Ibid., ¶2533, p. 743.

86. Ibid., ¶2532, p. 743.

87. Ibid., ¶¶258.3, 2501, 2503, 2524–2551, pp. 197, 721–22, 722–24, 737–63. Property owned *at level of its use* but held in trust to The United Methodist Church, so remains used for original purposes (¶2503).

88. Ibid., ¶141, p. 100. Even trustees are limited in control of uses of property (¶2532; sale/mortgage, and so on). If renovations of an existing building exceed 25 percent of the value of the existing structure or requires mortgage financing, approval must be obtained (changed in 2008; used to be 10%); note the detailed requirements for building program (¶2544, p. 752).

7. Conferences

1. See Wesley, "Sermon 16: The Means of Grace," in Outler, *Works*, vol. 1.

2. See Frank, *Polity, Practice and the Mission*, 289.

3. Russell E. Richey, *The Methodist Conference in America: A History* (Nashville: Kingswood Books, 1996), 45. After some conflict between early American Methodist leaders such as Francis Asbury, Thomas Coke, Jesse Lee, and James O'Kelly, what would become the first General Conference occurred in November 1792 in Baltimore.

4. 2012 *Discipline*, ¶501, p. 351.

5. Ibid., ¶8, p. 25: "There shall be a General Conference for the entire Church with such powers, duties, and privileges as are hereinafter set forth."

6. Ibid., ¶16, pp. 27–29.

7. Ibid., ¶¶17–22, pp. 29–30.

8. Ibid., ¶509.1, p. 355.

9. Ibid., ¶14, pp. 26–27.

10. For further explanation of the process for submitting petitions, see ibid., ¶507, 353–54.

11. Ibid., ¶511.4f, p. 358. The commission on the General Conference sets "the number of legislative committees and the assignment of legislative materials to those committees in consultation with the Secretary of the General Conference and Business Manager of the General Conference."

12. Ibid., ¶506, p. 507.

13. Ibid., ¶502.a, p. 351. This membership includes "delegates from The Methodist Church in Great Britain and other autonomous Methodist churches with which concordat agreements have been established providing for mutual election and seating of delegates in each other's highest legislative conferences" (¶502.b, p. 351). See also ¶13, p. 26: "In the case of The Methodist Church of Great Britain, mother church of Methodism, provision shall be made for The United Methodist Church to send two delegates annually to the British Methodist Conference, and The Methodist Church in Great Britain to send four delegates quadrennially to The United Methodist General Conference, the delegates of both conferences having vote and being evenly divided between clergy and laity."

14. Ibid., ¶502.2, p. 351.

15. Ibid., ¶502.3, pp. 351–52. Nominations for the secretary-designate are made by the Council of Bishops, though other nominations are permitted from the floor, for election by the General Conference (¶504). The secretary-designate assumes office immediately following adjournment of the General Conference. The secretary initiates procedures and prepares delegates for General Conference (¶504.3).

16. Ibid., ¶502, pp. 351–52.

17. Ibid., ¶13.1, p. 26: "The missionary conferences shall be considered as annual conferences for the purpose of this article."

18. *Happy Birthday!* (Nashville: General Council on Finance and Administration, The United Methodist Church, 2008), 3, quoted in Hendrik R. Pieterse, "A Worldwide United Methodist Church? Soundings toward a Connectional Theological Imagination," *Methodist Review* 5 (2013): 3–4.

19. Ibid.

20. Ibid.

21. 2012 *Discipline*, ¶9, p. 25.

22. For example, see ibid., ¶501, p. 351.

23. Ibid., ¶27, pp. 30–31.

24. James S. Thomas, *Methodism's Racial Dilemma: The Story of the Central Jurisdiction* (Nashville: Abingdon Press, 1992), 43.

25. Ibid., 52.

26. For a detailed discussion of the formation and dissolution of the Central Jurisdiction, see ibid.

27. 2012 *Discipline*, ¶24, p. 30: "The ratio of representation of the annual conferences and missionary conferences in the General Conference shall be the same for all jurisdictional conferences."

28. Ibid., ¶26, p. 30.

29. Ibid., ¶522, p. 362.

30. Ibid., ¶25, p. 30.

31. Ibid., ¶34, p. 34.

32. Ibid.

33. Ibid., ¶37, p. 35. See also ¶9, p. 35: "Provided that in The United Methodist Church there shall be no jurisdictional or central conference based on any ground other than geographical and regional division." This latter statement references the Central Jurisdiction, a

national body established to segregate African American members in 1939 with the organization of The Methodist Church. The Central Jurisdiction was disciplinarily dissolved in 1968, but operationally this dissolution was not implemented until 1972.

34. Ibid., ¶39, p. 36.

35. Ibid., ¶¶524 and 512, pp. 362–64, 359–61.

36. Ibid., ¶524.1, p. 362.

37. Ibid., ¶512, pp. 359–60.

38. Ibid., ¶524.3, pp. 363–64.

39. Ibid., ¶529, pp. 364–65.

40. Ibid., ¶¶530, 531, p. 365.

41. Ibid., ¶¶532–537, pp. 363–69.

42. Frank, *Polity, Practice, and the Mission*, 272.

43. Ibid.

44. 2012 *Discipline*, ¶28, p. 31: "There shall be central conferences for the work of the Church outside the United States of America with such duties, powers, and privileges as are hereinafter set forth."

45. Ibid., ¶31, pp. 31–32.

46. Ibid., ¶540.3, p. 370.

47. Ibid., ¶540.4, p. 370.

48. Ibid., ¶540.1, p. 370.

49. Ibid., ¶30, p. 31.

50. Ibid., ¶540.2, p. 370.

51. Ibid., ¶¶540–591.

52. Ibid., ¶543.8, p. 374.

53. Ibid., ¶543.7, 10, 12, 13, 14, 18-21, pp. 373–76.

54. Pieterse, "A Worldwide United Methodist Church?," 11.

55. Ibid.

56. 2012 *Discipline*, ¶543.9, p. 374.

57. Ibid., ¶543.12, p. 374.

58. Ibid., ¶543.13-14, pp. 374–75.

59. Ibid., ¶543.15-16, p. 375.

60. Ibid., ¶546.1, p. 376.

61. Ibid., ¶33, pp. 33–34.

62. Ibid., ¶601, p. 394.

63. Heitzenrater, *Wesley and the People Called Methodists*, 141–46.

64. Women began to receive ordination and full membership as elders in The United Methodist Church in 1956. Maud Keister Jenson was the first woman to be ordained in The United Methodist Church. For more information, see Jean Miller Schmidt, *Grace Sufficient: A History of Women in American Methodism* (Nashville: Abingdon Press, 1999), 281–83.

65. Frank, *Polity, Practice and the Mission*, 287.

66. Ibid.

67. 2012 *Discipline*, ¶32, p. 33.

68. Ibid., ¶603.3, p. 398.

69. Ibid., ¶603.2, p. 398.

70. Ibid., ¶603.5, p. 398.

71. Ibid., ¶¶603.9, 607, pp. 399, 406–7.

72. Ibid., ¶33, pp. 33–34.

73. Ibid., ¶¶35, 36, pp. 34–35.

74. Ibid., ¶33, pp. 33–34.

75. Ibid., ¶602.1-10, pp. 395–98.

76. Ibid., ¶604, pp. 399–401.

77. Ibid., ¶604.8-9, p. 401.

78. Ibid., ¶604.2, p. 400.

79. For a discussion of the recent historic evolution of annual conference organization see Frank, *Polity, Practice and the Mission*, 290–92.

80. 2012 *Discipline*, ¶613.3, p. 414.

81. Ibid., ¶611, p. 411.

82. Ibid., ¶586, p. 388.

83. Ibid., ¶587, p. 391.

84. Ibid., ¶585, p. 388.

85. Ibid.

86. Ibid., ¶589, pp. 391–92.

87. Ibid., ¶586.1, p. 389.

88. Ibid., ¶586.2, p. 389.

89. Ibid., ¶586.4a, p. 389.

90. Ibid.

91. Ibid., ¶42, p. 36.

92. Ibid., ¶658, p. 494.

93. Ibid., ¶¶658, 659, p. 494.

94. Ibid., ¶666, p. 497.

95. Ibid., ¶667, p. 499.

96. Ibid., ¶¶668, 670, 669, pp. 500–503.

97. Ibid., ¶¶671, 667, pp. 502–5, 499–500.

98. Ibid., ¶¶661, 662, 663, p. 496.

8. Councils and Agencies

1. 2012 *Discipline*, ¶701, p. 507.

2. Ibid., ¶2601, p. 765.

3. "About the Judicial Council," UMC.org, accessed February 4, 2013, http://www.umc.org/who-we-are/about-the-judicial-council. This text was adapted from an article by Robert Lear published in the *Interpreter* in 1996.

4. 2012 *Discipline*, ¶2707, p. 788.

5. Belton Joyner, "Judicial Council" (lecture, Duke Divinity School, Durham, NC, April 2012).

6. 2012 *Discipline*, ¶2707, p. 788.

7. Ibid., ¶55, p. 40.

8. Ibid., ¶56, pp. 40–41.

9. Ibid., ¶57, p. 41.

10. Ibid., ¶58, p. 41.

11. Sally C. AsKew, "A Brief History of the Judicial Council of The United Methodist Church," *Methodist History* 49, no. 2 (January 2011): 87.

12. Ibid., 86–98.

13. Ibid., 86.

14. Ibid.

15. Ibid.

16. Ibid.

17. *The Discipline of The Evangelical United Brethren Church* (Dayton, Ohio: Board of Publication of The Evangelical United Brethren Church, 1967), section 402, quoted in AsKew, "A Brief History of the Judicial Council," 86.

18. AsKew, "A Brief History of the Judicial Council," 87.

19. "About the Judicial Council."

20. 2012 *Discipline*, ¶2602.1, p. 765.

21. See "Rules of Practice and Procedure: The Judicial Council of The United Methodist Church," UMC.org, last modified July 2012, http://archives.umc.org/uploads/documents/Rules-%20Adopted-July%20-2012.pdf, 7.

22. 2012 *Discipline*, ¶2607, p. 767.

23. Ibid., ¶2602.1-2, pp. 765–66.

24. Ibid., ¶2602.2, p. 766. "Originally, the names and conference affiliation of each nominee were published in two issues of the *General*

Conference Daily Advocate; beginning in 1968 a biographical sketch of each nominee not exceeding 100 words was required" (AsKew, "A Brief History of the Judicial Council," 87.).

25. 2012 *Discipline*, ¶2602.2, p. 766.

26. "In 1940, the number of alternates was exactly the same as the membership, and their terms were eight years. The number of alternates has fluctuated, and in the *2008 Discipline* the number is six lay and six clergy" (AsKew, "A Brief History of the Judicial Council," 87–88.).

27. 2012 *Discipline*, ¶2603, p. 744. "In 1996 the terms for alternates became four years." AsKew goes on to point out, "Interestingly, from 1940 to 1988 once 'the exhaustion of the list of alternate members' had been reached, the Judicial Council had the authority to choose members for the remainder of the quadrennium" (AsKew, "A Brief History of the Judicial Council," 88.).

28. 2012 *Discipline*, ¶2606, p.767.

29. Ibid., ¶2608, p. 767.

30. Ibid., ¶2608.2, p. 768.

31. AsKew, "A Brief History of the Judicial Council," 88.

32. Ibid., 91. See also "Rules of Practice and Procedure," 6.

33. AsKew, "A Brief History of the Judicial Council," 90. See also "Rules of Practice and Procedure."

34. AsKew, "A Brief History of the Judicial Council," 91. See also "Rules of Practice and Procedure," 1.

35. AsKew, "A Brief History of the Judicial Council," 89. See also 2012 *Discipline*, ¶¶2609, 2610, pp. 768–72.

36. 2012 *Discipline*, ¶2610.2, p. 771.

37. "About the Judicial Council."

38. See "Rules of Practice and Procedure," 6.

39. AsKew, "A Brief History of the Judicial Council," 93–94.

40. Ibid., 89.

41. Ibid., 91. See also 2012 *Discipline*, ¶2715.7, p. 799.

42. 2012 *Discipline*, ¶2702.4, p. 777.

43. AsKew, "A Brief History of the Judicial Council," 88–89. For the current details on "Jurisdiction and Powers," see also 2012 *Discipline*, ¶2609, pp. 768–71.

44. AsKew, "A Brief History of the Judicial Council," 92.

45. Ibid.

46. Ibid. See also 2012 *Discipline*, ¶2610.3, p. 749.

47. AsKew, "A Brief History of the Judicial Council," 92.

48. See "Rules of Practice and Procedure," 6–7; 2012 *Discipline*, ¶2612.1, p. 772. For the archive of all decisions, see "Judicial Council Decisions," UMC.org, accessed February 14, 2013, http://archives .umc.org/interior_judicial.asp?mid=263.

49. AsKew, "A Brief History of the Judicial Council," 92–93. See also "Rules of Practice and Procedure," 2.

50. AsKew, "A Brief History of the Judicial Council," 92.

51. Ibid., 93.

52. 2012 *Discipline*, ¶363, p. 305–6.

53. Ibid., ¶360.1, p. 301.

54. Ibid., ¶362.1, p. 304.

55. Ibid., ¶360.2, p. 301.

56. Ibid., ¶363.1, p. 306.

57. Ibid., ¶363, p. 306–8

58. See ibid., ¶¶350–360. In 2012, these actions spread from ¶350 to ¶360, with ¶361 covering withdrawal; ¶362 in 2012 deals with fair hearing, and ¶363 with due process/just resolution. Honorable location is the discontinuing of itinerant status without retirement benefits. See ¶359, pp. 299–301.

59. Ibid., ¶2704.2.a, p. 780.

60. 2016 *Discipline*, ¶2702.1, p. 788–89.

61. Ibid., ¶2702.2, p. 789.

62. Ibid., ¶2702.3, p. 789.

63. See 2012 *Discipline*, ¶¶2702–2714, pp. 776–98.

64. Ibid., ¶422.1, p. 336.

65. Ibid., ¶47, p. 37.

66. Ibid., ¶422.3, p. 336.

67. Ibid., ¶50, p. 39.

68. Ibid., ¶¶422–423, pp. 335–36.

69. Ibid., ¶901, p. 572.

70. Ibid., ¶¶903, 904, p. 572.

71. "About the Connectional Table," UMC.org, accessed February 5, 2013, http://www.umc.org/who-we-are/about-connectional-table.

72. 2012 *Discipline*, ¶906, pp. 573–75.

73. 2012 *Discipline*, ¶906.1.a-h, pp. 573–74. The 2008 *Discipline* also included the president of the General Commission on Christian Unity and Interreligious Concerns. The 2012 *Discipline* added the ecumenical officer of the Council of Bishops.

74. "About the Connectional Table."

75. "Connectional Table: Structure and Membership," UMC.org, accessed February 5, 2013, http://www.umc.org/who-we-are/structure -and-membership. The task groups include: staff and planning advisory team, state of the church, worldwide nature of the church, evaluation and review, General Conference report, joint budget process committee, personnel, listening process team, finance committee, internal evaluation and review, legislation, and world service contingency funds. See the website for an organizational chart.

76. 2012 *Discipline*, ¶906.3, p. 575.

77. Ibid., ¶906.2, p. 575.

78. "About the Connectional Table."

79. Ibid.

80. "Connectional Table," UMC.org, accessed March 10, 2014, http://www.umc.org/who-we-are/connectional-table-main.

81. "Connectional Table: Our Work." UMC.org, accessed March 10, 2014, http://www.umc.org/who-we-are/connectional-table-our-work.

82. Ibid.

83. 2012 *Discipline*, ¶701, p. 507.

84. Frank, *Polity, Practice, and the Mission*, 275.

85. 2012 *Discipline*, ¶701, p. 507.

86. Ibid., ¶701.2, p. 507: "The term does not and is not meant to imply a master-servant or principal-agent relationship between these bodies and the conference or other body that creates them, except where the authority is specifically granted."

87. Ibid., ¶703, pp. 509–10.

88. Ibid., ¶¶702, 704, pp. 508, 511–12.

89. Ibid., ¶703.5, p. 510: "In all matters of accountability, epis-copal oversight as provided in ¶422 is assumed." The 2012 *Discipline* changed the status of the General Commission on Religion and Race, the General Commission on United Methodist Men, and the General Commission on the Status and Role of Women to program-related general agencies. In the 2008 *Discipline*, these general commissions were listed as administrative general agencies. The 2012 *Discipline* moved the Division on Ministries and Young People from the status of a program-related general agency, incorporating it into a division of the General Board of Discipleship (¶¶1201–1212).

90. Ibid., ¶703.6. The 2012 *Discipline* removed the Standing Com-mittee on Central Conference Matters and JUSTPEACE Center for Mediation and Conflict Transformation from the list of administrative agencies. The Standing Committee on Central Conference Matters is now described as "an independent coordinating body . . . to study the structure and supervision of The United Methodist Church in its work outside the United States and its territories and its relationships to other Church bodies" (¶2201, p. 714). It is facilitated by the Board of Global Ministries. JUSTPEACE is now described as "a mission of The

United Methodist Church," which acts as an "incorporated resource of The United Methodist Church." It is accountable to the General Conference and has the authority to create relationships with other UMC and non-UMC agencies and organizations, "while preserving its role as an impartial entity" (¶2401.1-2, p. 719).

91. Beth Adams Bowser, *Living the Vision: The University Senate of The Methodist Episcopal Church, The Methodist Church, and The United Methodist Church 1892–1991* (Nashville: General Board of Higher Education and Ministry, 1992), ix. This resource contains a detailed discussion of the University Senate's history and purpose.

92. Charles Wesley, "Hymn 461: For Children," in *The Bicentennial Edition of the Works of John Wesley*, vol. 7, *A Collection of Hymns for the Use of the People Called Methodists*, ed. Franz Hildebrandt and Oliver A. Beckerlegge with James Dale (Oxford: Oxford University Press, 1983), 644. Charles Wesley composed the lines for the Kingswood School.

Conclusion: Sent to the World

1. 2012 *Discipline*, ¶120, p. 91.

2. Wesley, "The 'Large' *Minutes*," in Rack, *Works*, 10:845.

3. "The Baptismal Covenant I" and "The Baptismal Covenant II," 35 and 40.

4. 2012 *Discipline*, ¶419, p. 333.

– Glossary –

1784 (Christmas Conference). The conference at which The Methodist Episcopal Church in America was established.

1844. The year The Methodist Episcopal Church split, forming The Methodist Episcopal Church and The Methodist Episcopal Church, South.

1939. The year The Methodist Episcopal Church, The Methodist Episcopal Church, South, and Methodist Protestant Church reunited to form The Methodist Church. With this reunion the Central Jurisdiction, a racially segregated national jurisdiction, was organized alongside five regional or geographic jurisdictions in the United States.

1946. The year the United Brethren in Christ merged with The Evangelical Association to form The Evangelical United Brethren.

1968. The year The Methodist Church joined with The Evangelical United Brethren Church to form The United Methodist Church. It is also the year the Central Jurisdiction, a racially segregated national jurisdiction, was formally dissolved.

affiliate members (local church). These members are individuals of another United Methodist local church who may be temporarily far from their home congregation and wish to connect with another congregation (¶227).

affiliated autonomous Methodist churches. According to the 2012 *Discipline* (¶570.2), "a self-governing Methodist church in whose establishment The United Methodist Church or one of its constituent members (The Evangelical United Brethren Church and The Methodist Church or its predecessors) has assisted and which by mutual agreement has entered into a Covenant of Relationship (in effect from 1968 to 1984) or an Act of Covenanting (see ¶573) with The United Methodist Church."

affiliated united church. This church is self-governing and is formed by the uniting of two or more denominations, at least one of which shall have been related to The United Methodist Church or one of its constituent members (The Evangelical United Brethren Church and The Methodist Church or their predecessors). Each affiliated united church shall be entitled to at least two delegates, one clergy and one layperson, to the General Conference of The United Methodist Church in accordance with ¶2403.1b (¶570.3).

annual conference. This body is the basic organizational unit of The United Methodist Church. A bishop, assigned to the episcopal area in which the annual conference is located, presides over the gathering of this regional body, which normally meets annually. The business session is composed of equal numbers of clergy and laity.

Articles of Religion, the. This collection of articles dates back to the formation of the Church of England in the 1500s. The articles express specific beliefs of Christian doctrine. John Wesley adopted the Articles of Religion for the early Methodist movement, revising those thirty-nine articles to twenty-five.

associate member (local church). These individuals have been baptized in another Christian denomination and wish not only to connect with a local United Methodist church but also to keep their current denominational membership rather than become professing members of The United Methodist Church (¶227).

associate membership. These members of annual conference are often local pastors who have completed at least four years of full-time service as a local pastor and the five year Course of Study, and have been approved by the board of ordained ministry and clergy session. They are not ordained but are licensed for pastoral ministry and are available for full-time service and are guaranteed an appointment within the annual conference. Associate members have voice and vote in every matter except constitutional amendments, ordination, and conference relations of clergy (¶¶321–23).

autonomous Methodist churches. Self-governing churches in the Wesleyan tradition that may or may not have entered into the act of covenanting with The United Methodist Church. Autonomous Methodist churches are not entitled to send delegates to the General Conference of The United Methodist Church (¶570.1).

baptism. Baptism is one of two sacraments recognized by Protestants, with Communion or the Lord's Supper. In baptism a person is cleansed by the Holy Spirit of original sin and initiated into the body of Christ— the church.

bishop. A bishop is one of two roles, with district superintendents, related to the superintendency of The United Methodist Church. Bishops are elected by lay and clergy delegates of jurisdictional conferences. United Methodism in the United States practices lifetime episcopacy. Many central conferences outside the United States practice term episcopacy. Bishops may oversee one or more annual or other conferences. Upon consecration bishops assume membership in the Council of Bishops. They serve as spiritual and administrative leaders for the denomination.

board of laity (annual conference). This body is charged with the responsibility of fostering awareness of the role of the laity throughout the ministry of the church (¶631).

board of ordained ministry. Each annual conference has a board of ordained ministry consisting of lay and clergy representatives appointed by the bishop. The board recruits, nurtures, and supports those preparing for licensed and ordained ministry as well as evaluates candidates' gifts and equipping for ministry. The board is the credentialing body for clergy in an annual conference and is responsible for continuing formation programs for clergy and for matters relating to changes in conference relationships (¶635).

board of trustees (local church). This body is charged with the care of the property and assets of the local church. The pastor may be a member if elected. Not all members need to hold local church membership (¶640).

***Book of Common Prayer, The* (BCP).** This is the official service book of the Anglican Communion or Church of England dating to 1549. It contains prayers and rites for use in public and private worship. John and Charles Wesley used the BCP in their worship leadership.

Book of Discipline, The. The *Discipline* is the authoritative and legally binding book of The United Methodist Church. Each General Conference amends the *Discipline*, and the actions of the General Conference are reflected in the quadrennial revision.

Book of Homilies, The. This text, a collection of sermons, was prepared and distributed by the Church of England for clergy use at Sunday services, special worship services, and in teaching. The first book was published in 1547. John and Charles Wesley referred to this book in their preaching ministries.

Book of Resolutions, The. Published every four years following General Conference, this book contains all resolutions adopted by the previous three General Conferences and collected over eight years. Resolutions may be renewed and are organized by the Social Principles.

candidate. A candidate is a baptized and professing member of a local church who participates in discernment with other laity and clergy for the purpose of possibly receiving credentials to serve in a set-apart ministry as a local pastor, deacon, or elder.

catechism. A document with the basic beliefs and principles of the Christian faith in a question-and-answer format used to initiate new church members, particularly children.

central conferences. Central conferences are similar to jurisdictional conferences, though outside the United States. They are also responsible for the election of bishops and setting of annual conference boundaries. The United Methodist Church has seven central conferences: Africa, Central and Southern Europe, Congo, Germany, Northern Europe and Eurasia, Philippines, and West Africa. (¶540–48).

Central Jurisdiction. The Central Jurisdiction was created at the 1939 General Conference by the merger of The Methodist Episcopal Church; The Methodist Episcopal Church, South; and The Methodist Protestant Church. This racially segregated jurisdiction for African American Methodists functioned as an administrative body until it was eliminated at the 1968 General Conference.

certification. Certification in The United Methodist Church is recognition by the General Board of Higher Education and Ministry of an individual's calling and formation to a specialized ministry by meeting the standards for training, experience, and continuing study required for certification in the specialized area.

certified lay minister. This role may involve all pastoral functions except for those duties that require ordination or licensing. Certified lay ministers are certified by the district committee on ordained ministry (¶271).

certified lay servant or local church lay servant. This role is approved by the district or conference committee on Lay Servant Ministries for service in the local church at the request of the pastor, district superintendent, or committee on Lay Servant Ministries. This role serves the local church through leading meetings, conducting or assisting in conducting worship (including preaching), relating to specific ministry areas, and assisting with the distribution of the Lord's Supper (¶266–68).

certified lay speakers. The duties of a certified lay speaker entail providing leadership at the local, district, and conference level; supporting program emphases of the church; and offering leadership in worship, prayer, study, training, and discussion groups. Most often, certified lay speakers serve in pulpit supply (¶266–69).

charge conference. The charge conference is the basic governing unit of each United Methodist local church and is composed of all members of the church council as well as retired ordained ministers, retired diaconal ministers, and others designated by the *Discipline*. All members of the charge conference must be members of the local church. The charge conference must meet at least once per year called by the pastor in consultation with the district superintendent or vice versa. The district superintendent, or a designate, is present. The charge conference reviews and evaluates the mission of the local church. The charge conference recommends candidates for ordained ministry as well as other lay roles such as lay speakers and lay ministers and sets the compensation for the pastor and others appointed by the bishop. (¶246–47)

church conference. A church conference is called to have broad participation of the members of the congregation and can replace the charge conference as needed. The church conference is most often called at the discretion of the district superintendent. The church conference elects local church leadership. A church conference must be called to receive approval for a building program (¶248–51).

church council. The church council is an administrative arm of the charge conference. It meets at least quarterly and may be called by the pastor or its chairperson, which is an office elected by the church conference. The church council plans and implements the programs and ministry of the local church (¶252).

Church of England, the (Anglicanism). The Church of England was founded by King Henry VIII in 1534 as a result of the refusal by the pope to annul Henry's marriage to Catherine of Aragon. The newly formed church maintained much of its Catholic identity and practices. The Church of England is the official state church of England.

Church of the United Brethren in Christ, the. Initially led by Philip Otterbein this denomination is one of the predecessor denominations of The United Methodist Church. It merged with The Evangelical Church in 1946 to form The Evangelical United Brethren Church, which then joined The Methodist Church in 1968 to form The United Methodist Church.

classes and bands. John Wesley implemented small groups, specifically classes in Bristol, England, to raise money for the Methodist renewal movement. Classes were usually geographical in organization with membership of ten to twelve. Bands, also a small group unit, were usually homogenous in nature organized around a common characteristic or situation (single, married, male, female) and consisted of six to eight participants. Classes and bands have served Methodism in the work of Christian education.

Contemporary classes vary in size depending on the congregation and continue to facilitate Christian spiritual formation.

commissioned minister. One who was elected to provisional membership (revised from probationary membership in the 2000 *Book of Discipline*) seeking ordination as elder or deacon and full membership in the annual conference. These persons are often licensed for pastoral ministry within an annual conference and serve in ministry with the supervision of the district superintendent and by appointment of the bishop.

committee on nominations and leadership development (local church). The purpose of this committee is to identify, develop, and evaluate Christian spiritual leadership for the local congregation. The pastor serves as chair and a layperson elected from the committee serves as vice-chair (¶258).

Communion or the Lord's Supper. This is one of two sacraments, with baptism, within Protestantism. It recalls the Last Supper of Jesus with the disciples as a celebration and remembrance of God's grace. Normally, ordained elders preside at this sacrament, though licensed local pastors appointed by the bishop and deacons in full connection with permission from the bishop may preside in specific contexts.

concordat churches. These churches have Methodist heritage in common with The United Methodist Church or one of its constituent members that have entered into concordat agreements, affirming the equal status of the churches, expressing mutual acceptance and respect, and creating opportunities for closer fellowship between the churches, especially on the leadership level (¶570.5).

Connectional Table, the. Its purpose is for the discernment and articulation of the vision of the church and the stewardship of the mission, ministries, and resources of The United Methodist Church as determined by the actions of the General Conference and in consultation with the Council of Bishops (¶904).

consecration. This is an act of blessing or dedication that may include the consecration of elements by an authorized representative of the church in the Lord's Supper or confer an office of ministry such as deaconess, home missioner, or bishop.

Constitution, the. The Constitution continues to be a defining legal document of The United Methodist Church that describes the basic structure of the church and its leadership. While the current Constitution was approved as part of the merger of The Evangelical United Brethren Church and The Methodist Church in 1968, it may be and has been revised.

constitutional standards. The constitutional standards of The United Methodist Church are the Articles of Religion, the Confession of Faith, the General Rules of Our United Societies, and though debated, John Wesley's *Sermons* and *Notes upon the New Testament.*

Council of Bishops. All active and retired bishops of The United Methodist Church constitute the Council of Bishops. The council meets at least twice a year.

Course of Study. An educational process administered by the General Board of Higher Education and Ministry in collaboration with some UM theological seminaries that enables local pastors to meet educational qualification for associate membership (after five years) or full membership and ordination as an elder (after four additional years) in an annual conference.

covenanting churches. These are autonomous Methodist churches, affiliated autonomous Methodist churches, affiliated united churches, or other Christian churches that have entered into a covenanting relationship with The United Methodist Church through an Act of Covenanting. The Act of Covenanting does not warrant that the covenanting churches shall be entitled to delegates at the General Conference of The United Methodist Church or at the equivalent body of the covenant partner (¶570.4).

Daily Christian Advocate, The. This is the periodical containing the official agenda, rules, petitions, and resolutions to be taken up by General Conference. Also included are reports from the general agencies/commissions as well as general information for delegates. An *Advanced Daily Christian Advocate* is distributed to all delegates prior to General Conference.

deacon. Deacons are ordained to lifetime ministry of word, service, compassion, and justice to community and congregation. In this capacity, they lead the church in relating the gathered life of Christians to their ministries in the world, thus connecting the church's worship with its service in the world. They are full members of the annual conference, called to a specialized nonitinerant ministry.

deaconess. A deaconess is a layperson who, in response to God's call and on recommendation of the General Board of Global Ministries, is commissioned by a bishop to share faith in Jesus Christ through ministries of love, justice, and service. Deaconesses form a covenant community rooted in scripture, informed by history, driven by mission, ecumenical in scope, and global in outreach. Deaconesses serve the church in any capacity not requiring full clergy rights. The office of deaconesses was initially recognized by The Methodist Episcopal Church in 1888.

diaconal minister. Initially established in 1976 by the *Book of Discipline*, this role allows a person, in response to God's call, to commit his or her life to serving and equipping others to serve Christ in a specialized form of ministry on behalf of The United Methodist Church. Many diaconal ministers transition to the office of ordained deacon, which was established in 1996.

district committee on ordained ministry. This committee evaluates, certifies, and recommends to the board of ordained ministry all those applying for licensed or ordained ministry. This committee, sometimes referred to as DCOM, oversees all candidates within that district and supervises all matters related to candidacy and licensing. The committee interviews candidates, recommends candidates for provisional membership, and approves all local pastors serving within the district (¶666).

district superintendent. This role serves as an extension of the bishop in overseeing the total ministry of the clergy. Duties include assisting in appointment of ministry personnel, developing systems of recruitment, examining, overseeing candidates for ordained and licensed ministry, and interpreting church law. District superintendents are the chief missional strategists for the denomination.

ecclesiology. This is the theological study of the church.

ecumenical. This term describes the cooperation or dialogue among Christian denominations with the hoped for goal of uniting all in one body of Christ. Both the World Council of Churches and the National Council of Churches are dedicated to such partnerships and dialogue.

elder. Elders are ordained to a lifetime ministry of service, word, sacrament, and order. They are authorized to preach and teach God's word, to administer the sacraments of baptism and Holy Communion, and to order the life of the church for mission and ministry. Elders are the generalists of the church as compared to the deacons who specialize in particular forms of ministry. As members of the order of elders, they make themselves available for appointment by the bishop and serve both within the local church and in settings that extend the ministry of the church.

endorsement. Endorsement increases accountability to the church and those serving in specialized settings. It provides important networking opportunities. Endorsement is available for deacons and elders who may be provisional, full, or associate members of their annual conference, Government agencies and some civilian agencies require endorsement. Endorsement may be required for certification by professional pastoral care organizations, for example, the Association of Professional

Chaplains (APC) and the American Association of Pastoral Counselors (AAPC). The United Methodist Endorsing Agency (UMEA) endorses chaplains (military and nonmilitary), pastoral counselors, and, most recently, life coaches. The UMEA has responsibility for recruitment, endorsement, and support of clergy in extension ministries beyond the local church, including chaplains in hospitals, prisons, and military service, and pastoral counselors. The UMEA also provides ministry to United Methodist laity outside the United States.

episcopacy. This term refers to the office of bishop in any Christian tradition.

episcopal area. The bishop is assigned to and lives within the bounds of the episcopal area and presides over the work of one or more annual conferences.

Evangelical Church, The. Initially led by Jacob Albright, this denomination is one of the predecessor denominations to The United Methodist Church. Its successor joined with the United Brethren in 1946 to form The Evangelical United Brethren Church, which then joined The Methodist Church in 1968 to form The United Methodist Church.

Evangelical United Brethren Confession of Faith. This is a statement of belief consisting of sixteen articles developed by The Evangelical United Brethren Church (EUB). During the formation of The United Methodist Church in 1968, the EUB Confession of Faith was adopted as one of the basic statements of the Christian faith and included among the constitutional standards of doctrine.

Evangelical United Brethren Church, The (EUB). This church formed in 1946 as a result of the union of the Church of the United Brethren in Christ and The Evangelical Church. In 1968 The Evangelical United Brethren Church and The Methodist Church joined to form The United Methodist Church.

evangelism. Evangelism is the sharing of the message of salvation, or gospel of Jesus Christ, through words and lives, and the initiation of Christian believers into the reign of God.

Explanatory Notes upon the New Testament. This historic text is an accompanying commentary prepared by John Wesley on the books of the New Testament and a debated, though recognized, constitutional standard of doctrine of The United Methodist Church.

extension ministries. This term refers to elders who serve in ministry outside of a local church setting. It includes settings such as conference administration, chaplaincy, pastoral counseling, and teaching. The bishop appoints elders to extension ministries (¶343–44).

finance committee (local church). The purpose of this committee is to provide the local church with financial guidance and strategy throughout the year. One of its responsibilities is to perform an annual audit of the local church's financial records (¶258).

full membership. This term refers to ordained elders and deacons elected to permanent membership in an annual conference who have committed to live within the covenantal relationships of the order of elders or order of deacons.

General Board of Church and Society (GBCS). The GBCS seeks to relate the gospel to the world guided by the Social Principles. It develops resources to inform, motivate, and train United Methodists on issues of social justice.

General Board of Discipleship (GBOD). This board assists annual conferences, districts, and local churches in their efforts of discipleship and Christian ministry. It provides leadership and resources in the areas of spiritual growth, devotional literature, curriculum resources, Christian education, evangelism, worship, stewardship, and ministry of the laity.

General Board of Global Ministries (GBGM). The GBGM serves as the missional instrument of The United Methodist Church. It seeks to witness throughout the world, to recruit and send missionaries, and to support persons in local churches for global missions.

General Board of Higher Education and Ministry (GBHEM). This board assists persons preparing for ministerial service. It provides general oversight for campus ministries and institutions of higher education.

General Board of Pension and Health Benefits (GBPHB). The GBPHB serves as the general supervisor and administrator of support, relief, assistance, and pensioning of clergy and lay workers within the Church.

General Commission on Archives and History (GCAH). This general commission promotes and cares for the historical interests of The United Methodist Church. It maintains archives and libraries to preserve records and supports historical work in annual conferences and jurisdictions.

General Commission on Christian Unity and Interreligious Concerns (GCCUIC). This general commission provides ecumenical leadership training and resources to committees on Christian unity, develops further resources, and pursues relationships with other Christian bodies.

General Commission on Communication (GCC). The General Commission on Communication provides leadership and services in communication, public relations, and promotions of the general funds and programs of the denomination. It is the official newsgathering and distribution agency of The United Methodist Church.

General Commission on Religion and Race (GCRR). This general commission seeks to challenge and equip the general agencies, institutions, and connectional structures of The United Methodist Church to practice full and equal participation in the church.

General Commission on the Status and Role of Women. This general commission challenges The United Methodist Church and its agencies, institutions, and connectional structures to continuing commitment to equal responsibility and participation of women as well as others in the total life and mission of the Church.

General Commission on United Methodist Men. The General Commission on United Methodist Men has primary oversight for the coordination and resourcing of men's ministry within The United Methodist Church. It declares centrality of Christ in every man's life; enhances evangelism, mission and spiritual life; and provides support services to promote growth of men's ministries.

General Conference. The highest legislative body of The United Methodist Church is composed of an equal number of lay and clergy delegates. It meets every four years and is the only body that can speak officially for the denomination.

General Council on Finance and Administration (GCFA). This general council administers finances and serves as the central treasurer of The United Methodist Church.

general evangelist. A general evangelist serves the church as a leader in the ministry of evangelism for people of all ages. He or she promotes, educates, provides guidance, and plans opportunities for evangelistic ministry. This person is recommended by the annual conference board of ordained ministry and the board of discipleship.

General Minutes, The. These are compiled and published annually by the General Council on Finance and Administration. Each volume contains statistical information of local churches and annual conferences for the previous year. The General Minutes contains the appointment list of pastors to their charges. The decisions of the Judicial Council for the year are also included in this publication.

General Rules, the. This is a set of rules composed in 1743 by John Wesley for his societies as a guide to holy living. Thomas Coke and Francis

Asbury prepared a revised edition, which has continued to be considered an authoritative constitutional doctrinal standard within the *Book of Discipline.*

home missioner. Established as an official position at the 2004 General Conference, home missioners are similar to deaconesses. They are professionally trained and devote their lives to service. They are approved by the General Board of Global Ministries and commissioned by a bishop. They may serve with any United Methodist agency or program or in agencies outside The United Methodist Church, provided that approval is given by the board in consultation with the bishop of the receiving area (¶1314).

itineracy. This is the system of The United Methodist Church by which ordained elders and licensed local pastors submit to the bishop's authority to appoint them to pastoral charges.

Judicial Council. The Judicial Council is the highest court of appeal within the denomination. It consists of a group of nine persons elected by General Conference. They are responsible for ruling on questions of constitutionality in matters of church law and practice.

jurisdictional conference. This is a regional meeting held every four years and attended by elected delegates. The business includes the election and assignment of bishops. The five geographic areas in the United States that correspond to the jurisdictional conferences, each composed of several annual conferences as determined by the General Conference, are North Central, Northeastern, South Central, Southeastern, and Western.

justification. Justification is an aspect of Christian salvation in which an individual receives assurance and pardon for sins as a result of the imputation of Jesus Christ's righteousness to the believer.

lectionary. The lectionary is a list of scripture readings distributed over a multiple year cycle, for example *The Revised Common Lectionary* provides readings from scripture over three years. While the lectionary does not include an exhaustive selection of scripture texts drawing from the whole of the canon, it provides a selection of texts that represent the major themes, narratives, and genres. The lectionary provides suggested readings for each Sunday as well as daily readings from the Old Testament, Psalms, New Testament, and Epistles and acknowledges the recognition of saints' days.

local pastor. A local pastor is licensed, approved annually by the district committee on ordained ministry, and authorized to perform all the duties of an ordained minister, including the sacraments, while assigned to a particular charge under the supervision of a district superintendent. A clergy mentor oversees the local pastor's work in the Course of Study for ordained ministry and advises on matters of pastoral responsibility.

means of grace. The means of grace are a broadly recognized set of practices within the Christian tradition dating to the early church and consist of both works of piety and works of mercy or charity. These practices are not pursued to earn salvation but rather in response to God's grace.

missionary annual conference. The United States includes three missionary annual conferences: Alaska, Oklahoma Indian, and Red Bird. These conferences present distinctive opportunities for ministry though often in the midst of limited resources.

National Council of the Churches of Christ. The United Methodist Church is a founding member of the National Council of the Churches of Christ through its predecessor denominations. The NCC is an ecumenical gathering with members from a range of Christian traditions including Roman Catholic, Orthodox, and Protestant denominations.

ordination. This is the act of conferring authority for ministry through the laying on of hands by a bishop. While United Methodism is arguably not a part of the apostolic succession, ordination alludes to the succession of those authorized to lead the church beginning with Jesus's identification of Peter.

pastoral charge. A pastoral charge is one or more local churches organized under a single charge conference and to which a minister or a local pastor is appointed.

prevenient grace. Prevenient grace is available to all and precedes a person's recognition of faith though allows one to acknowledge moral value (good from evil).

professing members (local church). These are baptized persons who have taken vows declaring the Christian faith. Professing members include all people who have come into local church membership by profession of faith or by transfer from other churches.

provisional membership. The United Methodist Church requires a provisional period of two years for those seeking ordination as full members. This process may begin when half the education requirements have been met, but must include at least two years following the completion of a seminary degree (¶326).

quadrennium. The official four-year period following each General Conference, during which The United Methodist Church implements General Conference legislation and action items.

Restrictive Rules, the. The Restrictive Rules were adopted at the 1808 General Conference to "restrict" the powers of some components of Methodism, particularly the General Conference in relationship to the Constitution, doctrinal standards, episcopacy, and the clergy's right to trial.

sanctification. Sanctification is an aspect of Christian salvation in which an individual receives the impartation of the Holy Spirit, being made new and holy often facilitated by participation in the means of grace.

scriptures. In the Christian faith, its scriptures, or the Bible, consist of the Old and New Testaments.

Social Principles, the. These make up a document setting forth the basic position of The United Methodist Church on important social issues. The Social Principles, while slightly revised at each General Conference, were adopted by a study commission appointed in 1968 and chaired by Bishop James Thomas (¶160–66).

staff/pastor-parish relations committee (local church). The committee in each church that assists clergy and staff in setting leadership and service priorities and evaluates and approves those beginning candidacy for licensed or ordained ministry from that congregation (¶258.2).

Standard Sermons of John Wesley, The. Forty-four sermons of Wesley published in the first four volumes of his sermons. *The Standard Sermons* set forth those doctrines Wesley embraced and taught. These sermons are included among United Methodist doctrines in the constitutional standards.

Thirty-Nine Articles, the. These historic resources were adopted in 1563 as the authoritative theological beliefs and principles of the Anglican Church. This document serves as the foundation for John Wesley's Articles of Religion, *The Book of Common Prayer*, and *The Book of Homilies*.

United Methodist Book of Worship, The. This is a book containing the rituals, sacraments, and orders of worship related to The United Methodist Church. The most recent text was approved by General Conference in 1992.

United Methodist Committee on Relief, the (UMCOR). A not-for-profit ministry of The United Methodist Church committed to alleviating human suffering throughout the world, UMCOR works in over eighty countries, including the United States. The committee provides long-term recovery as well as immediate relief.

United Methodist Hymnal, The. *The United Methodist Hymnal,* the most recent version published in 1988, is approved by the General Conference and serves as the guide for singing in worship across United Methodism and beyond.

University Senate. One of the oldest and longest serving accrediting bodies of higher education in the United States, dating to 1892, the University Senate represents those interests held in common by The United Methodist Church and its affiliated schools, colleges, universities, and graduate schools of theology. It conducts reviews for the educational institutions qualifying for affiliation with the denomination and for denominational support.

World Council of Churches (WCC). The WCC is a worldwide ecumenical association of Christian churches founded in 1948.

World Methodist Council (WMC). The WMC is a network of Wesleyan traditions founded in 1881 whose current headquarters are located in Lake Junaluska, North Carolina. It gathers every five years in a different international venue, most recently in 2011 in Durban, South Africa.